NEW DIRECTIONS
IN
MARITIME LAW 1984

editors

David J. Sharpe

Professor of Law
National Law Center
George Washington University
Washington, D.C.

and

W. Wylie Spicer

McInnes, Cooper & Robertson
Halifax, Nova Scotia

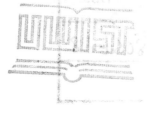

1985
CARSWELL • STEVENS
Toronto • London

Canadian Cataloguing in Publication Data

Main entry under title:

New directions in maritime law 1984

Papers given at the New Directions in Maritime Law Conference held in Halifax in May, 1984.
ISBN 0-459-37210-6

1. Maritime law – Canada – Congresses.
2. Maritime law – United States – Congresses.
3. Salvage – Congresses.   4. Shipping – Data processing – Congresses.   I. Sharpe, David J.   II. Spicer, W. Wylie (William Wylie), 1949-   III. New Directions in Maritime Law Conference (1984: Halifax, N.S.).

JX4411.N48 1985   341.7'566   C85-098011-9

Preface

The papers in this Volume were prepared for the New Directions in Maritime Law 1984 Conference at Halifax, Nova Scotia, co-sponsored by the Maritime Law Section of the Canadian Bar Association (Nova Scotia), the Canadian Maritime Law Association, and the Faculty of Law of Dalhousie University, Halifax.

Each biennial New Directions in Maritime Law Conference since 1976 has chosen topics for discussion which seemed to be of current interest to the maritime community. The 1984 Conference selected as its major topic the conflict of laws in maritime laws, about which very little has heretofore been written. The papers in this Volume should sum up what is known in the area and may assist in the making of new and better law. Papers were also given in other areas of topical interest, the impact of computer technology on shipping documents and the role of government in the provision of salvage services.

The 1984 Conference could not have been successful without the presence and participation of the authors of the papers in this Volume. It has been an easy task to edit their work. The cooperation of many authors, editors, and publisher's staff is gratefully acknowledged.

David J. Sharpe
Washington, D.C.

W. Wylie Spicer
Halifax, Nova Scotia

CONTENTS

THE RESOLUTION OF
CONFLICT OF LAWS
ISSUES IN MARITIME CLAIMS:
AN OVERVIEW

A COURSE CHANGE TO STARBOARD: NEW DIRECTIONS IN MARITIME CONFLICT RESOLUTION IN THE UNITED STATES

*Harold K. Watson**

The conference papers which comprise this collection of essays describe in detail the processes of resolution of the conflict of laws in particular areas of maritime law. This paper serves as an introduction to the collection by tracing the broad outlines of American maritime conflict jurisprudence, describing where the decisional and legislative trends have been, and trying to predict (or guess) where they are going.

The task of preparing such an introduction has both constricting and liberating aspects. On the one hand, it is often difficult to say much of anything about the law in general, as opposed to addressing certain legal problems in particular. On the other hand, being asked merely to provide a broad outline at least permits an author to attempt to avoid errors by relying on the nature of the assignment. When confronted with an obvious anomaly between real life and the model described, one can always respond, "Oh, that is just an exception, and I was only speaking of the general rule."

It is impossible to discuss general trends in American maritime conflict of laws jurisprudence without addressing some of the related problems which arise when a legal dispute has ties to more than one country. Very frequently, a single dispute will involve any number of related issues: subject matter jurisdiction, personal jurisdiction, choice of law, and appropriate forum. There are discrete concepts, although the

---

*Partner in Liddell, Sapp, Zivley, Brown & LaBoon, Houston, Texas. Mr. Watson is a Member of the Bar of the States of Texas and Louisiana, and has published articles in the Maritime Lawyer, Louisiana Law Review, Houston Law Review and The Journal of Maritime Law and Conference on various subjects of maritime law, including personal injury and death, carriage of goods, limitation of liability, and jurisdiction and choice of law.

courts have often blurred the distinctions among them. For example, the courts have at times addressed the question of whether the Jones Act or foreign law should apply to determine the substantive rights of the parties in terms of "jurisdiction,"[1] when, in fact, no jurisdictional problem is involved at all, since the federal courts of the United States have subject matter jurisdiction to adjudicate maritime disputes arising anywhere in the world.[2] The question in such a case is one of choice-of-law; or perhaps whether the court should exercise that jurisdiction, or decline in favor of adjudication in the courts of another country. Fortunately, the American courts have shown a growing tendency to distinguish these related problems, and to apply the appropriate analytical criteria to resolve them.[3]

Questions of "jurisdiction", be it subject matter jurisdiction or personal jurisdiction, are generally dealt with by American courts on constitutional or statutory bases. The Constitution of the United States and the Judicial Code give the federal courts the power to adjudicate all "cases of admiralty and maritime jurisdiction."[4] This means that the federal courts have subject matter jurisdiction over all matters arising on navigable waters[5] and bearing a "significant relationship to traditional maritime activity",[6] without regard to the citizenship of the parties or where the claim arose.[7] Questions of jurisdiction over the person also involve constitutional questions, since the due process clauses of the fifth and fourteenth amendments preclude an American court from asserting jurisdiction over a person unless the person has such "minimum contacts" with the forum "that the maintenance of the suit does not offend" traditional notions of "fair play and substantial justice."[8]

---

1   See, e.g., *Dassigienis v. Cosmos Carriers & Trading Corp.,* 1971 A.M.C. 1104, 1105 (2d Cir. 1971): "[T]he test of subject matter jurisdiction involves an analysis of various connecting factors which might justify the application of United States law to a particular claim." See also *Sanchez v. Caribbean Carriers, Ltd.,* 552 F.2d 70 (2d Cir. 1977); *Frangiskatos v. Konkar Maritime Enterprises, S.A.,* 1973 A.M.C. 333 (2d Cir. 1972).

2   See discussion at notes 4-7, *infra.*

3   See, e.g., *Union Ins. Co. of Canton, Ltd. v. S.S. Elikon,* 642 F.2d 721 (4th Cir. 1981). The Supreme Court has consistently rebuffed attempts to confuse these issues. See *Lauritzen v. Larsen,* 345 U.S. 571, 575 (1953); *Romero v. Int. Terminal Operating Co.,* 358 U.S. 354 (1959).

4   Article III, § 2; 28 U.S.C. § 1333(1).

5   See G. Gilmore & C. Black, *The Law of Admiralty,* § 1-11 (2d ed. 1975).

6   *Executive Jet Aviation, Inc. v. City of Cleveland,* 409 U.S. 249, 268 (1972).

7   *The Belgenland,* 114 U.S. 355 (1885).

8   *Int. Shoe Co. v. State of Washington,* 326 U.S. 310, 316 (1945), quoting from *Milliken v. Meyer,* 311 U.S. 457, 463 (1940).

Issues of the proper law and proper forum, on the other hand, usually do not turn on constitutional provisions,[9] but rather on judicial and legislative notions about the rightful role of American law and American courts in determining disputes with foreign connections. While the better view is that the criteria that should be used to determine applicable law are different from the criteria applicable to determine whether to exercise jurisdiction and adjudicate a particular dispute,[10] the same considerations underlie the analyses in both cases. Accordingly, this paper will treat them as different aspects of the same problem.

Like the ebb and flow of the tide, trends in judicial decision-making come and go. Perhaps nowhere is this more dramatically demonstrated than in maritime conflict of laws decisions in the United States courts. In the 1960's and early 1970's, the decisions of the federal courts in this area of law exhibited a pronounced nationalistic flavor, applying American law and exercising jurisdiction in many circumstances where American contacts and interests would appear to be minimal. Then, in less than a decade, the American courts made a change of course in both methodology and substance which is, to borrow from the Rules of the Road, "large enough to be readily apparent."[11]

It would probably be an oversimplification of the development of American maritime conflict law to view almost 200 years of jurisprudence as a battle between internationalist and nationalistic approaches, but this dualist approach has much to recommend it. The modern case law, in particular, appears to be a struggle over whether the maritime law will endeavor to accommodate the international nature of the industry it regulates, or adhere to a more nationalistic, result-oriented mode of decision-making.

To put these remarks and recent developments into context, it is necessary to digress a bit into the annals of history. It is probably safe to say that the sorts of problems that can give rise to conflict of laws were one of the primary reasons the constitutional convention of 1789 decided to vest the federal courts with admiralty jurisdiction.[12] Because of the potential for international incidents arising out of the adjudication of maritime disputes, which more often than not involve foreign nationals, it was felt that maritime litigation should best be handled on a federal, rather than state, level.

---

9   Occasionally, a forum may have so little contact with a transaction that application of forum law may constitute a deprivation of property without due process of law. See, e.g., *Home Ins. Co. v. Dick,* 281 U.S. 397 (1930).

10   See, e.g., *Fisher v. Agios Nicolaos V,* 628 F.2d 308 (5th Cir. 1980).

11   Rule 8(b), International Steering and Sailing Rules.

12   See authorities cited in D. Robertson, *Admiralty and Federalism* 2 n.1 (1970).

Despite the potential for conflicts-generating disputes, in the early days of the American republic, conflict of laws was not a matter given much consideration by the admiralty courts. Maritime law was viewed as part of the *jus gentium,* the law of nations, and was common to all civilized states. For example, none other than Chief Justice John Marshall said in *American Ins. Co. v. Canter,*[13] "a case in admiralty does not, in fact, arise under the Constitution or laws of the United States. These cases are as old as navigation itself; and the law, admiralty and maritime, as it has existed for ages, is applied by our Courts to the cases as they arise."[14]

With the advent of nationalism and positivism, however, different views began to prevail. The maritime law came to be viewed as national law, applicable only to the extent that some appropriate organ of the United States government, be it the courts or the Congress, chose to adopt it.[15] During this positivist period, the United States courts were particularly averse to the application of foreign law in instances where the Congress had spoken. For example, in *The Titanic,*[16] the Court held that the British owners of that ill-fated vessel were entitled to limit their liability pursuant to American law, even as to the claims of British subjects. To Justice Holmes, the question was simply one of statutory construction.

Legislative activity relating to maritime affairs took a similar nationalistic bent during this period. For example, section 4 of the Seamen's Act of March 4, 1915,[17] entitles seamen to one-half of their wages earned at every port where the vessel calls, and goes on to provide that it applies "to seamen on foreign vessels while in harbors of the United States," and that "the courts of the United States shall be open to such seamen for its enforcement." The legislative history of this act makes it clear that it was intended to apply to foreign seamen when in American ports to equalize the operating expenses of foreign shipowners with American vessel operators by giving foreign seamen "the right to leave the ship when in a safe harbor."[18] This legislation was

---

13   26 U.S. (1 Pet.) 511, 545 (1828).
14   *Ibid.* at 545-6.
15   Perhaps the classic statement of this view was given by Justice Holmes in *The Western Maid,* 257 U.S. 419, 432 (1922):

   There is no mystic over-law to which even the United States must bow. When a case is said to be governed by foreign law or by general maritime law that is only a short way of saying that for this purpose the sovereign power takes up a rule suggested from without and makes it part of its own rules.
16   *Oceanic Steam Navigation Co. v. Mellor,* 233 U.S. 718 (1914).
17   46 U.S.C. § 597.
18   H.R. Rep. No. 645, pt. 1, 62 Cong., 2d Sess. 7 (1912).

upheld in *Strathearn Steamship Company v. Dillon*,[19] despite a vigorous *amicus curiae* argument on behalf of the British Government that the act was contrary to international law.[20]

Similarly, the Harter Act,[21] passed in 1893 to regulate certain aspects of ocean bills of lading, applies by its terms to all voyages to or from the United States, without regard to the flag of the vessel or the citizenship or domicile of the shipper or shipowner.[22] Congress took the same approach when adopting the Hague Rules in the American Carriage of Goods by Sea Act in 1936.[23] Not only did these legislative enactments contain their own conflicts provisions, but the courts held that no other factors normally given consideration in conflict analysis, such as party autonomy, could be considered.[24]

The modern retreat from nationalistic conflicts adjudication really begins with the decision of the Supreme Court of the United States in *The Norwalk Victory*.[25] This case arose out of a collision between the United States flag *Norwalk Victory* and the British flag *Merganser* in the Schelde River in Belgium. Suits were filed in the United States, and the owner of the *Norwalk Victory* instituted limitation proceedings, posting a bond in the appropriate amount under Belgian law, which was less than required by American law. The lower courts dismissed for failure to post a bond in the appropriate amount.[26] In an opinion that has been described as "extraordinarily obscure",[27] the Court reversed, suggesting that Belgian law might be applicable and hinting that a complete conflict of laws analysis rather than slavish adherence to statutory language might be appropriate:

> Whether they are in fact considerations of domestic policy which deserve to be measured against application of the *lex loci delicti* and whether such considerations are as significant where the foreign limitation is lower than our own as where it is higher – these too are questions not now before us in view of the fact that the case is here merely on exceptions to the petition for limitation of liability.[28]

---

19   252 U.S. 348 (1920).
20   *See* Symeonides, "Maritime Conflicts of Law from the Perspective of Modern Choice of Law Methodology", (1982), 7 Mar. Lawyer 223 at 228.
21   46 U.S.C. § 190-196.
22   46 U.S.C. § 190; *Knott v. Botany Worsted Mills*, 179 U.S. 69 (1898).
23   46 U.S.C. § 1300.
24   *Knott v. Botany Worsted Mills*, 179 U.S. 69 (1900); *Gen. Motors Overseas Operation v. S.S. Goettingen*, 225 F. Supp. 902 (S.D.N.Y. 1964).
25   *Black Diamond S.S. Corp. v. Robert Stewart & Sons, Ltd.*, 336 U.S. 386 (1949).
26   *In re Black Diamond S.S. Corp. and U.S.*, 1948 A.M.C. 816 (E.D.N.Y. 1947); *U.S. and Black Diamond S.S. Corp. v. Robert Stewart & Sons, Ltd.*, 167 F.2d 308 (2d Cir. 1948).
27   G. Gilmore & C. Black, *The Law of Admiralty* § 10-44 at 941 (2d ed. 1975).
28   336 U.S. at 396-6.

The analytical, internationalist approach to maritime conflict problems suggested in *The Norwalk Victory* was expressly adopted by the Supreme Court in *Lauritzen v. Larsen.*[29] *Lauritzen* arose out of the injury to a Danish seaman aboard a Danish flag vessel in Havana harbor. The vessel was owned by a Danish subject, and the seaman had signed articles providing that the rights of crew members would be governed by Danish law and by the collective bargaining agreement entered into between the Danish Seaman's Union, of which the seaman was a member, and the employer. The only ties with the United States were the facts that the seaman had signed articles and joined the ship while temporarily in New York, and that the suit was filed in the Southern District of New York.

The Supreme Court reversed the decision of the lower court[30] that the pertinent American legislation, the Jones Act, applied. The Court reviewed the problem not as one of simple statutory construction, but of a balancing of interests, and stated that American law should "apply only to areas and transactions in which American law would be operative under prevalent doctrines of international law."[31]

The Court set forth seven factors it believed worthy of consideration in determining whether to apply American maritime law. The place of the wrongful act was mentioned in view of the traditional vitality of *lex loci delicti commissi,* but was said to have "limited application to shipboard torts, because of the varieties of legal authority over waters she [the ship] may navigate . . . ."[32] Similarly, the Court placed little importance on the place of the contract, viewing this also as a fortuitous event.[33] The Court felt that "the territorial standard is so unfitted to an enterprise conducted under many territorial rules and under none that it usually is modified by the more constant law of the flag,"[34] which was said to be of "cardinal importance."[35] Since the flag of the vessel was one of the few constants by which parties could plan their actions, and because the law of the flag had traditionally been given preeminent importance, the Court felt that the law of the flag "must prevail unless some heavy counterweight appears."[36]

The Court recognized the practice of registering vessels under flags of convenience, however, and indicated that it might be appropriate in

---

29   345 U.S. 571 (1953).
30   *Larsen v. Lauritzen,* 196 F.2d 220 (2d Cir. 1952).
31   345 U.S. at 577.
32   *Ibid.* at 583.
33   *Ibid.* at 588.
34   *Ibid.* at 589.
35   *Ibid.*
36   *Ibid.*

certain instances to "go beyond the formalities of more or less nominal foreign registration to enforce against American shipowners the obligations which our law places upon them,"[37] thus placing some importance on the allegiance of the shipowner. The allegiance or domicile of the injured party was also mentioned as a factor that could, at times, have considerable importance.[38]

Finally, the Court mentioned, but again minimized, the questions of accessibility of a foreign forum and the law of the forum. The question of whether a foreign forum was accessible might well be a factor in determining whether to retain jurisdiction or dismiss a case pursuant to the doctrine of *forum non conveniens,* but had no relationship to applicable law.[39] Similarly, the law of the forum had little relevance, since "[t]he purpose of a conflict-of-laws doctrine is to assure that a case will be treated in the same way under the appropriate law regardless of the fortuitous circumstances which often determine the forum."[40]

The next foray of the Supreme Court into maritime conflict of laws came in *Romero v. International Terminal Operating Company.*[41] This was another Jones Act and general maritime law claim by a foreign seaman injured aboard a foreign flag vessel. The only additional American contact was the fact that the injury had occurred in the port of Hoboken, New Jersey. Applying the rationale of *Lauritzen,* the Supreme Court held that both the Jones Act and the general maritime law of the United States were inapplicable.

The nationalistic tendencies prevalent during the 19th and the first half of the 20th century did not die so easily, however. The seeds for a turn away from internationalist philosophy were being sown almost contemporaneously with the *Lauritzen* and *Romero* decisions. In *Bartholomew v. Universe Tank Ships, Inc.,*[42] a permanent resident alien of the United States who was injured on a Liberian flag vessel owned and operated by a Liberian corporation brought suit under the Jones Act. Based upon the beneficial ownership of the vessel by American citizens (the stock of the Liberian corporation was held by a Panamanian corporation, the stock of which was in turn owned by citizens of the United States), the court held that American law was applicable.

In view of the plaintiff's residence in the United States and the interest of the country of domicile in protecting itself from having to support injured workers, the application of American law seems wholly

---

37   *Ibid.* at 587.
38   *Ibid.* at 586.
39   *Ibid.* at 589-90.
40   *Ibid.* at 591.
41   358 U.S. 354 (1959).
42   263 F.2d 437 (2d Cir. 1959).

appropriate. The problem arises from the methodology used. In the words of an old song, "It ain't so much as wot 'e said As the narsty w'y 'e said it."[43] Contrary to the approach taken in *Lauritzen,* the court approached the problem simply as one of statutory construction, stating that "traditional choice of law techniques may be more misleading than helpful."[44]

> Hence it must be said that in a particular case something between minimal and preponderant contacts is necessary if the Jones Act is to be applied. Thus we conclude that the test is that "substantial" contacts are necessary.[45]

In other words, the court thought it was only necessary to see if American contacts were sufficient to justify application of American law, and not to weigh the foreign contacts.

The *Bartholomew* approach was approved by the Supreme Court in *Hellenic Lines, Ltd. v. Rhoditis.*[46] There, suit was brought by a Greek seaman injured aboard a Greek ship in a U.S. port. The ship was owned and managed by a Greek corporation that had its largest office in New York. Almost all of the stock of the Greek corporation was owned by a Greek subject who had lived in the United States for almost 25 years. The vessel and its sister ships were frequent visitors to the U.S. ports. On these facts, the Court held the Jones Act was applicable. The Court stated that the *Lauritzen* test was not "mechanical"[47] and that the shipowner's "base of operations"[48] was also a significant factor. Perhaps more significantly, the Supreme Court espoused the notion that the purpose of the analysis is to effectuate "the liberal purposes of the Jones Act."[49]

The Court's reliance in *Rhoditis* on *Bartholomew* was to make the notion of "base of operations" not only a significant factor in resolving maritime conflict of laws issues, but the only factor, at least in the personal injury sphere. In the Second Circuit Court of Appeals (in New York), the courts went so far as to hold that American law was applicable if "at least some of the stockholders of the shipowner . . . are American citizens."[50] The analysis had turned from balancing of the contacts as called for in *Lauritzen* to determining whether there was some tie "to support jurisdiction under the Jones Act [sic]."[51] Similarly, in *Fisher v.*

---

43   Hough, "Admiralty Jurisdiction – of Late Years" (1924), 37 Harv. L. Rev. 529 at 543.
44   263 F.2d at 440.
45   *Ibid.* at 440-441.
46   398 U.S. 306 (1970).
47   *Ibid.* at 308.
48   *Ibid.* at 309.
49   *Ibid.* at 310.
50   *Antypas v. Compania Maritima San Basilio, S.A.,* 541 F.2d 307, 310 (2d Cir. 1976).
51   *Ibid.*

Agios Nicolaos V,[52] the Fifth Circuit (in New Orleans) held that American law was applicable to a death claim by the beneficiaries of a Greek citizen and domiciliary killed aboard a Greek flag ship wholly owned and operated by Greek nationals and domiciliaries. This decision was based solely upon the fact that the accident occurred in the United States and that the vessel was on her maiden voyage under her present ownership and that thus her "entire business activity prior to the accident had been in the United States."[53]

That parochialism was lingering on outside the field of maritime personal injury law was made evident in *Carbon Black Export, Inc. v. The Monrosa*.[54] There, the Court refused to enforce a forum selection clause in bills of lading, relying in part upon the notion that the parties could not "oust" the court of jurisdiction.

The personal injury decisions probably stand as the highwater mark of xenophobic judicial methodology. It is clear now, however, that the trend is in the opposite direction and towards a much more internationalistic approach to conflicts resolution.

The first evidence that the Supreme Court was to reject this parochial view in such matters came in *M/S Bremen v. Zapata Off-Shore Company*.[55] There, the owner of a mobile drilling rig contracted to have the rig towed from the Gulf of Mexico to the Adriatic. The contract contained an exculpatory provision exonerating the towing company and the towing vessel from any liability resulting from their negligence, and a forum selection clause calling for all disputes arising out of the contract to be litigated in London. The Fifth Circuit, relying on its earlier *Monrosa*[56] decision, held that the forum selection clause was invalid. The Supreme Court reversed, enforced the forum selection clause, and ordered the case dismissed so that proceedings could go forward in London.

The *Bremen* case is notable, and not simply because of the open-minded approach of the Court toward requiring parties to litigate abroad when they have agreed to do so, even if the foreign forum is not the most convenient one available. In requiring the parties to litigate their differences in London, the Supreme Court was consigning the plaintiff to a forum that would honor the exculpatory provisions in the towage contract, despite a long series of Supreme Court decisions that had, in no uncertain terms, declared that such provisions were contrary

---

52   628 F.2d 308 (5th Cir. 1980).
53   *Ibid.* at 318.
54   254 F.2d 297 (1958), cert. dismissed, 359 U.S. 180 (1959).
55   407 U.S. 1 (1972).
56   Note 54, *supra*.

to the public policy of the United States and unenforceable.[57] The willingness of the Court to effect a change of law as well as a change of forum was to set the tone for further developments.

The change of course in personal injury litigation came in *De Mateos v. Texaco Inc.*[58] There, suit was filed by the beneficiary of a Panamanian seaman who became ill on board a Liberian flag vessel and subsequently died. The ship was owned by a Panamanian subsidiary of a U.S. corporation and managed by a British subsidiary of the same U.S. company. The Third Circuit (in Philadelphia) held that American law was inapplicable. The statutory construction approach set forth in *Bartholomew-Rhoditis,* was rejected as "social jingoism."[59] The Court viewed its task as one of determining whether American or foreign law was more appropriate in view of the totality of the contacts with the United States and the foreign jurisdiction, and rejected the notion that beneficial ownership alone was sufficient to call for the application of American law.

The *De Mateos* case has been followed and expanded upon in cases dealing with the offshore petroleum industry.[60] Claims for the application of American law by foreign nationals injured while engaging in foreign offshore operations have received little sympathy from the American courts, even when the vessels involved were owned by American corporations and registered under American law.[61] Moreover, in 1982 Congress amended the Jones Act expressly to limit the right of foreign nationals not domiciled in the United States to bring claims for injuries incurred while engaged in the offshore industry.[62]

This trend has also extended to the related doctrine of *forum non conveniens.* Here, a number of seemingly well-established principles that restricted the application of the doctrine, and made it difficult in many instances to obtain dismissal so that litigation could go forward in a foreign forum, have been overturned.

It had long been held that "the consequences of a decision that American law applies are ... conclusive on the issue [of *forum non*

---

57 *Bisso v. Inland Waterways Corp.,* 349 U.S. 85 (1955); *Boston Metal Co. v. The Winding Gulf,* 349 U.S. 122 (1955); *Dixilyn Drilling Corp. v. Crescent Towing and Salvage Co.,* 372 U.S. 697 (1963).
58 562 F.2d 895 (3d Cir. 1977).
59 *Ibid.* at 902.
60 *de Oliveira v. Delta Marine Drilling Co.,* 707 F.2d 843 (5th Cir. 1983); *Bailey v. Dolphin Int., Inc.,* 697 F.2d 1268 (5th Cir. 1983); *Zekir v. Reading & Bates Drilling Co.,* 680 F.2d 1107 (5th Cir. 1982); *Chiazor v. Transworld Drilling Co., Ltd.,* 648 F.2d 1015 (5th Cir. 1981); *Phillips v. Amoco Trinidad Oil Co.,* 632 F.2d 82 (9th Cir. 1980).
61 Phillips, note 60, *supra.*
62 Pub. L. 97-389, Title V, § 503(a), 96 Stat. 1955, Dec. 29, 1982, amending 46 U.S.C. § 688.

conveniens]."[63] Of course, this notion would appear to conflict with the entire notion of the doctrine of conflict of laws. In *Lauritzen,* the Court expressly stated that "the purpose of a conflict-of-laws doctrine is to assure that a case will be treated the same way under the appropriate law regardless of the fortuitous circumstances which often determine the forum."[64] Thus, assuming that all of the courts involved apply enlightened conflict principles, the same law should be applicable in any number of fora. Nonetheless, American courts often felt that if American law were applied by an American court, dismissal on the basis of *forum non conveniens* would be inappropriate.

Tied up in this analysis was the fear that the foreign court would not apply American law. In *Piper Aircraft Company v. Reyno,*[65] the Supreme Court expressly rejected this notion, holding that "[t]he possibility of a change in substantive law should ordinarily not be given conclusive or even substantial weight in the *forum non conveniens* inquiry."[66] This holding severely undercuts the notion that a suit cannot be dismissed in favor of a more convenient forum simply because the American court would apply American law. Following this decision, the courts have indicated that personal injury claims may be dismissed on the basis of *forum non conveniens,* even if the Jones Act is applicable.[67] Similarly, the courts have held that an American citizen has no absolute right to an American forum, and may be consigned to a foreign court under the doctrine of *forum non conveniens.*[68] Such notions would have been anathema in the early seventies.

The growing willingness of American courts to apply foreign law and to dismiss under the doctrine of *forum non conveniens* have merged in limitation of liability litigation arising out of disasters in Canadian waters. In the *Arctic Explorer,* limitation proceedings pending in the United States, the lower courts have indicated a willingness to apply foreign limitation provisions, and to use the jurisdiction granted by American procedural aspects of the limitation proceeding to require claimants to litigate their claims elsewhere.[69]

Despite these developments, there is a substantial body of scholarly opinion that would approve of the tendency at times exhibited by

---

63   *Fisher v. Agios Nicolaos V,* 628 F.2d 308, 315 (5th Cir. 1980).
64   345 U.S. at 591.
65   454 U.S. 235 (1981).
66   *Ibid.* at 247.
67   *Cruz v. Maritime Co. of the Philippines,* 702 F.2d 47 (2d Cir. 1983).
68   *Alcoa S.S. Co. v. M/V Nordic Regent,* 654 F.2d 147 (2d Cir. 1980) (en banc), cert. denied, 440 U.S. 840 (1980).
69   *In re Geophysical Services, Inc.,* S.D. Tex. C.A. No. H-81-3381, minute entry dated January 22, 1983.

American courts to seek to apply American law in all conceivable situations. The historical survey that has been put forth should be addressed in light of these theories.

The first theory that is sometimes espoused as a conflict resolution tool is Professor Leflar's "application of the better rule of law" principle.[70] This, of course, is only another way of saying that conflict of law analysis is merely analogous to statutory construction, *i.e.,* the only question is to determine whether the policy of the forum is such that forum law should be applied. Along this line, the noted conflict scholar Brainerd Currie once argued that when an American court chooses to apply foreign law "it is holding the policy, or interest of its own state inferior and preferring the policy or interest of the foreign state," "a political function of a very high order; . . . a function that should not be committed to courts in a democracy."[71] Other commentators have even been so bold as to put this theory in terms of a "plaintiff favoring rule" which states that conflict resolution should always result in the application of the law which favors the plaintiff.[72]

The *Rhoditis-Bartholomew* line of decisions would appear to be children of this methodology. There, as we have noted, the courts viewed the conflict decision as merely one of determining whether the law of the forum, legislatively declared to be "the best" law, should be applied. The lengths that some of these decisions go to apply liberal American standards of recovery would even lead one cynically to conclude that some of these courts have adopted the "plaintiff-always-wins" approach alluded to above.

These approaches also find support in the interstate conflict of laws decisions of the United States Supreme Court. For example, the recent decision in *Allstate Insurance Company v. Hague,*[73] the Court permitted one state to apply its own laws as to stacking of uninsured motorists' coverages under Leflar's "better law approach" despite the fact that the plaintiff was a domiciliary of another state, the policies were issued in the other state, and the injury arose out of an injury in the other state.

It is perhaps presumptuous for a practitioner of the trade to take issue with such renowned legal scholars. Nevertheless, it would appear to this author that there are serious logical problems with the methodology espoused by these writers.

First, it can be said with tongue only partly in cheek that this methodology, if adopted, would put these conflict scholars out of a job,

---

70   See articles cited in Symeonides, "Maritime Conflicts of Law from the Perspective of Modern Choice of Law Methodology" (1982), 7 Mar. Lawyer 223 at 259 n. 133.

71   B. Currie, *Selected Essays on the Conflicts of Laws* 182 (1963).

72   R. Weintraub, *Commentary on the Conflict of Laws* 345-47 (2d ed. 1980).

73   449 U.S. 302 (1981).

for if the only consideration is the interest of the forum and a determination of the applicability of its laws, the whole field of conflict of laws is effectively at an end. If the interest of other nations are not to be afforded due regard, we only need studies in statutory construction, and not in private international law.

Secondly, and more seriously, the views espoused, particularly the "single plaintiff favoring rule", would appear to be the epitome of result-oriented decision-making that the rule of law is designed to prevent. If principled legal decision-making means anything, it requires that no class of litigant be given this sort of preferential treatment, and that each legal issue be judged on its merits.

This writer takes some solace in criticizing these views in the fact that the Supreme Court in recent years in maritime conflicts resolution has consistently rejected the methodology urged by these academics. *Lauritzen v. Larsen*[74] itself expressly rejected the notion that the proper analytical approach was merely one of determining the applicability of the law of the forum without due regard for the interests of other countries involved: "The purpose of a conflict-of-laws doctrine is to ensure that a case be treated in the same way under the appropriate law regardless of the fortuitous circumstances which often determine the forum."[75]

Secondly, the Supreme Court has also consistently rejected the notion that the substance of foreign law is a valid consideration in determining whether American or foreign law should be applied. In both *The Bremen*[76] and *Piper Aircraft v. Reyno,*[77] the Court ordered dismissal of actions in favor of litigation elsewhere, despite the clear implication that the result of the dismissals was to deny the plaintiffs any recovery whatsoever. The substance of the foreign laws may be relevant to determine the policies of the foreign forum, and to determine the strength of the foreign state's contacts to and interest in the transaction. However, in the absence of a showing that a foreign legal system is barbarous or completely irrational, which American courts have generally been reluctant to find,[78] the fact that another country has chosen to resolve a particular dispute in a different way should be simply of no consequence in the determination of applicable law.

Reliance on the interstate jurisprudence is also questionable. The decisions upholding a state's application of forum law under "better rule

---

74   *Supra* at note 29.
75   *Ibid.* at 591.
76   *Supra* at note 55.
77   *Supra* at note 65.
78   See, e.g., *Allianz Versicherungs–Aktiengesellschaft Munich Reinsurance Co. v. S.S. Eskisehir,* 353 F. Supp. 84 (S.D.N.Y. 1972).

of law" theories and the like are more accurately attributed to an aberration in American law whereby conflict of laws decisions are relegated to the states, rather than determined as a matter of federal law.[79] Thus, decisions such as *Hague*[80] stand for the proposition that these theories are constitutionally acceptable in a federal system, but not that they are the Supreme Court's conflict theories of choice. Only in *Rhoditis*[81] has the Supreme Court suggested in recent years that international maritime conflict of laws decisions can be made without giving full regard to principles of international law, and the other decisions show a strong internationalist approach.

This writer is firmly of the opinion that a trend towards careful analytical study of which country has the greater interest in providing substantive rules of decision, and in determining which is the most convenient forum, is to be welcomed. The demise of a "best law" approach that determines the answers to conflict questions by a predetermined notion of which party should win a lawsuit is to be heralded. In view of recent developments, it would appear, at least for the present, that American courts will approach these issues with an open and inquiring mind, eschewing mechanical solutions and embracing the internationalist approach that has traditionally characterized the development of the maritime law.

---

79   *Klaxon Co. v. Stentor Electric Mfg. Co.*, 313 U.S. 487 (1941).

80   *Supra* note 73.

81   *Supra* note 46.

ONE IF BY LAND, TWO IF BY SEA: OLD DIRECTIONS IN MARITIME LAW

*Vaughan Black**

1. INTRODUCTION

This paper examines briefly the nature of choice-of-law problems and the two main approaches which Anglo-Canadian courts take to them. Certain aspects of the heritage of maritime law give maritime courts and lawyers an advantage over their land-locked counterparts in dealing with cases with territorially-complex facts. They can use this to avoid some of the pitfalls that presently plague domestic conflicts jurisprudence. Perhaps in the process they can set a helpful example for non-maritime lawyers.

2. NATURE OF CHOICE-OF-LAW PROBLEMS

Problems in the conflict of laws come about mainly because domestic rules of law – whether stated in statutes, regulations, judicial opinions

*Assistant Professor of Law, Dalhousie University. My colleagues Chuck Arymowicz, Alastair Bisset-Johnson, David Fraser, Norman Letalik, Wade MacLauchlan and Wylie Spicer provided helpful comments on an earlier draft of this paper. Two students at the Dalhousie Law School, Caroll Daniels and Susannah Rowley, gave me useful editorial assistance. This paper also owes a special debt to the writings of Professor Moffatt Hancock and John Swan.

or simply proffered by counsel in the course of argument – are commonly phrased in terms of great generality, if not universality. That is, taken literally,[1] many rules would apply to an extremely broad class of factual occurrences. Brainerd Currie said it best:

> Lawgivers, legislative and judicial, are accustomed to speak in terms of unqualified generality. Apart from the imperatives, the words most inevitably found in rules of law are words like "all," "every," "no," "any," and "whoever." In part, perhaps, this propensity is traceable to the fact that there lurks in all of us some vestige of the superstition that laws have an inherent quality of universality, derived from their association with Justice and Right Reason.[2]

Whatever the explanation may be of the generality of lawgivers' speech, it is one of the daily tasks of law appliers to limit that language. In the course of deciding cases judges are forever finding, either expressly or implicitly, that "every" only means "some," that "all" just means "most" and so on. Even legal propositions not replete with universals present those who must apply such statements of law with the need to restrict (and sometimes extend) their ambit. Take, for example, the following provision from Ontario's *Highway Traffic Act:*

> Notwithstanding the provisions of subsection 1, the owner or driver of a motor vehicle, other than a vehicle operated in the business of carrying passengers for compensation, shall not be liable for any loss or damage resulting from bodily injury to, or the death of any person being carried in, or upon, or entering, or getting on to, or alighting from such motor vehicle.[3]

Although the section seems phrased in fairly specific terms, it, like numerous other statutory provisions, had to be limited and extended in a number of ways, many of which may not have been foreseen by the legislators who voted in its favour.[4] One of the contexts in which this

---

1   I realize that the unqualified use of the phrase "taken literally" begs a host of questions. Since John Willis wrote "Statute Interpretation in a Nutshell" (1938), 16 Can. Bar Rev. 1, it has been obvious that the mere fact that a court purports to apply the literal or plain meaning approach to a statute by no means leads to certainty of interpretation. More recently, Stanley Fish has written about the impossibility of ever directly and uncontroversially apprehending a text. See S. Fish, *Is There a Text in This Class? The Authority of Interpretive Communities* (1980), especially at pp. 303-37. For the most part this question and other similar ones will be begged throughout this paper. The details and difficulties of statutory construction are beyond the scope of this discussion.

2   Currie, "Married Women's Contracts: A Study in Conflict-of-Laws Method" (1958), 25 U. Chi. L. Rev. 227 at 230. Reprinted in B. Currie, *Selected Essays on the Conflict of Laws* (1963), p. 81.

3   R.S.O. 1937, c. 288, s. 47(2). The provision has been repealed.

4   Generally speaking, the provision was unpopular and it was the tendency of courts to constrict its scope. For an example see *Lemieux v. Bédard,* [1953] O.R. 837, [1953] 4 D.L.R. 252 (C.A.).

process of interpretation took place was the geographic one. With drivers from Ontario crossing its frontiers into other provinces and countries, and foreign drivers coming into Ontario, various courts eventually had to consider whether the provision should be applied to foreign passengers bringing suit against foreign drivers for accidents in Ontario, to passengers who were Ontario residents bringing suit against resident Ontario drivers for accidents in other countries, and so forth.[5] With a large number of possible factual permutations and little express guidance in the statute, the courts' tasks were not enviable ones and it is little wonder that decisions made in relation to this section have attracted considerable critical comment. Yet, whether the choice was simple or difficult, it had to be made.

At times, of course, the specificity of lawgivers is greater. Detailed subsections and definition provisions can simplify the task of the application of general rules, shrinking considerably the areas in which there are grounds for legitimate differences of opinion. This process can, and most commonly does, occur in relation to non-geographical problems. Sometimes, however, lawgivers foresee conflict-of-laws situations and incorporate in their propositions some measure of territorial specificity. This can limit doubt about a statute's breadth but, as with other areas of the law, the uncertainty will seldom disappear entirely. For example, s. 10(4) of Newfoundland's *Worker's Compensation Act,*[6] which was in force at the time of the Ocean Ranger disaster, reads: "Subject to this section compensation is not payable under this Part where an accident to a worker happens while he is employed out of Newfoundland." Speculation as to the effect of this provision on claims by workers injured on offshore oil platforms made it obvious that there was real doubt as to the subsection's applicability. However at least the argument could proceed by focussing on what Newfoundland's Legislature might have meant by the phrase "out of Newfoundland," and on whether one who signed an employment contract in St. John's to work on a rig on the Hibernia field was employed in or out of Newfoundland.[7]

---

5   In fact this particular subsection has probably given rise to more influential conflict-of-laws litigation than any other subsection in North American legislation. Among the conflicts cases that have considered s. 47(2), or one of its progeny in later versions of the Ontario *Highway Traffic Act,* are: *Lieff v. Palmer* (1937), 63 Qué. K.B. 278; *McLean v. Pettigrew,* [1945] S.C.R. 62, [1945] 2 D.L.R. 65; *Babcock v. Jackson,* 12 N.Y. 2d 473, 191 N.E. 2d 279 (1963, C.A.); *Macey v. Rozbicki,* 18 N.Y. 2d 289, 221 N.E. 2d 380 (1966, C.A.); *Neumeier v. Kuehner,* 31 N.Y. 2d 121, 286 N.E. 2d 454 (1972); and *Milkovich v. Saari,* 295 Minn. 203, N.W. 2d 408 (1973, C.A.).

6   R.S.Nfld. 1970, c. 403.

7   See, for instance, Mendes, "Newfoundland's Workers' Compensation Legislation: Constitutional and Conflict of Laws Issues Arising from Offshore Oil and Gas Exploration" (1983), 21 Alta. L. Rev. 1 at 5-11.

Quite properly, at least in Canada and the United States, this inquiry is seen as having two aspects: first, is it the purpose of the rule in question to apply to the particular (geographically-complex) factual situation before the court? An important part of this first issue may be an investigation of whether a broad application of the rule would violate some norm of public international law or offend the principle of the comity of nations; this concern may be raised to the level of a presumption against the extra-territorial application of statutes.[8] Secondly, if the rule is intended to apply to a factual situation with foreign elements, is such an application constitutional? In the case of provincial legislation this may involve an examination of the meaning of the phrase "in the province" which limits several heads of provincial legislative competence.[9]

3.   APPROACHES TO GEOGRAPHICALLY-COMPLEX CASES

In fact, however, not all cases of geographical complexity are approached in this manner by Canadian courts. Instead of the process of statutory construction just described, many such cases are handled by applying choice-of-law rules; a process which might, and sometimes does, have the effect of ignoring the purpose of underlying rules of substantive law and occasionally of threatening constitutional values as well.

At this point it might be useful to draw a distinction – familiar to conflicts lawyers – between two approaches to cases with geographically-complex facts. I shall label one the jurisdiction-selecting and the other the interpretive approach. These two approaches or methodologies are by no means unrelated and some judicial decisions are mixtures of the two, or at least display aspects of both approaches at some stage of the decision. Nevertheless, they are distinct.

---

8   "[A]n act of Congress ought never to be construed to violate the law of nations if any other possible construction remains . . .": *The Charming Betsy,* 6 U.S. (2 Cranch) 64, 118 (1804).

9   See, e.g., Edinger, "Territorial Limitations on Provincial Powers" (1982), 14 Ottawa L. Rev. 57 and, in the context of the example in the text, de Mestral, "The Law Applicable to the Canadian East-Coast Offshore" (1983), 21 Alta. L. Rev. 63. A similar question arises when courts have to consider the territorial reach of legislation of American states, though there the constitutional limitations are different. For a comparison of Canadian and American approaches here, see Hertz, "The Constitution and the Conflict of Laws: Approaches in Canadian and American Law" (1977), 27 U. Tor. L.J. 1.

(a) Jurisdiction-Selecting Approach

The jurisdiction-selecting[10] approach to choice-of-law problems proceeds by characterizing the situation before the court as, for example, a contracts case, a torts problem or a succession case, and then selecting the choice-of-law rule which governs that class of decision. The choice-of-law rules typically proffer one or more connecting factors (for example, domicile of the deceased) for the court to fill in with the appropriate findings of fact which will then point to the domestic laws of a given jurisdiction as the rules which should properly apply to the dispute. Once the jurisdiction is selected, the conflicts aspect of the case drops away and is forgotten. The matter then normally proceeds as though all factual occurrences took place with the jurisdiction whose domestic law has been chosen. "Private International Law, whatever its underlying purpose, has no material content. It does not offer any immediate solution for a particular dispute but operates indirectly. It only indicates the legal system which is to provide the rules to be applied in determining the particular issue."[11]

Theoretically the interposition of jurisdiction-selecting rules between the facts of the dispute and the actual rules of decision means that the choice-of-law decision is made "blind." The content of the competing substantive rules is not made known to the court. In Professor Castel's words:

> The relevant conflicts rule of the forum enables the court to select the law of a particular country or jurisdiction applicable to that legal category or issue without first having to ascertain how that law would decide the case. The jurisdiction-selecting choice of law rule makes a state or country the object of the choice. It does not consider the contents of the applicable law.[12]

---

10   David Cavers coined the term. See Cavers, "A Critique of the Choice-of-Law Problem" (1933), 47 Harv. L. Rev. 173 at 193. In *The Choice-of-Law Process* (1965), p. 9, note 24, Cavers summarizes what he meant by the phrase: "The jurisdiction-selecting rule makes a *state* the object of choice, in theory it is only after the rule has selected the governing state by reference to the 'contact' prescribed in the rule that the court ascertains the content of the state's law."

11   K. Lipstein, *Principles of the Conflict of Law, National and International* (1981), p. 2. It will be noted that this permits choice-of-law rules to be phrased with the same generality (the choice-of-law rule for torts applies to all conflicts/tort cases, no matter what the tort) as substantive rules of decision are. They can consequently seek to attain the same sort of appeal derived from transcendant grounding that inheres in broadly-phrased domestic rules. Of course sometimes legal disputes have a number of facets and different choice-of-law rules may apply to different aspects of the same case, a process known to conflicts lawyers as *dépeçage*. I do not believe the existence of *dépeçage* undermines any of the observations in this paper.

12   J.-G. Castel, *Canadian Conflicts of Law*, (1975), Vol. II, p. 14.

In actual fact, of course, this is not the way it works at all, because the contents of the competing rules of decision are normally included in the parties' pleadings. Moreover it is not the way it is meant to work. A more realistic description of the entire process is again found in the writings of one of its most enthusiastic adherents, Professor Castel:

> To say that the courts choose a law without considering how that choice will affect the controversy is not accurate. The lawyer representing one side or the other in a case characterizes ... the problem in such a way that it will, by virtue of the relevant conflict of law rules, ultimately call for the application of a law supporting his client's contention. Obviously he has examined the contents of the potentially applicable laws before presenting his characterization to the court. Similarly, before endorsing this characterization and applying the law which it calls for, the court will examine the contents of all the potentially applicable laws. If the court feels that it would lead to an unjust result to apply the law called for by the suggested characterization, it will reject such characterization, or use other techniques such as *renvoi,* public policy, and so on in order to apply a different law and reach a different result. As will be noted, characterization is not a purely mechanical process. If more than one characterization is available for a set of facts, the choice between the characterizations may turn upon the court's desire to achieve justice in the particular case or preference for one rule of law over another.
>
> Under the traditional approach the court is able to concern itself with the contents of the foreign laws among which it has to choose and of the policies behind them before selecting the one state whose law will be applied, even though the court does not phrase its opinion in those terms.[13]

It is an understatement to say that "characterization is not a purely mechanical process"; it is in fact barely principled at all.[14] Nevertheless I will defer criticism of the jurisdiction-selecting method here, pausing only to leave Karl Llewellyn with the final word once again: "Covert tools are never reliable tools."[15]

(b) Interpretive Approach

In clear contrast to the jurisdiction-selecting method, interpretive approaches to the conflict of laws face directly the difficulties posed by cases with territorially-complex facts. A court taking an interpretive route tries to resolve a conflicts problem by ascertaining the purposes of the competing local laws and applying the law which most appropriately

---

13   J.-G. Castel, *Conflict of Laws: Cases, Notes and Materials* (5th ed., 1984), p. 1-15.
14   For an example of the difficulties that can be posed by the need to characterize a geographically-complex problem before finding the law applicable to it, see *Sayers v. Internat. Drilling Co. N.V.,* [1971] W.L.R. 1176, [1971] 3 All E.R. 163 (C.A.). There the court grappled with the problem of whether a suit brought by an injured oil platform worker who had an exemption clause in his employment contract required the court to look to the choice-of-law rule for tort cases or for contract cases.
15   Llewellyn, "Book Review," (1939), 52 Harv. L. Rev. 700 at 703. Most criticisms of jurisdiction-selecting approaches are essentially elaborations of this insight.

governs the fact situation or transaction in question. One of the advantages of such a procedure is that problems of characterization disappear. Since the approach is the same whether the suit is classified as a contracts case, a torts case or whatever, results will not depend on what label is assigned to a given action.[16] Just as there is disagreement among adherents of the jurisdiction-selecting approach as to what the best choice-of-law rules are, there is no unanimity among interpretivists as to the best method for discovering and resolving competing local policies. David Cavers has his "principles of preference"[17], and Brainerd Currie his governmental interest analysis.[18] Arthur von Mehren and Donald Trautman believe that Currie's approach errs in focussing only on domestic policies and ignoring multi-state policies derived from the existence of a community of concerned jurisdictions.[19] The *American Restatement (Second) of Conflict of Laws* (1971) makes an effort to take into account all of the above and more.[20]

(c) Present Status of Approaches

Debates among these approaches and others are the main preoccupation of current American conflicts jurisprudence, but it is not my purpose here to join that important and difficult discussion. I wish instead to assess the present status of jurisdiction-selecting and interpretive approaches to choice of law in Canada and to argue for the usefulness of an interpretive approach, at least for maritime conflicts of law.

---

16   E.g., in *Brodin v. A/R Seljan,* 1973 S.L.T. 198, the Court of Session considered a case which was very similar to *Sayers v. Internat. Drilling Co. N.V., supra* note 14. The Scottish court proceeded in an essentially interpretivist manner and avoided lengthy disputes as to whether the choice-of-law rule for torts cases or for contracts cases should govern.

17   D. Cavers, *The Choice-of-Law Process* (1965).

18   B. Currie, *supra* note 2.

19   A. Von Mehren and D. Trautman, *The Law of Multistate Problems* (1965), pp. 76-9 and 406-8.

20   Section 6(2) of the *Second Restatement* sets out the factors deemed normally relevant to the choice of the applicable rule of law. They are: (a) the needs of the interstate and international system, (b) the relevant policies of the forum, (c) the relevant policies of other interested states and the relative interests of those states in the determination of the particular issue, (d) the protection of justified expectations, (e) the basic policies underlying the particular field of law, (f) certainty, predictability and uniformity of result, and (g) ease in the determination and application of the law to be applied. These principles are to be applied in the light of factual contacts (such as the place of the injury and the residence of the parties) to point to the appropriate local law. The *Second Restatement* makes everything relevant but gives courts little guidance on how to weigh conflicting and competing factors.

Although a brief look at the reported cases would indicate that jurisdiction-selecting methodology is the dominant one in Anglo-Canadian courts, interpretive-style decisions are not unknown. A description of two cases will serve to provide examples of both approaches and to give some sense of the relationship between them.

In *The Assunzione*,[21] the English Court of Appeal faced the task of deciding which law was applicable to a claim by cargo owners against the owners of a ship. The action was for damage to, and short delivery of, a shipment of wheat. The competing laws were those of France and Italy, but the report of the case gives no indication as to the relevant difference between them. We can only presume that, since the plaintiffs argued for the applicability of French law, it favoured them, and that Italian law benefitted the defendants in this dispute. The court first characterized the case as sounding in contract and then set off in search of the proper law of the contract; the law which the parties intended to apply. Since no express choice-of-law clause was to be found, the court had to gather the parties' presumed intentions from the whole of the facts. The circumstances which Singleton L.J. thought relevant were that the ship was an Italian one owned by two Italians, it flew an Italian flag, the master was an Italian, the cargo was to be discharged at an Italian port, the currency of payment was the lira and the bills of lading were endorsed by Italian consignees before the ship's arrival in Venice.[22] Supporting the plaintiffs' argument in favour of the applicability of French law were the facts that the charterparty was made and the bills of lading were issued there; furthermore the charterers were a French organization, the bills of lading were in the French language and the goods in question were shipped from a French port.[23] Singleton L.J. thought that the form and place of payment were very important factors in a case of this sort and concluded: ". . . the scale comes down in favour of the application of Italian law."[24]

The approach has the advantage of appearing on its face to be a rational choice between competing legal rules, free from bias in favour of the law of the forum and connected with the real issues in dispute. Since we never learn the content of the competing laws there is no way to evaluate the result in *The Assunzione* as either just or unjust, unless we are prepared to assume that following this procedure will always yield a just result.

In contrast to this jurisdiction-selecting handling of a geographically-complex contracts dispute, there is the interpretive approach

---

21   [1954] P. 150, [1954] 1 All E.R. 278 (C.A.).
22   *Ibid.* at 177-8 (P.), 291 (All E.R.).
23   *Ibid.* at 176 (P.), 290 (All E.R.).
24   *Ibid.* at 179 (P.), 292 (All E.R.).

displayed in *Harold Meyers Travel Service v. Magid.*[25] There the plaintiff sued in an Ontario court to recover money alleged to be owing to it by virtue of its having paid the defendant's gambling debts in the Bahamas, where gambling was legal. The defendant pleaded the provisions of Ontario's *Gaming Act*[26] which barred suits to recover such debts. A jurisdiction-selecting approach would have required the court to characterize the case (presumably as a contracts dispute), repeat the appropriate choice-of-law rule (the proper law of the contract, ascertained by finding the jurisdiction with which the contract had its closest and most real connection) and tote up the various connecting factors to arrive at the answer. On the Ontario side of the scale we would have the residence of the plaintiff and of the defendant, the place of the formation of the relationship between the two and the place of the making of the promissory note at issue in the suit. On the Bahamian arm of the balance we would find the place where the underlying gambling debt arose. However, instead of engaging in such a process, the court proceeded to investigate the Ontario legislation pleaded by the defendant. It looked at a number of non-conflicts decisions under the statute and its predecessors, and came to the conclusion that the provision relied on by the defendant did ". . . not catch such contracts or agreements made abroad where gambling is legally permissible."[27]

It is not easy to account for the difference between the approach in *The Assunzione* and that in *Harold Meyers*. It may be argued that they are different sorts of cases and call for different approaches, but it is not quite clear how this is so. Each is a dispute over a contract with factual matters arising in more than one jurisdiction. Either case could have been dealt with by the manner employed in the other. Moreover, neither court even addressed the issue of the appropriate approach to the case at hand. Both simply charged straight ahead.

In any event it is clear from the reported cases that the jurisdiction-selecting approach to choice-of-law problems is presently the more common one in current Anglo-Canadian courts. The curious co-existence between it and the interpretive approach may be made easier by the fact that cases like *Harold Meyers* are not always recognized as conflict-of-laws cases. (In neither of the reports in which *Harold Meyers* appears is it indexed as a conflict-of-laws case. It is simply labelled as a contracts case.) I want to suggest that, in spite of the example of *The Assunzione*, interpretive approaches to choice-of-law have life in courts hearing

---

25   (1975), 9 O.R. (2d) 200, 60 D.L.R. (3d) 42 (H.C.), affirmed 16 O.R. (2d) 1, 77 D.L.R. (3d) 32 (C.A.).

26   R.S.O. 1970, c. 187 [now R.S.O. 1980, c. 183].

27   *Supra* note 25 at p. 215 (O.R.), p. 57 (D.L.R.).

maritime disputes and that maritime lawyers would do well to foster such approaches, if only because they would lead to greater rationality and predictability in choice-of-law cases.

4. HISTORY OF INTERPRETIVE APPROACH

In spite of the fact that interpretive methodologies do not dominate current Anglo-Canadian approaches to choice-of-law issues, an argument on their behalf in the area of maritime law is not as radical as it might appear. Although the list of interpretivists cited above[28] could give the impression that this approach to conflicts problems is a modern phenomenon – a product of the recent American choice-of-law revolution – that is not the case at all. The 12th-century Italian glossators, whose work represents the true birth of the conflict of laws as we know it,[29] began with interpretive approaches, such as applying the better local law or searching the text of competing local statutes to determine their true reach. Policy-based methods actually pre-date jurisdiction-selecting rules.[30]

More importantly for the purposes here, interpretive methods have played a significant role in the development of conflicts jurisprudence in English Admiralty Courts. It is well known that the conflict of laws was a late-developing area in the common law. Due to England's unitary legal system, intra-national conflicts cases seldom arose there,[31] and, because for a long time the common-law courts would not entertain cases arising outside England, they did not develop a method for dealing with conflicts between English and foreign laws. The exceptions to this were the admiralty and commercial law judges who, in their special courts, heard cases which might have arisen beyond England's shores. In so doing they purported neither to apply the common law of England nor to choose the appropriate law by means of choice-of-law rules (which were being developed on the continent). They applied instead a species of *ius gentium* or general law of nations. In the case of the admiralty judges this was the general maritime law and in the case of the mercantile courts, the law merchant or *lex mercatoria*. Whether or not these bodies of law truly had a widely-shared, supra-national character is less important for our

---

28   See notes 14, 15, and 16.

29   Juenger, "A Page of History" (1984), 35 Mercer L. Rev. 419 at 427.

30   Y. Loussouarn and P. Bourel, *Droit international privé* (1978), pp. 117-9 and 126.

31   The personal union of England and Scotland which accompanied the 1603 accession of James I to the English throne precipitated some conflict-of-laws cases. *Calvin's Case* (1608), 7 Co. Rep. la, 77 E.R. 377 (Ex. Ch.) was an English/Scottish dispute and may well have been the first conflict-of-laws case heard by an English court. These English/Scottish cases were not numerous and appear to have had little important effect on English jurisprudence.

purposes than the fact that the English courts just mentioned thought, or at least behaved, as if they did. For if that were the case then this generally-applicable, transcendent law obviated the need for choice-of-law rules. The substantive rules of decision had a spatial reach that was theoretically infinite (because they were based on natural reason) so they applied directly.

The persistence of this notion of a general maritime law had crucial consequences for the development of maritime choice-of-law. The rise of nationalism eventually destroyed these cosmopolitan systems of law. In the case of the law merchant, the notion of a supra-national law did not persist into the 19th century. After the English common-law courts, under the leadership of Lord Mansfield, absorbed the law merchant into the common law of England in the 18th century,[32] it soon became clear that the mercantile law applied in English courts was different from that applied in French ones. English statutes affecting commercial matters accentuated this difference, since broadly-shared commercial custom could no longer be appealed to as the sole source of authority. The common-law courts developed the capacity to try disputes which had arisen outside of England and, faced with their first real choice-of-law problems, responded by employing jurisdiction-selecting rules; borrowing those already developed in continental (mainly Dutch) jurisdictions.[33]

The Admiralty Court, on the other hand, remained separate from the common-law courts throughout most of the 19th century and was free to preserve the notion of a *ius gentium* – the general maritime law. Choice-of-law rules did not appear to be required. Nevertheless, with an increasing number of English statutes which bore on maritime matters, the Admiralty Court was faced with what were, in fact, choice-of-law problems. If matters arising on the high seas were brought before the Admiralty Court and there was English legislation which (at least in general terms) appeared to apply to the dispute, true conflicts issues might be presented if, for instance, the parties to the dispute were foreign owners of foreign ships. Should the governing law be the general law of nations or should it be that law as modified by English statutes? It is clear

---

32 See W. Holdsworth, *A History of English Law* (1938), XII. pp. 524-36 and L. Trakman, *The Law Merchant: The Evolution of Commercial Law* (1983), pp. 27-33.

33 The best account of the reception in England of continental choice-of-law maxims is in the introduction to Westlake's *Private International Law*. See J. Westlake, *A Treatise on Private International Law* (7th ed., Bentwich ed.) pp. 19-22. Its account of how "[i]mperfect acquaintance with the continental literature of the subject" (p. 20) and the unfortunate combination of civil law rules and English *stare decisis* got modern English private international law off on the wrong track explains in part why jurisdiction-selecting rules have not served Anglo-Canadian courts well (or vice versa).

that this could be a difficult question and equally clear that choice-of-law rules – at least of the sort which had been developed on the continent – were ill-suited to handle it. It was not much use saying, for example, that the law of the place of the wrong governed, for even if the place of the wrong was the high seas (which might appear to dictate the applicability of the general maritime law), it was obvious that some of the English legislation in question purported to affect matters arising on the high seas. Some method of choosing between competing substantive rules of decision was required. The Court of Admiralty in the 19th century responded to this matter in what we would today call an interpretive manner. It sought to find out whether it was the intent of Parliament to have its legislation apply to cases which might arise on the high seas and which might involve foreign vessels. It did this by the familiar practice of construing the English statute in question, probing it to find its true purpose.

We can see the continued use of the interpretive approach in actions brought for collisions at sea before the English Court of Admiralty in the last century. Traditionally, the applicable law in such cases was the general maritime law as understood in the British courts. Parliament's enactment of legislation to limit the liability of shipowners for damage done by their ships confronted the Admiralty Court with the question of the territorial scope of such legislation. The first general limitation statute, the Act of 53 Geo. 3[34] contained no express statements as to its geographical scope. It did not on its face confine its applicability to any particular class of ships, nationality of owner, flag of the plaintiff ship, place of accident or place of forum. All this was left to judicial determination.

The Carl Johan,[35] a case arising shortly after the statute's enactment, gave Lord Stowell the opportunity to set the tone of choice-of-law decisions under it. The case concerned the liability of the owners of a Swedish vessel which had negligently run down an English ship off the coast of Norfolk. Lord Stowell remarked that

> . . . anciently the owners were, under the general law, civilly answerable for the total loss occasioned by the negligence or unskilfullness of the persons they employed; but the avowed purpose of the relaxation of this rule of law, was to protect the interests of those engaged in the mercantile shipping of the state, and to remove the terrors which would otherwise discourage people from embarking in the maritime commerce of a

---

34   An Act to Limit the Responsibility of Ship Owners, in Certain Cases, 1813. c. 159.

35   (1821). The case is not reported but is cited in argument in *The Dundee* (1823), 1 Hagg. 109, 166 E.R. 39 (Adm.) and in the judgment in *The Girolamo* (1834). 3 Hagg. 169, 166 E.R. 368 (Adm.). A more extended analysis of *The Carl Johan* and the following 19th-century cases can be found in G. Sundström. *Foreign Ships and Foreign Waters* (1971), pp. 36-57.

country, in consequence of the indefinite responsibility which the ancient rule attached upon them. It was a measure evidently of policy, and established by countries for the encouragement of their own maritime interests.[36]

Lord Stowell held that the English statute was intended to apply to British ships, but not to foreign ships or foreign owners. However, he went on to say that it might have been possible to apply a liability-limiting rule if both England and Sweden had adopted similar ones. He therefore held the owners liable to make good the full amount of the damage.

No single connecting factor or group of connecting factors was found to point abstractly to a given body of law (in this case either the general maritime law or the general maritime law as modified by English statute). Rather, the contending rules were analyzed in light of their purposes and the intent of Parliament was ascertained and implemented.

Between the decision in *The Carl Johan* and the *Merchant Shipping Amendment Act, 1862*,[37] when the British Parliament began expressly to spell out the scope of its liability limitation provisions, there arose a series of cases which addressed many of the factual permutations which might arise under liability limitation provisions. The reversals and elaborations in which the Admiralty Court engaged reveal a pattern of statutory interpretation which is not remarkable for its consistency. Indeed a perusal of the cases may remind some readers of the struggles of the New York courts applying Brainerd Currie's interest analysis to guest passenger statutes in automobile collision cases.[38] But the method of attack throughout is to divine the purpose of the competing rules of law and to apply to the case at hand the rule that Parliament intended to govern.

Cope v. Doherty,[39] an 1858 case of a collision on the high seas between two American ships, with the owners of the negligent vessel

---

36   1 Hagg. 109 at 113, 166 E.R. 39 at 41.

37   25 & 26 Vict., c. 63. Section 54 of that Act expressly stated that it applied to "the owners of any ship, whether British or foreign."

38   The series of New York cases dealing with guest passenger statutes is well known to students of the conflict of laws, mainly for the erratic explanations offered by the courts as the rationale of such legislation. Five decisions of New York Court of Appeals – *Babcock v. Jackson,* 12 N.Y. 2d 473, 191 N.E. 2d 279 (1963, C.A.); *Dym v. Gordon,* 16 N.Y. 2d 120, 209 N.E. 2d 792 (1965, C.A.); *Macey v. Rozbicki,* N.E. 2d 394 (1969, C.A.); *Tooker v. Lopez,* 24 N.Y. 2d 569, N.E. 2d 394 (1969, C.A.); and *Neumeier v. Kuehner,* 31 N.Y. 2d 121, 286 N.E. 2d 454 (1972, C.A.) – as well as a number of lower court cases comprise this series. They have been discussed many times but perhaps the most comprehensive analysis is that of Korn, "The Choice-of-Law Revolution: A Critique" (1983), 83 Colum. L. Rev. 72.

39   27 L.J. Ch. 600, 6 W.R. 695. Citations are from the former report.

seeking to limit their liability before the English courts under s. 514 of the *Merchant Shipping Act,* 1854,[40] was treated from start to finish as a case of statutory construction. Since both the law of the flag of both vessels and the law of the forum had statutory provisions limiting liability, one might have thought that the words of Lord Stowell in *The Carl Johan* would have argued convincingly in favour of some measure of limitation. Yet that was not the result. At trial Wood V.C. spoke at length about principles of statutory interpretation – about the ability of the court to look at the words of the relevant section, at the preamble to the statute, at the circumstances attending the passing of the Act and at the entire purport and scope of the statute in order to find the intention of the legislature. In a case of this sort, Wood V.C. thought that this process required the court to consider not only the purpose of the statute but whether the British Parliament would have the right to restrict the applicability of the general maritime law of foreign shipowners.[41] The results of his inquiry led him to distinguish *The Carl Johan,* and to find in the 1854 statute "a strong indication of what the intention of the legislature was in laying down rules for the restriction of damages, *viz.,* that it should be applicable to British shipping and to British shipping only."[42] By this he meant that it would apply, at least in cases of collisions on the high seas, only to collisions between two British vessels.

The decision was upheld on appeal[43] where both Knight Bruce and Turner LL.J. treated the issue as a matter of finding the necessary geographical limits to the general words of the statute. Knight Bruce L.J. reserved consideration of the proper result in the case of a high seas collision between a British and a foreign ship.

Two years after *Cope v. Doherty,* such a case as was reserved by Knight Bruce L.J. came before Wood V.C. in *Gen. Iron Screw Collier Co. v. Schurmanns,*[44] with the owners of the negligent English ship seeking to limit their liability to the owners of the Belgian ship which had been totally lost in a collision two-and-a-half miles off the English coast. The court again viewed the question as a matter of statutory construction. Its judgment is as pure an example of interest analysis as Brainerd Currie could have wished to see. The court examined the type of statute in question and found their purpose to be as follows: "They are for the advancement of British shipping; for the security and promotion of the

---

40   17 & 18 Vict., c. 104.
41   *Supra* note 39, p. 602 (L.J. Ch.). This parallels the concern with constitutional concerns mentioned in the text at note 9, *supra.*
42   *Supra* note 39, at p. 606.
43   *Supra* note 39, at p. 607.
44   (1860), 29 L.J. Ch. 877, 1 John. 8 H. 180, 70 E.R. 712, 8 W.R. 732.

commerce of this country, by encouraging British shipping in every possible way."[45]

The court then found that not to apply the Act in the case where a British vessel sought to limit its liability to a foreign one for a collision near the English coast would be, considering the enormous coasting trade of England, a most unreasonable construction of the Act. And, since the common law of nations – the rules of public international law – permitted national legislation to operate to a distance of three miles from a country's shore, there could be no objection to the *Merchant Shipping Act's* governing this case.

Two years later, in *The Wild Ranger*,[46] Dr. Lushington had occasion to consider the same statute's applicability. The owner of an American ship, which was entitled to a limitation of liability by American law, sought to avail himself of the limitations provisions of the English Act to curtail his liability before the English courts for a collision on the high seas with an English ship. The American owner argued that, if the English ship had been at fault, its owners would have been entitled to limit their liability before the English courts. To fail to extend him the same right would be inequitable. Dr. Lushington was not prepared to express an opinion on the proper result in the factual variation posed by the American owner but found that in the case before him the statute did not apply to foreign ships on the high seas.[47]

Judicial consideration of this statutory provision was curtailed before English courts had the opportunity to consider the factual variant proposed in *The Wild Ranger* when Parliament enacted s. 54 of the *Merchant Shipping Amendment Act, 1862*.[48] This legislation replaced the general words in the earlier Act's limitation provision with the words "the owners of any ship, whether British or Foreign." The amendment thus provided that foreign shipowners might avail themselves of the limitation provisions. The statute was passed just in time, for the following year in the case of *The Amalia*,[49] the Privy Council was faced with a case in which British shipowners, whose ship was at fault in a collision with a Belgian ship in the Mediterranean Sea, sought to limit their liability before the English courts. The owners of the lost Belgian vessel argued that Parliament had no power to restrict the natural rights of foreigners in respect of matters occurring outside British territory and that, in order to give the statute its intended meaning, some limiting words would have to be implied. However, the Privy Council could see

---

45   *Ibid.,* at 880 (L.J. Ch.).
46   (1862), Lush. 553, 7 L.T. 725, 167 E.R. 249 (Adm.).
47   *Ibid.* at 565 (Lush.), 256 (E.R.).
48   *Supra* note 37.
49   *Cail v. Papayanni; The Amalia* (1863), 1 Moo. P.C. (N.S.) 471, 15 E.R. 778.

no reason for such a restrictive interpretation and construed the statute so as to apply to all collisions on the high seas proper.

Other instances of the Admiralty Court's handling of conflicts issues could be given, but these examples are representative of its approach, at least in the last century. The actual interpretive stance taken was unfortunate at times. It was generally very unilateralist in nature, refusing to enter upon an inquiry of the purpose of competing foreign statutes and failing to take account of multi-state concerns. Yet, whatever its deficiencies, the Admiralty Court's understanding of its task in these cases – a choice between an over-arching general law of nations and the statute law of England – generally sheltered it from the need to adopt, or even consider, continental choice-of-law rules.

The 1873 consolidation of the High Court of Admiralty with the other courts of England to form the Supreme Court of Judicature made it more difficult for admiralty judges to preserve their distinct approach to conflicts matters. Causes of a maritime nature were thereafter heard in the Probate, Divorce, and Admiralty Division. The concept of a general maritime law of nations underwent the same sort of change that the law merchant did when it was absorbed by the common-law courts a century earlier; it blurred and essentially disappeared. For judges faced with cases with geographically-complex facts, this meant a choice between the domestic rules of nation states and, since by this time the common law had developed choice-of-law rules to deal with such matters, those rules began to be applied in maritime disputes, displacing or obscuring the interpretive approach.

5.   CURRENT CONFLICT-OF-LAWS PROBLEMS

The interpretivist heritage of Admiralty conflicts jurisprudence has not disappeared altogether however. Many of the old cases are still "good law". In fact there is great uncertainty as to how to approach maritime choice-of-law matters today, mainly because of the existence of essentially incompatible methods: the interpretive approach which is the heritage of 19th century courts and the overlay of jurisdiction-selecting rules.

I wish to take two specific examples of current conflict-of-laws problems – contractual choice-of-law clauses and personal injury actions – and to suggest that the best way forward for maritime courts and lawyers faced with territorially-complex cases is to go back to the interpretive manner of analysis commonly employed in the last century.

(a)   Contractual Choice-of-Law Problems

Decisions dealing with choice-of-law and choice-of-forum clauses in contracts are an area in which the split between courts following the jurisdiction-selecting and the interpretive approaches to conflicts matters is evident. The *locus classicus* in Anglo-Canadian law has been, at least until recently, the decision of the Privy Council in *Vita Food Products Inc. v. Unus Shipping Co.*[50] In delivering the unanimous judgment of their Lordships, Lord Wright wrote the words that were to become the touchstone for numerous later decisions concerning choice-of-law clauses. He said that the parties' choice of the applicable law would be upheld

> ... where there is an express statement by the parties of their intention to select the law of the contract ... provided the intention expressed is *bona fide* and legal, and provided there is no reason for avoiding the choice on the ground of public policy.[51]

The decision is a curious one because it concerned a choice-of-law clause in a bill of lading covering goods shipped from Newfoundland, and the dispute concerned the parties' ability to contract out of the limitations of liability spelled out in the Newfoundland *Carriage of Goods by Sea Act.*[52] Section 1 of that Act stipulated that the rules in question should have effect in relation to and in connection with the carriage of goods by sea in ships carrying goods from any port in Newfoundland. The statute also provided that every bill of lading should contain express statements that the bill should be subject to the liability rules set out in the Act. The bill of lading in question contained no such statement but did have a choice-of-law clause in favour of English law, which by statute had exactly the same mandatory liability rules as did Newfoundland (The Hague Rules). It is obvious then that, whether or not the Privy Council could be persuaded to give effect to the choice-of-law clause, the result would be the same.[53] Nevertheless, Lord Wright made the statement above, and lower courts have been struggling with it ever since, trying to give meaningful content to the terms "legal" and "public policy."

The Privy Council would have done much better simply to interpret the Newfoundland statute before it and apply it to the facts. Had it done so, it could not have failed to see that Newfoundland's *Carriage of Goods by Sea Act* was mandatory in nature. Parties could not contract out of its standard liability provisions directly and the court would never have allowed them to choose another law if that law had been of a

---

50   [1939] 2 D.L.R. 1, [1939] A.C. 277, [1939] 1 W.W.R. 433, 48 C.R.C. 262.

51   *Ibid.* at 8 (D.L.R.), 290 (A.C.), 440-1 (W.W.R.), 270 (C.R.C.).

52   S.Nfld. 1932, c. 18.

53   The owners of the goods wanted to avoid the effect of both England's and Newfoundland's limitations of the carrier's liability by contending that, since the bill in question did not expressly state that it was subject to the statutory provisions, the contract was illegal and the carrier was fully liable for its negligence. This is nonsense and the courts held against the owners of the goods at every level.

jurisdiction which did not, like England and Newfoundland, subscribe to the Hague Rules. It might be argued that, if the parties had in fact stipulated for the law of such a nation, the court could have disallowed the choice by finding that it was not *bona fide* or legal or that it was against public policy. But if that would be the result, there would be no reason to pretend that the court was ever truly allowing the parties to choose their own law or their own allocation of risk.

In fact the terms *"bona fide"* and "legal" have not, in later cases applying *Vita Foods,* been applied so as to reach results consistent with any interpretive approach to choice-of-law problems. As a consequence, contracting parties have been permitted to evade quite improperly the application of rules which legislatures intended to apply to them. Incorrect results have been reached by assuming that a jurisdiction-selecting approach to contracts cases can provide justice.

There is evidence in some recent maritime choice-of-law decisions in this area of a return to an interpretive approach. Before examining them, however, it may be useful to look at a typical example of Lord Wright's *Vita Foods* formula to choice-of-law clauses in contracts. In *Greenshields Inc. v. Johnston,*[54] the Alberta Court of Queen's Bench was called upon to rule on the validity of a guarantee which did not meet the formal requirements of the *Guarantees Acknowledgement Act.*[55] That statute provides that no guarantee has any effect unless the person entering into the obligation appears before a notary public, acknowledges to that official that she executed the guarantee and, in the presence of the notary, signs a statement that she is aware of the contents of the guarantee and understands it. The Act's terms are typically universal; it contains no express statements about its geographical scope. In *Greenshields,* the defendant Johnston was an Alberta resident who had signed the guarantee in question in Alberta and given it to the plaintiff there. The plaintiff was a corporation with its head office in Toronto, but it had a business office in Edmonton with which the defendant dealt. The guarantee was given to cover the liability of Johnston's company which bought and sold securities through the plaintiff's Edmonton office. However the guarantee contained a clause stating that it was to be construed in accordance with the laws of the province of Ontario, and that province had no legislation similar in effect to the *Guarantees Acknowledgment Act* of Alberta; Ontario law required only that guarantees be in writing.

The court relied on Lord Wright's statement in *Vita Foods* that choice-of-law clauses would be given effect if they were *bona fide,* legal

---

54   [1981] 3 W.W.R. 313, 28 A.R. 1, 119 D.L.R. (3d) 714 (Q.B.), affirmed 17 Alta. L.R. (2d) 318, [1982] 2 W.W.R. 97, 131 D.L.R. (3d) 234, 35 A.R. 487 (C.A.).

55   R.S.A. 1970, c. 163 [now R.S.A. 1980, c. G-12].

and not against public policy. It pointed out that the transaction had a real connection with Ontario in that the plaintiff's head office was there, the orders received in Edmonton were relayed by the plaintiff to Toronto and confirmation vouchers were sent directly from Toronto to the defendant. Finding that the clause did not offend against Alberta's public policy (in the sense that it in no way was founded on moral turpitude and did not offend against Alberta's essential public or moral interest),[56] the court gave effect to the clause and held the guarantee valid, stating: "It cannot be said that this choice-of-law clause was inserted for the purpose of evading the Alberta statute."[57]

The decision is wrong, or at least wrong-headed. Irrespective of whether the clause was inserted for the *purpose* of evading the Alberta statute, the Alberta Court, in employing this jurisdiction-selecting approach, gave the clause precisely that effect. At least this is true if we can conclude that the purpose of the Alberta legislation was to protect Albertans who might otherwise be pressured or deceived into contractual arrangements, the serious consequences of which they might fail to appreciate. It is true that difficulties might arise in instances where Alberta residents gave guarantees while temporarily outside Alberta, or where non-Albertans gave non-complying guarantees while temporarily within Alberta's borders. When an Albertan gives a guarantee in Alberta, however, there can be little doubt that it is the purpose of the statute to stipulate mandatory formal requirements for its effectiveness. There should have been no uncertainty about the geographical scope of the statute and, since there were no extraterritorial connections suffi-

---

56   The court's use of the concept of public policy here is the correct one. Even if the choice-of-law process (be it interpretive or jurisdiction-selecting) points to a rule of foreign law as the proper one to decide a dispute, a domestic court may refuse to apply such a rule if to do so would offend the public policy of the forum. This use of the concept of public policy should be kept within very narrow bounds, however. It should be invoked only when the foreign rule of decision is so repugnant to domestic ideas of justice that to apply such a rule would bring the administration of justice into disrepute. The concept of public policy thus operates as a kind of trump card in favour of forum law. A court refuses to apply the indicated foreign rule for much the same reason as it might refuse to enforce an illegal contract; justice might not be done between the parties but at a certain point the court has its own reputation to consider. The area of choice-of-law clauses has been one in which some courts have been inclined to use the concept of public policy in a weaker sense. They have construed "public policy" to mean legislative intent, thus smuggling in an interpretive approach by the back door when the jurisdiction-selecting rules "point the wrong way". When used in this sense public policy appears as a sort of *deus ex machina* to sort out the failings of jurisdiction-selecting rules; but its appearance is erratic and Llewellyn's assessment of covert tools is applicable here.

57   119 D.L.R. (3d) at 722.

cient to raise constitutional infirmities, no choice-of-law clause should have been permitted to subvert the statute's policy.[58]

We might look at this question another way by wondering how the court would treat the same case if, in place of the choice-of-law clause, the guarantee in question had simply provided that the parties waived the protections of the *Guarantees Acknowledgement Act*. No court should give effect to such a clause, even if the guarantee was given in favour of a company whose head office was in Toronto. Yet in giving effect to the choice-of-law clause, the Alberta court did exactly that, allowing the parties to do indirectly what they would not have been permitted to do directly.[59]

In contrast to *Greenshields,* the recent decision in *Agro Co. of Can. Ltd. v. The "Regal Scout"*[60] shows that maritime courts, by returning to

---

58   It is of course possible to argue that the Alberta statute was not intended to apply to this situation, but that argument seems weak. If the Alberta legislature would be content to have foreign corporations enter Alberta and take effective non-complying guarantees from Albertans, then the decision is correct. A choice-of-law clause in such a guarantee might then be a useful device for the parties to make clear their intent not to be bound by the statute. Even if Alberta was concerned with subversion of its policy by choice-of-law clauses it might be possible for courts taking an interpretive approach to uphold choice-of-law clauses in certain instances. For example, if the foreign jurisdiction indicated in the contract had a rule which sought to protect unsophisticated guarantors and if that rule had been complied with, then an interpretive approach concerned with multi-state values might uphold the guarantee. In *Greenshields,* however, the only requirement of Ontario law was that guarantees be in writing and it is difficult to see how the formal requirement adequately meets the policy concerns expressed in the Alberta *Guarantees Acknowledgement Act.*

59   In fairness it should be pointed out that the defendant, Johnston, was an experienced businessman who clearly understood the effect of the guarantee he gave and was merely trying to evade the consequences of his company's unfortunate dealings, somewhat in the manner of someone trying to rely on the Statute of Frauds to avoid an oral agreement which everyone admits was made. He was not, it may be presumed, among the class of persons with whom the Alberta legislature was most concerned when it enacted the legislation in question. Yet unless the court would be prepared to reach the same result in the case of a sophisticated Alberta guarantor who gave a non-complying guarantee without a choice-of-law clause (for instance, by saying that in spite of the statute's generality of phrasing the legislature could never have meant it to apply to such guarantors) the decision in *Greenshields* is still incorrect. The court should either be prepared to hold Johnston liable or to face the issue squarely and proclaim that the Act does not protect experienced guarantors such as him. In any case *Greenshields* is not an isolated case. In *Bank of Montreal v. Snoxell* (1982), 143 D.L.R. (3d) 349, 44 A.R. 224 (Alta. Q.B.), *Greenshields* and *Vita Foods* were relied on to uphold another non-complying guarantee executed by an Albertan in Alberta. *Snoxell* is an enforcement-of-judgments case so the concerns are somewhat different, but there is no information in the report as to whether the guarantor was an experienced businessman and it may well have been that the result as well as the approach was wrong.

60   (1983), 148 D.L.R. (3d) 412 (Fed. T.D.). Hereafter, *The Regal Scout.*

an interpretive approach, have rediscovered the correct path here. In *The Regal Scout* the defendant had moved for an order staying proceedings before the Federal Court, relying heavily on a clause in a bill of lading which read:

> 3. JURISDICTION. Any dispute arising under this Bill of Lading shall be decided in the Tokyo District Court in Japan according to Japanese law, except only as otherwise agreed herein or as otherwise determined by controlling foreign law.[61]

There was no disagreement that, should the case be heard in Tokyo, Japanese substantive law would be applied and the result would be much different than if the Canadian *Carriage of Goods by Water Act*[62] governed. Noting that the statute in question was expressly made applicable to shipments of goods by water from any port in Canada[63] (as was the case here) and that bills of lading issued in connection with such shipment were expressly and mandatorily made subject to the Hague Rules, Cattanach J. refused to grant the requested stay. He noted that the application of Japanese law would have the effect of altering the limitations on liability for loss and that it was the purpose of the *Carriage of Goods by Water Act* not to permit that. That which could not be done directly should not be done with a choice-of-law clause.[64]

In some respects the judicial task in *The Regal Scout* was simpler than that in *Greenshields*. The statute before the court in the former case contained both an express delineation of its geographical scope ("carriage of goods by water in ships carrying goods from any port in Canada to any other port whether in or outside Canada")[65] and a stipulation that it was not to be contracted out of.[66] Moreover the Federal Court had before it the example set by the House of Lords in *The Morviken*.[67] That case was similar to *The Regal Scout* and, in refusing to let an express choice-of-law provision take effect, their Lordships employed what was essentially an interpretive approach. They also voiced some dissatisfaction with *Vita Foods*. The *Greenshields* court had none of that assistance.[68]

---

61   *Ibid.* at 414.
62   R.S.C. 1970, c. C-15.
63   Just as the statute in *Vita Foods* was. In *The Regal Scout* a Canadian cargo owner employed a Japanese shipper to carry goods from British Columbia to Japan.
64   The clause in question here was both a choice-of-law and a choice-of-jurisdiction clause, but it was not the inconvenience of the Japanese forum that convinced the court to refuse to stay Canadian proceedings; it was the fact that, if the case was heard in Japan, Japanese law would be applied.
65   R.S.C. 1970, c. C-15, s. 2.
66   *Ibid.,* Art. III, s. 8.
67   [1983] 1 Lloyd's Rep. 1.
68   An interpretive approach to this problem does not in the least foreclose the ability of the parties to allocate risks and form obligations by means of a choice-of-law clause.

Yet the tasks of the *Greenshields* and *The Regal Scout* courts were the same: to ascertain by the usual practice of interpretation the intended scope of the legal rule(s) in question and apply them to the case at hand. Only the court in the maritime dispute did this. There is no reason why, if a statute or other legal rule contains *some* specifications as to its intended territorial scope it should be dealt with in an interpretive manner, while if it contains *none* courts should refuse to interpret it and should interpose jurisdiction-selecting choice-of-law rules. In any event no statute could ever truly be said to be without clues as to its intended geographical scope since courts' and lawyers' general knowledge of the purpose of most statutes is quite broadly shared. Even where interpretations differ there will be bases – preambles, analogous statutes, appeals to consequences and so on – for courts and counsel to explore in the usual manner the breadth which a rule is to be accorded. Engaging in this process only where a legal rule contains some express statements of its geographical scope is comparable to a practice in a wholly domestic sphere of deciding that, if a statute contains some qualifications of its generality, its applicability in an individual case will be determined by interpretation, but that, if it is phrased entirely in general and universal terms,[69] its applicability will be judged by some set of neutral and "content-blind" rules. Not even the most formalistic application of rules of construction, such as the *ejusdem generis* rule, dictates such a practice.

(b) Personal Injury Actions

But before Canadian maritime courts and lawyers become too complacent in their superior handling of conflict-of-laws issues, they should look at a second issue in conflict of laws, one in which their casual

---

If there is an area in which parties are free to stipulate their contractual obligations without worrying about the effect of mandatory implied terms then an express contractual choice-of-law clause may add certainty to that process. With bills of lading one such area still left open to private autonomy is that of the carrier's responsibility for loss before loading and after discharge (an area frequently subject to wide exemptions on behalf of the carrier). Should the parties wish to include in their contractual provisions with respect to this risk a choice-of-law clause, then there could be no reason for not paying attention to it. Choice-of-law clauses should be given effect here because they are a kind of legal shorthand, an incorporation by reference of suppletive legal rules similar in effect to the incorporation of the rules of a trade association.

69   Admittedly it is difficult to imagine a legal rule phrased *entirely* in universal terms ("everyone is liable to everyone for everything"?). Article 1053 of Quebec's Civil Code may come as close as any: "Every person capable of discerning right from wrong is responsible for the damage caused by his fault to another, whether by positive act, imprudence, neglect or want of skill."

abandonment of the interpretive approach which is their birthright in favour of choice-of-law rules developed for non-maritime claims has caused them to stray far off the track of both predictability and justice. I am speaking of maritime torts and, in particular, personal injury claims.

The abandonment referred to here has been quite unnecessary, since a brief glance at the American model will show that courts in that country have led the way in developing an interpretive approach to such claims. The decision of the Supreme Court of the United States in *Lauritzen v. Larsen,*[70] though it has been superseded and modified by later decisions of that body, has set the tone for approaches to the judicial handling of maritime personal injury claims that pose conflict-of-laws questions. In *Lauritzen* a Danish seaman, who while temporarily in New York had joined the crew of a ship of Danish flag and registry, had been negligently injured in the course of his employment in Havana harbour. He brought an *in personam* claim against the Danish owner of the vessel in the United States. In unanimously dismissing the plaintiff's suit, the Supreme Court noted that "Denmark has enacted a comprehensive code to govern the relations of her shipowners to her seagoing labor which by its terms and intentions controls this claim"[71] and that "allowance of an additional remedy under our Jones Act would sharply conflict with the policy and letter of Danish law."[72]

The relevant provisions of the *Jones Act,*[73] the American statute dealing with maritime personal injury claims, bore no express clues as to its territorial limitations (assuming it had any). Its terms were quite universal and, if read literally, conferred an American right of action on any sailor of any nationality who should suffer personal injury in the course of his or her employment, whether or not there were any factual elements to connect the dispute to the United States. It would apply to Chinese sailors hired in Hong Kong to work on a Japanese ship, even if the injury took place on the high seas. Of course such an interpretation would appeal to an absurd idea of legislative intent. The Supreme Court's response to the whole problem was to say that it was

> ... simply dealing with a problem of statutory construction rather commonplace in a federal system by which courts often have to decide whether "any" or "every" reaches to the limits of the enacting authority's usual scope or is to be applied to foreign events or transactions.[74]

The court then set about the task of finding the geographical limit of the *Jones Act* by, among other methods, examining the statute's pre-

---

70   345 U.S. 571 (1953).
71   *Ibid.* at 575.
72   *Ibid.* at 575.
73   46 U.S.C. §688.
74   *Supra* note 70, at pp. 578-9.

decessors, noting, for instance, that the title of one of them began: "An Act to promote the welfare of American seamen in the merchant marine of the United States."

Although the *Lauritzen* case is well known for setting out a number of connecting factors for courts to evaluate when considering whether or not to permit a *Jones Act* claim to proceed in a case involving foreign elements,[75] it is most important to remember that the court said that the significance of these various connecting factors had to be weighed in the light of the national interest served by the assertion of the legal rule in question (that is, the decision could not be made "blind") and that in fact it stated that some of the factors would not normally be of much importance. Thus, although recent decisions have modified *Lauritzen* in some respects and have in fact added new connecting factors,[76] the method of determining the applicability of the *Jones Act* to geographically-complex cases remains essentially one of engaging in the practice of statutory interpretation. The approach is clearly not a jurisdiction-selecting one.

This is not the case with similar claims in Canada. Although there are uncertainties about how our courts might approach a maritime choice-of-law decision today, there is no doubt that the general choice-of-law rule in all tort claims, the rule in *Phillips v. Eyre*,[77] would play a central part in any such decision. The general and oft-repeated statement of the rule in *Phillips v. Eyre* is found in the following words of Willes J. (which do not even seem to be the *ratio* of the famous case):

> As a general rule, in order to found a suit in England for a wrong alleged to have been committed abroad, two conditions must be fulfilled. – First, the wrong must be of such a character that it would have been actionable if committed in England. . . . Secondly, the act must not have been justifiable by the law of the place where it was done.[78]

This double-barrelled rule is without parallel in other areas of the conflict of laws. We permit our courts to entertain claims in contract which would not succeed if all of the factual elements had occurred in their jurisdiction. Yet when it comes to tort claims, the plaintiff who comes to our courts with a cause of action which would entitle her to

---

75   Namely the following seven: the place of the wrongful act, the law of the flag, the allegiance or domicile of the injured person, the allegiance of the defendant shipowner, the place of the contract, the inaccessability of the foreign forum and the law of the forum.

76   The most significant alteration to *Lauritzen* is *Hellenic Lines Ltd. v. Rhoditis,* 398 U.S. 306 (1970). There the Supreme Court added a new connecting factor, the place of the shipowner's base of operations, thus increasing the number of potentially significant factors to eight. And it noted that there might be others.

77   (1870), L.R. 6 Q.B. 1, 40 L.J.Q.B. 28 (Ex. Ct.).

78   *Ibid.* at 28-9 (L.R.Q.B.), 40 (L.J.Q.B.).

relief in the courts where that cause of action arose will be turned away if the claim is not actionable here. Canadian courts have never offered a clear reason why this should be the case, and the true explanation for the bar can likely be traced to a misunderstanding of the basis of the Privy Council's decision in *The Halley*.[79] As for the advisability of allowing that decision to have any effect on modern choice-of-law decisions, I throw in my lot with the assessment made by Moffat Hancock in 1942:

> It seems incredible that because in 1868 the Privy Council refused to enforce a particular rule of Belgian law, the courts of Canadian provinces should refuse to enforce any law of a sister province which happens to differ slightly from their own. Yet this appears to be the prevailing doctrine in Canada today. One would look far to find a more striking example of "mechanical jurisprudence", blind adherence to a verbal formula without any regard for policies or consequences.[80]

Although the flexibility and ability to achieve just results which Castel claims for the traditional, jurisdiction-selecting approach would appear to have failed here, and although this failure has led at times to legal decisions which are preposterous,[81] I do not wish to enter upon a

---

79   *Liverpool, Brazil & River Plate Steam Navigation Co. v. Benham; The Halley* (1868), L.R. 2 P.C. 193, 5 Moo. P.C. N.S. 362, 16 E.R. 514. It seems likely that the Privy Council in *The Halley* refused to apply foreign law because it thought the specific foreign rule in question to be contrary to the public policy of England. It appears unlikely that their Lordships intended to decide that no rule of foreign tort law should ever be applied by an English court. For an analysis of this aspect of *The Halley*, see Yntema, "Book Review" (1949), Can. Bar Rev. 116; Kahn-Freund, "Reflections on Public Policy in the English Conflict of Laws" (1953), 39 Tr. Grot. Soc. 39; and Gerber, "Tort Liability in the Conflict of Laws" (1966), 40 Aust. L.J. 44. There is also an analysis of how the decision on *The Halley* is attributable to a misunderstanding of *dicta* in *The Amalia, supra* note 49: Hancock, "Torts Problems in Conflict of Laws Resolved by Statutory Construction: *The Halley* and Other Older Cases Revisited" (1968), 18 U. Tor. L.J. 331.

80   M. Hancock, *Torts in the Conflict of Laws* (1949), p. 89. Hancock has also commented cryptically on the second limb of the rule in *Phillips v. Eyre*, the one which requires the acts complained of to be non-justifiable by the law of the place where they were done. The Supreme Court of Canada adopted a version of this rule in *McLean v. Pettigrew*, a case involving Ontario's guest passenger rule (see note 4, *supra*). Hancock's two-sentence case comment at (1945), 23 Can. Bar Rev. 348 is among the most accurate that journal has printed: "Students of conflict of laws will no doubt be interested to note that the decision of the English Court of Appeal in *Machado v. Fontes* (1897), disapproved by judges in Scotland, Victoria, Saskatchewan and Quebec, and criticized by Beale, Cheshire, Goodrich, Pollock, Wharton, Keith, Minor and Robertson, has been followed by the Supreme Court of Canada without any discussion of the problem involved. This conclusion of the Court was supported by drawing a quite unnecessary implication from a statement made by Chief Justice Duff in a previous case and by a quotation from Dicey on Conflict of Laws." (Footnotes have been omitted.)

81   See *M'Elroy v. M'Allister*, 1949 S.C. 110, 1949 S.L.T. 139 and *Simonson v. Can. Nor. Ry.* (1914), 24 Man. R. 267, 6 W.W.R. 898, 17 D.L.R. 516, 28 W.L.R. 310 (C.A.) for examples of both inferior reasoning and brutal results.

general assessment of the rule in *Phillips v. Eyre.*[82] However its applicability in the field of maritime personal injury claims is of interest. In that context it is important to note that in both maritime and non-maritime claims the rule in *Phillips v. Eyre* has not simply been applied as a common-law choice-of-law rule for the purpose of choosing the proper, underlying common law of torts. It has been applied as well to statutory rules affecting tort claims. For instance, in the case of *O'Connor v. Wray,*[83] a leading Canadian decision on the choice-of-law rule in tort, the Supreme Court heard a claim by Ontario victims of an Ontario traffic accident against the Quebec owner of the vehicle which injured them. The Quebec car owner had not himself come into Ontario, but he had loaned his vehicle to an employee to take a weekend trip into that province. Ontario's *Highway Traffic Act*[84] provided for the vicarious liability of car owners if the driver of the car had possession of the car with the owner's consent. On the other hand Quebec law, although it provided for vicarious liability of automobile owners in certain circumstances, would not have placed liability on the defendant in this case if all of the events had taken place in Quebec. The Supreme Court of Canada made no attempt to determine the geographic scope of either Ontario or Quebec law. Although it might have entered upon an inquiry as to whether it was the purpose of the Ontario statute to impose vicarious liability on car owners who did not themselves come into the province, although their cars did, the court did not perform such a task. Nor did it inquire whether it was the purpose of the Quebec law to protect Quebec owners from liability in those instances in which they loaned their automobiles to persons whom they knew were driving into another jurisdiction.[85] No interpretive effort was made. The rule in *Phillips v. Eyre* was assumed to apply to choices between different statutes and, since the action had been brought before the Quebec courts and was not actionable there, the plaintiffs' claim foundered on the second aspect of the rule and was dismissed.

---

82   Canadian courts' supine acceptance of English choice-of-law rules in the earlier part of this century caused them to adopt the rule in *Phillips v. Eyre.* Now that this rule has been abandoned or at least favourably modified by the House of Lords (see *Chaplin v. Boys*, [1971] A.C. 356, [1969] 2 All E.R. 1085 (H.L.)) Canada remains virtually singular in clinging to it.

83   *O'Connor v. Wray; Boyd v. Wray*, [1930] S.C.R. 231, [1930] 2 D.L.R. 899.

84   S.O. 1923, c. 48.

85   If the court had found that the purpose of either statute was extra-territorial in effect, it would then have had to decide whether that proposed effect was constitutional. The constitutional question arises no matter which way the court approaches the issue, and in the jurisdiction-selecting approach which the Supreme Court actually took, the court did not in fact recognize that its decision gave the Quebec law a certain extra-territorial effect. The jurisdiction-selecting effect of *Phillips v. Eyre* masks important constitutional concerns.

One can only speculate as to how the Supreme Court would have approached the case if either of the statutes in question, instead of being phrased in the usual territorially unlimited language, had contained express clues as to its geographical reach, as does the *Carriage of Goods by Water Act.* If Ontario's *Highway Traffic Act* had expressly stated that its vicarious liability rule applied to claims arising out of all accidents within Ontario borders, would *Phillips v. Eyre* still have defeated the plaintiffs' claim? If the legislation had gone further and stated that it applied regardless of whether the owner sought to be made vicariously liable had ever entered Ontario, would the court then have perceived that its task in deciding the case was to determine the territorial scope of competing rules of law, or would *Phillips v. Eyre* still persist in dictating that the case be decided for the defendant? And if Quebec's law said that it applied only to accidents within that province, would the interpretive approach have been adopted at that point?

These questions must remain matters of pure speculation. Similar questions which could be asked about other choice-of-law decisions in non-maritime cases will also generally remain speculative, since non-maritime domestic rules of tort law, statutory and judicial, contain few expressions of their intended territorial scope. It is therefore easy and natural (though still, of course, entirely incorrect) for courts to cling to the jurisdiction-selecting approach to choice-of-law problems. But when we turn to maritime personal injury claims the matter is in some respects different, for statutes dealing with maritime matters typically foresee issues of geographical complexity and make some attempt to give express guidance as to their proper resolution.[86] For instance, s. 274 of the *Canada Shipping Act*[87] provides:

> Where in any matter relating to a ship or to a person belonging to a ship there appears to be a conflict of laws, then if there is in this Part any provision on the subject that is hereby expressly made to extend to that ship, the case shall be governed by that provision; but if there is no such provision, the case shall be governed by the law of the port at which the ship is registered.

Although certain other sections of the Part of the *Canada Shipping Act* dealing with seamen do in fact contain precise stipulations regarding geographical complexity,[88] such provisions are relatively few. Section 274 would appear to make the law of the flag relevant to most claims by

---

86 See, e.g., the discussion of the application of the express liability provisions in the *Carriage of Goods by Water Act, supra.*

87 R.S.C. 1970, c. S-9.

88 For example, there are provisions dealing with deserters from foreign ships (s. 246), the formalities of seamen's contracts entered into in other countries (s. 166) and substantive contractual matters arising relating to the engagement of seamen out of Canada (s. 181).

seamen, including those arising out of personal injury or death in the course of employment. This is confirmed by the leading decision of the Supreme Court of Canada in this area, but the way in which the court tells us to handle the section is a curious one. In *C.N. SS. Co. v. Watson,*[89] suit was brought in Quebec in respect of a personal injury to a seaman on a British-owned vessel which was registered in Vancouver. The accident had happened on the high seas on a ship destined for Charlottetown. The decision of the majority, written by Duff C.J.C., made it clear that the court thought the dispute was governed by the predecessor of the current s. 274,[90] yet it did not follow the section and apply the law of the port of registry. Instead, and quite inexplicably, the Supreme Court viewed the plaintiff's claim as being subject to the common-law choice-of-law rule in *Phillips v. Eyre.* Rather than apply the law of the port at which the ship was registered, the court assumed that, since suit was being brought at a place other than that where the tort was allegedly committed, it should proceed by first assigning a *lex loci delicti* to the case and seeing whether the claim was justifiable there. It did this by assuming that the statute in question made the place of registry into the place of the accident, and that consequently the court was faced with a tort case in which the tort took place in Vancouver and suit was brought in Quebec. Thus for the plaintiff to succeed he would have to show that the act complained of was not justifiable by the law of British Columbia and was actionable by the law of Quebec. The jurisdiction-selecting approach survived in the face of an express statutory instruction as to the applicable law in such instances.

The fruits of this approach have been described by one writer as "a legal 'Catch-22,' "[91] and when we consider the possible consequences of this approach for claims by injured offshore-drilling-platform workers, its error becomes clear. Such workers might well have no claim under provincial workers' compensation legislation, either because it is not the purpose of such legislation to apply to such claims, or because such an intended extra-territorial application is unconstitutional.[92] Nor is it

---

89   [1939] S.C.R. 11, [1939] 1 D.L.R. 273. Although just nine years separate this case from *O'Connor v. Wray,* none of the members of the court which heard that case was among those who heard the appeal in *Watson.*

90   S. 265 of the *Merchant Shipping Act,* 57 & 58 Vict., c. 60. The discussion that follows draws heavily on case comments on *Watson* by John Falconbridge in (1939), 17 Can. Bar Rev. 546 and (1940), 18 Can. Bar Rev. 308. The two comments appear in a revised and condensed form in Falconbridge's *Essays on the Conflict of Laws* (2nd ed., 1954), at pp. 823-8.

91   Mendes, *supra,* note 7, at p. 11.

92   See *Workmen's Comp. Bd. v. C.P.R.,* [1920] A.C. 184, [1919] 3 W.W.R. 167, 48 D.L.R. 218 (P.C.) for a discussion of the constitutional aspects of extra-territorial application of provincial workers' compensation statutes.

likely that drilling-platform workers would have a claim under the federal *Merchant Seamen Compensation Act,*[93] since s. 2 of that statute states that the Act only applies when the ship in question is on a foreign or home-trade voyage and it is not likely that an offshore platform is on either. What would remain then would be an action in tort in a Canadian court, and, since drilling-platform workers are seamen within the definition of that term in the Canada Shipping Act, s. 274 would apply to their claim. If, for example, the platform in question were flying the American flag, the claim could not proceed unless the acts complained of were not justifiable under American law. So far so good. But the effect of the *Watson* decision would mean that the claim would fail unless it was actionable by the law of the forum and, since Canadian provinces have workers' compensation legislation taking away injured workers' causes of action, the platform worker's claim could fail. The worker would not have a cause of action if all of the acts complained of had taken place within a Canadian province. Such a worker, who might well be a Canadian Citizen, would have no claim for monetary compensation of any sort before the courts of this country.

Such a result is absurd.[94] Whatever the merits of the argument between jurisdiction-selecting and interpretive approaches in other contexts, the Canada *Shipping Act* expressly tells us that the law of the place of registry is to govern. This should eliminate the need to haul out the rule in *Phillips v. Eyre.* If the drilling platform is registered in an American port then the law of that port – presumably the *Jones Act* – should be applied by Canadian courts. American rules of liability and of damages would apply.[95]

6. CONCLUSION

Obviously the adoption of an interpretive approach is no panacea. It is not even an answer, merely a different way of posing the question. One hopes that it is a more *useful* way to ask the question – that Currie's observation that "[w]e would be better off without choice-of-law

---

93   R.S.C. 1970, c. M-11.
94   And it is an absurdity too crucial to be buried in a footnote as does Mendes, *supra* note 7, at p. 13, fn 51. The decision of the Court of Session in *MacKinnon v. Iberia Shipping Co.,* [1954] 2 Lloyd's Rep. 372, confirms that this absurdity could become a reality. See especially the judgment of Lord Carmont.
95   I realize that there is an argument that damages are a procedural matter and should therefore always be awarded in accordance with the law of the forum, but that is largely a function of jurisdiction-selecting rules, and if a court adopts an interpretive approach it might well find that it was the purpose of the rule in question that it apply not only to liability but to remedies as well.

rules"[96] is correct – but still it does no more than permit courts and counsel to face more directly the problems posed by cases with territorially-complex fact patterns. And those problems can be tough ones. In dealing with them, the first and most important step is to realize the true consequences of an interpretive approach: there is no such thing as a choice-of-law case.[97] Not only was a case like *Harold Meyers* handled in a useful fashion, with counsel making rational arguments about the proper scope of the competing rules of decision, it was also properly indexed. It was a contracts dispute and nothing else. Under an interpretive approach there can only be contracts cases, torts cases, lien cases and so on. Some of these will have geographically-complex facts and some will not, but where a legal question arises it will always be solved by the familiar process of rule interpretation and application.

Of course when the competing rules of decision come from different jurisdictions, some new wrinkles are presented. In a purely domestic case, when opposing counsel contend for the application of different rules, the methods of judicial resolution are well known. If both rules are common-law rules, the court must decide which one properly governs the facts at hand. If one is a common-law rule and the other a constitutionally valid statute of the domestic legislature, the court must determine whether it is the purpose of the statute to govern the facts at hand. If both competing rules are local statutes, the court must again discover their purpose. If the rules lead to different results, they cannot both govern and a court must find a way to "eliminate" one of them. There are a number of familiar methods: the more specific provision prevails over the more general, the one enacted later impliedly repeals the earlier, and so on. When the rules are both constitutionally valid rules of *different* states, new techniques are needed, but they should not differ fundamentally from methods of rule application in purely domestic cases.

I will not attempt here to elaborate a comprehensive interpretive approach, but I think Currie's governmental interest analysis offers a useful way forward:

> 1. Normally, even in cases involving foreign elements, the court should be expected, as a matter of course, to apply the rule of decision found in the law of the forum.
> 2. When it is suggested that the law of a foreign state should furnish the rule of decision, the court should, first of all, determine the governmental policy expressed in the law of the forum. It should then inquire whether the relation of the forum to the

---

96   Currie, "Notes on Methods and Objectives in the Conflict of Laws," [1959] Duke L.J. 171 at 177, reprinted in B. Currie, *Selected Essays on the Conflict of Laws* (1963), p. 183.

97   Either that or all legal disputes are choice-of-law cases. It amounts to the same thing.

case is such as to provide a legitimate basis for the assertion of an interest in the application of that policy. This process is essentially the familiar one of construction or interpretation. Just as we determine by that process how a statute applies in time, and how it applies to marginal domestic situations, so we may determine how it should be applied to cases involving foreign elements in order to effectuate the legislative purpose.

3. If necessary, the court should similarly determine the policy expressed by the foreign law, and whether the foreign state has an interest in the application of its policy.

4. If the court finds that the forum state has no interest in the application of its policy, but that the foreign state has, it should apply the foreign law.

5. If the court finds that the forum state has an interest in the application of its policy, it should apply the law of the forum, even though the foreign state also has an interest in the application of its contrary policy, and, a fortiori, it should apply the law of the forum if the foreign state has no such interest.[98]

This is not a complete solution. It does not tell a court how to proceed when neither of the competing rules of decision is a rule of the forum, as was the case in *The Assunzione*. Its forum bias, while suitable for true international disputes, might be inappropriate when the competing rules are those of two Canadian provinces, expecially if the forum was the Federal Court. But these problems exist no matter which approach we take; the jurisdiction-selecting approach serves only to mask them, while an interpretive approach permits their candid exploration.

Currie's approach and others like it have gained favour in American courts and I think we would do well to pursue them in Canada. While this might be difficult to do in all instances, the obstacles seem smaller in maritime cases than elsewhere. Having given some reasons why I think such a course is preferable, here is why I think it it is possible. First, although jurisdiction-selecting approaches are dominant in all Canadian courts, moving aside the weight of precedent in maritime disputes may not be the Sisyphean task it would be elsewhere. The heritage of 19th-century jurisprudence is available. The old cases have considerable appeal and some weight. Secondly, as mentioned above, when it comes to problems of geographic complexity, many maritime statutes are not nearly so Delphic as most non-maritime ones are. Some of the problems of multi-state fact patterns have been foreseen and addressed.[99] This invites interpretation in a way that broadly-phrased domestic statutes do not. Choice-of-law decisions in Canadian maritime cases present us with a valuable opportunity to get the whole of Canadian conflict-of-laws jurisprudence back on course.

---

98 Currie, "Notes on Methods and Objectives in the Conflict of Laws," [1959] Duke L.J. 171 at 178, reprinted in B. Currie, *Selected Essays on the Conflict of Laws* (1963), at pp. 183-4.

99 E.g., s. 274 of *The Canada Shipping Act*.

THE RESOLUTION OF CONFLICT OF LAWS ISSUES

IN MARITIME PERSONAL INJURY AND DEATH CLAIMS

CONFLICT OF LAWS AND FORUM NON CONVENIENS DETERMINATIONS IN MARITIME PERSONAL INJURY AND DEATH CASES IN UNITED STATES COURTS

*David W. Robertson**

1. INTRODUCTION: "A TEXAS STYLE CLAIM"

Traditional seamen, offshore-oil-and-gas workers, other maritime workers and passengers on vessels and airplanes[1] may suffer injury or

---

*Albert Sidney Burleson Professor of Law, University of Texas. Professor Robertson is the author of *Admiralty and Federalism* and of more than 30 law review articles on maritime and personal injury law. He is a member of the American Law Institute, the Maritime Law Association of the United States, and the Washington, D.C., Louisiana, and Texas Bars.

1 U.S. admiralty jurisdiction extends to crashes of land-based aircraft on the high seas and to injuries occurring on planes flying over the high seas, even though there is no

death on any of the world's navigable waters under circumstances that will support litigation in the courts of the United States. United States courts are attractive to such litigants for a variety of reasons. Attention has focussed on plaintiffs' expectations of more generous damages under American law.[2] Other advantages include the frequent prospect of more favorable liability principles,[3] the perceived advantages of jury trial, the availability of contingency-fee financing of the litigation and the wide-ranging discovery procedures available in United States courts.

Defensive interests are currently as aggressive as plaintiffs in pursuit of a favorable forum. Just as plaintiffs and their lawyers seek the best forum and the best law by bringing suit in the United States and seeking recovery under American law, so do defendants and their lawyers seek the best forum and the best law by resisting American jurisdiction and the application of American law, by seeking dismissal of the United States action on the basis of the discretionary doctrine of *forum non conveniens,* and occasionally by moving a tribunal outside the United States to enjoin plaintiff from litigating in the chosen forum.[4]

Because the stakes are high, an international forum-shopping battle can easily become protracted and bitter, and commentators have occasionally portrayed the plaintiff's pursuit of American rights as somehow unseemly or improper.[5] The recent *Castanho* litigation is illustrative.

---

contact with the water. It also extends to such occurrences on or over the territorial waters of foreign nations. See *Re Air Crash Disaster Near Bombay,* 531 F. Supp. 1175, 1182-84 (W.D. Wash. 1982); *Hammill v. Olympic Airways, S.A.,* 398 F. Supp. 829 (D.D.C. 1975); Symeonides, "Maritime Conflicts of Law From the Perspective of Modern Choice of Law Methodology" (1982), 7 The Mar. Lawyer 223 at 235, n. 51 (1979); Thomas, "Maritime Aviation Losses and Conflict of Laws" (1979), 45 J. Air L. & Comm. 61 at 72, 84.

2 See, *e.g.,* Lord Denning's hyperbole in *Smith Kline & French Laboratories Ltd. v. Bloch,* [1983] 2 All E.R. 72 at 74, [1983] 1 W.L.R. 370 (C.A.): "As a moth is drawn to the light, so is a litigant drawn to the United States. If he can only get his case into their courts, he stands to win a fortune."

3 See *Piper Aircraft Co. v. Reyno,* 454 U.S. 235 at 252 and nn. 18, 19 (1981).

4 It is hornbook law that a court has inherent power to protect its jurisdiction by enjoining parties subject to its jurisdiction from proceeding elsewhere: A. Ehrenzweig, *Conflict of Laws* (1962), §36, p. 129. See also *Re Unterweser Reederei, GMBH,* 428 F. 2d 888 at 890 (5th Cir. 1970), affirmed mem. en banc. 446 F. 2d 907 (5th Cir. 1971), vacated on other grounds (*sub nom. The Bremen v. Zapata Offshore Co.*) 407 U.S. 1 (1972). However, whether a court in another country will honor such an injunction is a matter of comity; there is no legal compulsion to do so: *Castanho v. Jackson Marine, Inc.,* 484 F. Supp. 201 at 208 (E.D. Tex. 1980), affirmed 650 F. 2d 546 (5th Cir. 1981). See generally Watson, "Transnational Maritime Litigation: Selected Problems" (1983), 8 The Mar. Lawyer 87 at 114-16.

5 In much of the early periodical literature that was influential in securing the establishment of the *forum non conveniens* doctrine in U.S. jurisprudence, "foreign

Castanho was a Portuguese seaman, injured aboard a North Sea oilfield supply ship in an English harbor. He initially proceeded in the courts of England, and as a result of that litigation received interim payments and an admission of liability. Subsequently he retained American counsel and sought to discontinue the English litigation and institute suit in the United States. The trial court in England refused to permit the English proceedings to be discontinued and enjoined plaintiff from proceeding in the United States.[6] The Court of Appeal, over Lord Denning's vehement dissent, reversed, concluding that plaintiff was entitled to pursue the "legitimate advantage" of American litigation.[7] The House of Lords affirmed the Court of Appeal's determination.[8]

In the United States court, defendants sought a stay, *forum non conveniens* dismissal and an injunction against plaintiff's proceeding elsewhere in the United States. All these motions were denied by the trial judge,[9] who also refused to certify his refusal to dismiss the case as proper matter for an interlocutory appeal. The Fifth Circuit held that, on the limited review available by *mandamus,* the trial court's refusal to dismiss the case should be upheld, and also affirmed the trial court's other rulings.[10] The American litigation was subsequently settled for a reported payment by defendants of $2.75 million.[11]

In the English Court of Appeal, Lord Denning, dissenting, was irate at plaintiff's efforts to discontinue the English litigation in order to pursue American rights:

> "A Texas-style claim is big business." That is how the newspaper put it. The managers of the business are two attorneys of Houston, Texas. They keep a look-out for men

---

ambulance chasing" was a favorite theme. See Foster, "Place of Trial in Civil Actions" (1930), 43 Harv. L. Rev. 1217 at 1239, 1245; Foster, "Place of Trial – Interstate Application of Intrastate Methods of Adjustment" (1931), 44 Harv. L. Rev. 41 at 59; Blair, "The Doctrine of Forum Non Conveniens in Anglo-American Law" (1929), 29 Colum. L. Rev. 1.

6 *Castanho v. Brown & Root (U.K.) Ltd.,* [1980] 1 All E.R. 689 (Q.B.). The English trial judge also cited the U.S. lawyers for contempt. According to Lord Denning's dissenting opinion in the Court of Appeal ([1980] 1 W.L.R. 833 at 856): "In our present case the defendants' solicitors applied to a judge in chamber, for leave to serve a summons for contempt on [the Texan attorneys], in Houston, Texas. The judge granted leave and in pursuance of it we are told that summonses for contempt of the English court were served in the streets of Houston, Texas, on [the Texan attorneys]. They asked for them to be committed to Pentonville Prison here in London, England. That cannot be right."

7 [1980] 3 All E.R. 72, [1980] 1 W.L.R. 833 at 847 (C.A.).

8 [1981] 1 All E.R. 143, [1980] 3 W.L.R. 991 (H.L.).

9 *Castanho v. Jackson Marine, Inc., supra* note 4.

10 *Castanho, supra* note 4.

11 It should be noted that, under the recent amendment to the U.S. *Jones Act,* 46 U.S.C. §688, discussed *infra* at notes 139-150, U.S. relief would probably no longer be available to a worker like Castanho.

injured on the North Sea oil rigs. The worse a man is injured, the better for business. Especially when he has been rendered a quadriplegic and his employers have no answer to his claim. Their look-out man tells the Texan attorneys. They come across to England. They see the injured man and say to him: "Do not bring your action in England or Scotland. You will only get £150,000 there. Let us bring it in Texas. We can get you £2,500,000 in Texas." If he agrees, they get him to sign a power of attorney which provides for their reward. Under it the attorneys are to get 40 per cent of any damages recovered. That is 1,200,000 pounds for themselves. Big business indeed![12]

Denning went on to conclude that virtually everything connected with plaintiff's efforts to pursue American litigation was improper, and stated in no uncertain terms that he would insist that the litigation remain and be concluded in the English courts.

Lord Shaw, on the winning side in the English Court of Appeal, had a different perspective. In his view, this grievously-injured plaintiff's pursuit of maximum satisfaction should be applauded rather than condemned, and it would be "less than humane" to deny plaintiff that right.[13] Yet, said Lord Shaw, denying him that right is exactly what defendants, the lower court, and Lord Denning wanted to accomplish. Lord Shaw observed that "the unattractive aspects [of this litigation] are by no means all on one side".[14] He pointed out that defendants must have been delighted when litigation was initially instituted in England, and that they spared no effort to keep it there:

One can almost hear the sigh of mingled astonishment and relief breathed by those concerned for the insurers for [defendants] when proceedings were proposed in England. No better policy could be pursued from the insurers' point of view than to encourage the issue of those proceedings in this country and to confine them there.[15]

Lord Shaw went on to describe defendants' efforts to "confine" the proceedings to English courts. Before suit was filed, defendants offered plaintiff an interim payment, provided he instituted proceedings in England. Once that had resulted, however, defendants resisted making any further interim payments. In light of the fact that liability was conceded and the total interim payment sought by plaintiff was far less than even the lowest conceivable award of damages by an English court, Lord Shaw thought it "at least peculiar" that defendants resisted paying it, and stated:

It permits at least the surmise that the earlier show of solicitude had not been disinterested and was tactical rather than humanitarian. Now that the action was tied (or apparently so) to the courts of this country, there was no point in providing any more carrots.[16]

---

12 *Castanho, supra* note 7, at p. 849.
13 *Ibid.* at 858.
14 *Ibid.* at 858.
15 *Ibid.* at 859.
16 *Ibid.* at 861.

Finally, Lord Shaw turned to the charges of impropriety that had been made against the American attorneys, including allegations of "champerty" and "maintenance". These words, said Lord Shaw, "have ugly connotations in English law",[17] but should not be permitted to obscure the realities of the situation:

> The allegations of impropriety were yet another desperate and disingenuous effort to keep the plaintiff's claim within the relatively moderate limits now current in the courts of England. Fortunately American corporations, like their insurers, are aware of the scale of damages in the United States and they arrange their policies and the premiums accordingly.
>
> This is a case about money, not morality.[18]

Lord Shaw's perspective seems demonstrably superior to Lord Denning's. Given the realities of litigation and of lawyers' perceived obligations to their clients, claims of moral superiority by either side of an international forum-shopping battle are almost always misplaced. These cases are about money, not morality.

2. TRANSNATIONAL MARITIME PERSONAL INJURY AND DEATH LITIGATION IN THE UNITED STATES FEDERAL COURTS: THE DOCTRINAL BATTLEGROUNDS

While some of these cases find their way into state courts in the United States, the great majority have been brought in or removed to federal courts. This paper concentrates on litigation in the federal courts.[19] The doctrines that control the availability of United States forum jurisdiction and United States law are outlined below.

(a) Subject-Matter and Personal Jurisdiction

Any plaintiff seeking redress in a United States federal court must first establish subject-matter jurisdiction. The United States district courts exercise subject-matter jurisdiction under three major headings. Federal question jurisdiction is present if the case arises under the Constitution, laws or treaties of the United States.[20] Diversity jurisdiction is present if the matter in controversy exceeds $10,000 and the suit

---

17 *Ibid.* at 866.
18 *Ibid.* at 866.
19 Because the U.S. federal courts are using the *forum non conveniens* doctrine in increasingly restrictive ways, plaintiffs in the future may seek relief in state courts in the U.S. with more frequency. See generally Dué, "Rights of Foreign Seamen in American Courts – The Law Into The 80's" (1982), 7 The Mar. Lawyer 265 at 277-80.
20 28 U.S.C. §1331.

is between citizens of different states or between citizens of a state and citizens or subjects of a foreign state.[21] Admiralty jurisdiction is present if the occurrence took place on navigable waters and involved a significant relationship to traditional maritime activity.[22]

A maritime personal injury or death case may afford plaintiff the opportunity of invoking one or more of the foregoing bases of subject-matter jurisdiction. For seaman plaintiffs, the *Jones Act*[23] provides a cause of action for employer negligence which will lie under the federal question jurisdiction or under admiralty jurisdiction, at plaintiff's option.[24] In actions brought on the federal question basis, jury trial is available. A plaintiff bringing his *Jones Act* suit as a federal question action may join his claims under the general maritime law for maintenance and cure and for relief under the doctrine of unseaworthiness, and the *Jones Act* claim will take the entire case to the jury.[25] Most other maritime personal injury and death claims do not present a basis for federal question jurisdiction. Diversity jurisdiction, if present, will also provide a basis for jury trial. Admiralty jurisdiction – if specifically invoked by plaintiff or if it is the only available basis for federal court subject-matter jurisdiction[26] – will result in bench trial.

Plaintiff in a United States court must also establish the requisites of jurisdiction over the person of the defendant and satisfy the procedures for serving process on the defendant. As a broad generalization it can be said that the existence of personal jurisdiction turns in major part on whether there are "minimum contacts" between defendant and

---

21   28 U.S.C. §1332.
22   28 U.S.C. §1333; *Executive Jet Aviation, Inc. v. City of Cleveland,* 409 U.S. 249 (1972).
23   *Supra* note 11.
24   *Panama R.R. Co. v. Johnson,* 264 U.S. 375 (1924).
25   *Fitzgerald v. U.S. Lines Co.,* 374 U.S. 16 (1963); *Romero v. Internat. Terminal Operating Co.,* 358 U.S. 354 (1959).
26   Fed. R. Civ. Pro. 9(h). If *in rem* relief is sought, admiralty jurisdiction is exclusive. Further, certain actions are confined by statute to the admiralty jurisdiction, including suits against the United States under the *Suits in Admiralty Act,* 46 U.S.C. §§741 *et seq.,* or the *Public Vessels Act,* 46 U.S.C. §§781 *et seq.;* actions under the *Foreign Sovereign Immunities Act,* 28 U.S.C. §1330; and proceedings for *Limitation of Liability,* 46 U.S.C. §§183 *et seq.*

While the matter is not free from doubt, the weight of authority holds that actions under the *Death on the High Seas Act,* 46 U.S.C. §§761-68 (*DHSA*), are cognizable only under the admiralty jurisdiction. See, *e.g., Hammill v. Olympic Airways, S.A.,* 398 F. Supp. 829 at 836-37 (D.D.C. 1975). In wrongful death cases involving victims other than seamen and arising beyond a marine league from the shores of the United States, the *DHSA* is the only available U.S. remedy: *Mobil Oil Corp. v. Higginbotham,* 436 U.S. 618 (1978). Further, a seaman's wrongful death claim arising beyond a marine league in which unseaworthiness is an asserted basis of liability would have to invoke the *DHSA.*

the forum.[27] While many defendants in transnational maritime personal injury litigation can make valid objections to personal jurisdiction,[28] that topic is not further treated in this paper.[29]

(b) Major Lines of Defence: Choice of Law and Forum Non Conveniens

Defendants in transnational maritime injury and death cases have four major lines of defence: they may contest subject-matter jurisdiction, personal jurisdiction, and/or the existence of a cause of action under United States law, and they may also seek a dismissal of the action under the discretionary doctrine of *forum non conveniens.*

The transnational dimensions of the case do not alter the basic tests for subject-matter jurisdiction, and the existence of subject-matter jurisdiction is rarely a legitimate issue in these cases. A transnational maritime personal injury or death claimant can as easily assert subject-matter jurisdiction under one or more of the three above-discussed headings as can a domestic plaintiff. The Supreme Court has tried to make it clear that in transnational cases the assertion of jurisdiction under any one of the foregoing headings, coupled with a colourable assertion of the existence of rights under American law, establishes

---

27 *Int. Shoe Co. v. Washington,* 326 U.S. 310, 316 (1945). *International Shoe* involved the Fourteenth Amendment due process standards, applicable to State Courts and to Federal Courts exercising diversity jurisdiction. The test for personal jurisdiction under the Fifth Amendment, applicable to Federal Court cases grounded in federal question or admiralty jurisdiction, may be broader. See, e.g., *Handley v. Indiana & Washington Elec. Co.,* 732 F. 2d 1265 (6th Cir. 1984).

28 See generally *DeJames v. Magnificence Carriers, Inc.,* 654 F. 2d 280 (3d Cir. 1981), cert. denied, 454 U.S. 1085 (1981); *Koupetoris v. Konkar Intrepid Corp.,* 535 F. 2d 1392 at 1395-96 (2d Cir. 1976); *Grammenos v. Lemos,* 457 F. 2d 1067 (2d Cir. 1972).

On April 24, 1984, the U.S. Supreme Court handed down its decision in *Helicopeteros Nacionales de Colombia, S.A. v. Hall,* 52 U.S.L.W. 4491, holding that a Texas state court's assertion of personal jurisdiction over a Colombian corporation in litigation arising from an air crash in Peru offended the due process requirements of the Fourteenth Amendment. The reasoning in *Helicopeteros* may suggest some narrowing in the court's view of the permissible reach of personal jurisdiction.

29 This paper also omits direct treatment of the topic of venue. In general, venue in an admiralty action in a U.S. court is proper if the court has personal jurisdiction. However, there are some special venue provisions for certain types of admiralty actions. See, *e.g.,* Fed. R. Civ. Pro. F(9), providing venue rules for *Limitation of Liability* proceedings. *Jones Act* suits brought as actions at law must be brought "in the district in which the defendant employer resides or in which his principal office is located": 46 U.S.C. §688. But *Jones Act* cases brought as admiralty claims fall under the general admiralty rule legitimating venue wherever personal jurisdiction can be obtained.

Improper venue is challenged by a motion under Fed. R. Civ. Pro. 12(b)(3). Only if venue is proper can *forum non conveniens* issues arise.

subject-matter jurisdiction.[30] What this means is that defendant is usually mistaken, as a technical matter, in couching the choice-of-law argument (the argument that applicable choice-of-law principles preclude plaintiff from invoking the benefits of American law) in the form of an objection to subject-matter jurisdiction; the correct procedural devices for asserting that argument are a pre-answer motion to dismiss for failure to state a claim on which relief can be granted under Federal Rule of Civil Procedure 12(b)(6), a motion for summary judgment on the same basis or assertion of the same defensive matter in the answer.[31] Nevertheless, defendants continue to put their choice-of-law arguments in the form of objections to the courts' subject-matter jurisdiction, and courts sometimes state that they are dismissing cases (in which defendants succeed with that argument) on the basis of a lack of subject-matter jurisdiction.[32] The importance of this technical distinction may be small in most cases, but a court's conclusion that it lacks subject-matter jurisdiction is generally not accorded *res judicata* effect,[33] and one commentator has suggested that plaintiff, on suffering a dismissal on the stated basis of a lack of subject-matter jurisdiction, should simply present the case to another judge.[34]

In addition to contending that United States law is inapplicable to the case under applicable choice-of-law principles, defendant may also contend that the United States court should in no event retain jurisdiction over the case but should dismiss it on the basis of the doctrine of *forum non conveniens*. *Forum non conveniens* is a discretionary doctrine whereby a court in which subject-matter and personal jurisdiction are admittedly proper may nevertheless refuse to entertain the action because trial elsewhere would be greatly more convenient than trial in the chosen forum. Transnational maritime personal injury and death cases are a fertile ground for *forum non conveniens* arguments, which are often

---

30 *Romero v. Internat. Terminal Operating Co., supra* note 25, at p. 359; *Lauritzen v. Larsen,* 345 U.S. 571 at 575 (1953).

31 See Albritton, "Choice of Law in a Maritime Personal Injury Setting: The Domestic Jurisprudence" (1983), 43 La. L. Rev. 879 at 880. *Cf.* Carlson, "The Jones Act and Choice of Law" (1981), 15 Int. L. 49 at 50 and n. 10, arguing that a R. 12(b)(6) motion is not a proper vehicle for raising the choice-of-law defence. Carlson's view seems idiosyncratic.

32 See, *e.g., Rodriguez v. Flota Mercante Grancolombiana, S.A.,* 703 F. 2d 1069 (9th Cir.), cert. denied, 104 S. Ct. 84 (U.S. 1983); *Blanco v. Carigulf Lines,* 632 F. 2d 656 (5th Cir. 1980); *Avila v. M/V Toluca,* No. 79-2921 (5th Cir., May 30, 1980) (unpublished opinion made an appendix to Judge Brown's dissent from denial of rehearing in *Fisher v. Agios Nicolaos V,* 636 F. 2d at 1112 (5th Cir. 1981)); cases cited in Watson, "Applicable Law in Suits by Foreign Offshore Oil Workers" (1981), 41 La. L. Rev. 827 at 828 n. 5.

33 See 5 Wright & Miller, *Fed. Prac. & Pro.* §1350, p. 543 n. 54 (1969).

34 See Carlson, *supra* note 31 at p. 59 n. 10.

intertwined and confused with choice-of-law arguments. A major part of this paper addresses the requisites of a successful *forum non conveniens* defence, and attempts to distinguish that defence from the choice-of-law issue.

3. THE RELATIONSHIP BETWEEN CHOICE OF LAW AND FORUM NON CONVENIENS

A personal injury or death claimant who pleads the requisites of federal question, diversity or admiralty jurisdiction and who asserts a colorable claim for relief under United States law has properly invoked the court's subject-matter jurisdiction. As indicated above, in transnational cases the relevant issues usually do not involve subject-matter jurisdiction, but rather (i) whether plaintiff has stated a claim under United States law upon which relief can be granted, and (ii) whether in any event the court should dismiss the case on the basis of *forum non conveniens*.[35]

The choice-of-law and *forum non conveniens* issues are analytically distinct. The choice-of-law issue addresses the question whether American law should govern the case. The *forum non conveniens* issue addresses whether there is another forum, other than the United States court chosen by plaintiff, where trial would be much more appropriate. The analytical distinction between the two issues is such that, in a case in which both defences are raised, four outcomes are theoretically possible. The court could decide that:

1. United States law governs the case and it should be tried in the United States court.

---

35 If plaintiff has pleaded causes of action based on U.S. law alone and the court concludes on choice-of-law principles that U.S. law is inapplicable, dismissal under Fed. R. Civ. Pro. 12(b)(6) or summary judgment is the appropriate response. As a technical matter, a case in the foregoing posture would not present a *forum non conveniens* issue; once it is concluded that U.S. law does not apply, the case is over if U.S. law is the only basis for the asserted cause(s) of action. See *Chiazor v. Transworld Drilling Co.*, 648 F. 2d 1015 at 1020 n. 7 (5th Cir. 1981), cert. denied, 455 U.S. 1019 (1982). On the other hand, if the court decides that U.S. law should govern the case, ordinarily *forum non conveniens* dismissal is unavailable. See text and notes 40-46, *infra*.

If plaintiff has asserted in the alternative a cause of action based on some other country's laws, the U.S. court concluding that U.S. law does not apply will then address the *forum non conveniens* issue, *i.e.*, whether the foreign-law claim should be tried in the United States forum. Usually the conclusion is negative.

Even in cases in which plaintiff has not asserted a foreign-law claim, the courts frequently go from the choice-of-law determination – United States law does not apply – to the *forum non conveniens* analysis. See, *e.g.*, *Chiazor, supra*.

2. United States law does not govern the case and it should be tried elsewhere.
3. United States law governs the case but it should be tried elsewhere.[36]
4. United States law does not govern the case but it should be tried in the United States court.[37]

As a practical matter, however, the choice-of-law and *forum non conveniens* issues are intertwined in such complex ways that ordinarily only one or the other of the first two theoretically possible options makes practical sense. If possible, courts would prefer to avoid deciding cases on the basis of foreign law, so the conclusion that American law does not govern the case is a strong factor weighing in favor of *forum non conveniens* dismissal.[38] Conversely, because it is often unrealistic to expect that a foreign forum will arrive at the same choice-of-law conclusions as the American forum, an American court concluding that American law should control the case should ordinarily retain jurisdiction.[39]

There is an abundance of authority for the proposition that, at least in cases brought on behalf of seamen, the conclusion that United States law applies means that the United States court must retain jurisdiction.[40] Under that view, *forum non conveniens* would not even be

---

36 *Piper Aircraft Co. v. Reyno,* 454 U.S. 235 (1981), was not a maritime case but its relevance is clear. The action was on behalf of Scottish victims of a plane crash in Scotland, against U.S. manufacturers. The Court of Appeal had held that U.S. courts would probably apply U.S. law to the case whereas British courts would apply British law, and that *forum non conveniens* dismissal should not occur when the result would be to remit plaintiffs to less favorable law than that available in the chosen forum: 630 F. 2d 149 (3d Cir. 1980). The Supreme Court reversed, holding, *inter alia,* that avoiding subjecting plaintiffs to less favorable substantive law is not a legitimate factor weighing against *forum non conveniens* dismissal.

37 See Gilmore and Black, *The Law of Admiralty* (2d ed., 1975), pp. 478, 482-83, suggesting that a court so concluding may well assume, at least in the absence of a strong showing to the contrary, that the maritime law of the foreign nation is more or less the same as U.S. maritime law. But see Watson, *supra* note 4, at pp. 99-102, discussing the ease of proving foreign law under Fed. R. Civ. Pro. 44.1.

38 But see *Re Air Crash Disaster Near Bombay,* 531 F. Supp. 1175 (W.D. Wash. 1982), holding Indian law applicable, but refusing to dismiss the case on the basis of *forum non conveniens* because it appeared that the Indian courts would hold the action irrevocably time-barred.

39 But see *Piper Aircraft, supra* note 36.

40 See *Koke v. Phillips Petroleum Co.,* 730 F. 2d 211 at 218 (5th Cir. 1984); *Gahr Dev. v. Nedlloyd Lijnen, B.V.,* 723 F. 2d 1190 at 1192 (5th Cir. 1984); *Diaz v. Humboldt,* 722 F. 2d 1216 at 1217 (5th Cir. 1984); *Needham v. Phillips Petroleum Co. of Norway,* 719 F. 2d 1481 at 1483 (10th Cir. 1983); *La Seguridad v. Transytur Line,* 707 F. 2d 1304 at 1310, n. 10 (11th Cir. 1983); *De Oliveira v. Delta Marine Drilling Co.,* 707 F. 2d 843 at 845 (5th Cir. 1983); *Szumlicz v. Norwegian America Line,* 698 F. 2d 1192 at 1195 (11th Cir. 1983); *Bailey v. Dolphin Internat. Inc.,* 697 F. 2d 1268 at 1274 (5th Cir.

addressed unless the court had first concluded that United States law should not apply. Despite the wealth of authority, however, the issue remains unsettled.[41] *Piper Aircraft Co. v. Reyno*[42] was a Supreme Court decision in a non-maritime context indicating that *forum non conveniens* dismissal may be proper even if the United States court believes that American law should apply.[43] Several commentators have suggested that *Piper* casts doubt on the proposition that the applicability of American law in a seaman's case means *forum non conveniens* dismissal is inappropriate.[44] Furthermore, in a case decided after *Piper* but not relying on it, the Second Circuit Court of Appeals repudiated its earlier decisions and indicated that a seaman's case calling for the application of United States law may nevertheless be dismissible under *forum non conveniens* considerations.[45] Nevertheless, a number of Court of Appeals decisions handed down since *Piper* have reiterated that the applicability of United States law to a seaman's case means that *forum non conveniens* dismissal is inappropriate.[46]

1983); *Vaz Borralho v. Keydril Co.,* 696 F. 2d 379 at 384 (5th Cir. 1983); *Chiazor v. Transworld Drilling Co., supra* note 35, at p. 1018; *Fisher v. Agios Nicolaos V,* 628 F. 2d 308 at 313, 315 (5th Cir. 1980), rehearing denied, 636 F. 2d 1107 (5th Cir.), cert. denied, 454 U.S. 816 (1981); *De Mateos v. Texaco, Inc.,* 562 F. 2d 895 at 899 (3d Cir. 1977), cert. denied, 435 U.S. 904 (1978); *Antypas v. Campania Maritima SanBasilio, S.A.,* 541 F. 2d 307 at 310 (2nd Cir. 1976), cert. denied, 429 U.S. 1098 (1977); *Bartholomew v. Universe Tankships, Inc.,* 263 F. 2d 437 at 443 (2d Cir.), cert. denied, 359 U.S. 1000 (1959); *Dalla v. Atlas Maritime Co.,* 562 F. Supp. 752 at 757 (C.D. Cal. 1983); *Allan v. Brown & Root, Inc.,* 491 F. Supp. 398 at 403 (S.D. Tex. 1980); *Mattes v. Nat. Hellenic Amer. Line, S.A.,* 427 F. Supp. 619 at 629 (S.D.N.Y. 1977); *Ying Shiue Jye Fen v. Sanko Kisen (USA),* 1977 A.M.C. 1224 at 1226 n. 2 (S.D.N.Y. 1977); Albritton, *supra* note 31, at p. 881; Sutterfield, "Foreign Offshore Worker Injuries In Foreign Waters – Why a United States Forum?" (1981), 48 Ins. L.J. 472 at 473.

41   See Watson, *supra* note 32, at pp. 829-39 and n. 18, suggesting that the recent decision of the Second Circuit Court of Appeals in *Alcoa S.S. Co. v. M/V Nordic Regent,* 654 F. 2d 147 (2d Cir.) (en banc), cert. denied, 449 U.S. 890 (1980) – holding that a case brought by a U.S. citizen should be dismissed for trial abroad under the *forum non conveniens* doctrine – casts doubt on the traditional view that the applicability of U.S. law means the case should be tried in the U.S.

42   *Supra* note 36.

43   See discussion in note 36, *supra.*

44   See Tate, "Fisher v. Agios Nicolaos V and Choice of Law: What Was All The Fuss About? And What the Fuss Should Have Been About (Maybe)" (1982), 7 The Mar. Lawyer 199 at 208 and n. 54, apparently agreeing with the cases holding that the applicability of U.S. law means U.S. jurisdiction should be retained but acknowledging that *Piper* calls that into question; and see Watson, *supra* note 4, at pp. 90-91, criticizing the idea that the applicability of U.S. law means U.S. jurisdiction should be retained and stating that *Piper* changes that.

45   *Cruz v. Maritime Co. of Philippines,* 702 F. 2d 47 at 48 (2d Cir. 1983).

46   See the 1982, 1983, and 1984 decisions cited in note 40, *supra.*

The foregoing confusion – as to whether the applicability of United States law to a seaman's case forecloses the question of *forum non conveniens* – is magnified by differences among the Circuit Courts of Appeals as to the appropriate scope of appellate review in these cases. The Fifth Circuit has repeatedly held that the choice-of-law issue should be addressed by the trial judge before entering into the *forum non conveniens* analysis,[47] and that the choice-of-law determination is subject to full or *de novo* appellate review as a question of law, whereas the *forum non conveniens* determination is reviewable only under an abuse of discretion standard.[48] The Court of Appeals for the Tenth Circuit agrees with the Fifth.[49] On the other hand, the Courts of Appeals for the District of Columbia,[50] Third[51] and Eighth Circuits[52] seem to treat the choice-of-law decision as provisional only, and as an integral part of the *forum non conveniens* analysis, holding that appellate review is limited to determining whether the trial court's *forum non conveniens* decision was an abuse of discretion. In the Eleventh Circuit, the court has stated that the choice-of-law determination should be made first and that a determination that American law applies means that jurisdiction should be retained without further inquiry into the *forum non conveniens* factors, but indicated in the same case that the scope of review of the entire matter is under the abuse of discretion standard.[53]

In the final analysis, the jurisprudence does not permit the confident conclusion that the choice-of-law and *forum non conveniens* issues are truly separate bases for refusing United States relief to a maritime injury or death plaintiff. Rather, the two doctrines, while analytically distinct, seem in recent cases to be treated by the courts as more or less interchangeable bases for declining relief. Under the next two headings, this paper introduces the relevant choice-of-law and *forum non conveniens* principles. The subsequent material treats the recent maritime

---

47   The choice-of-law issue should be determined first on the view that concluding that U.S. law is applicable means the case should remain in the United States, thereby foreclosing any necessity for a subsequent *forum non conveniens* inquiry.

48   *Koke v. Phillips Petroleum Co., supra* note 40, at p. 218; *Diaz v. Humboldt, supra* note 40, at pp. 1218, 1219; *Bailey v. Dolphin Internat., Inc., supra* note 40, at p. 1274; *Vaz Borralho v. Keydril Co., supra* note 40, at p. 384, reh'g denied, 710 F. 2d 207 (5th Circ. 1983). But see *Fisher v. Agios Nicolaos V., supra* note 40, at pp. 317-18, suggesting that the choice-of-law determination may sometimes turn on a finding of fact as to the existence of sufficient U.S. contacts, reviewable under the clearly erroneous standard. See explanation of the *Fisher* case by Judge Tate, *supra* note 44.

49   *Needham v. Phillips Petroleum Co. of Norway, supra* note 40, at p. 1483.

50   *Pain v. United Technologies Corp.*, 637 F. 2d 775 at 779, 791-92 (D.C. Cir. 1980), cert. denied, 454 U.S. 1128 (1981).

51   *Dahl v. United Technologies Corp.*, 632 F. 2d 1027 at 1029, 1032 (3d Cir. 1980).

52   *Lehman v. Humphrey Cayman, Ltd.*, 713 F. 2d 339 at 340-41, 345 (8th Cir. 1983).

53   *Szumlicz v. Norwegian Amer. Line*, 698 F. 2d 1192 at 1195, 1196 (11th Cir. 1983).

injury jurisprudence, with emphasis on the results obtaining and the factual particulars that seem to be most influential in convincing American courts that plaintiff should not have relief in the United States.

4. JUDICIAL DEVELOPMENT OF MARITIME CHOICE-OF-LAW PRINCIPLES IN SEAMEN'S INJURY CASES

Most of the reported transnational maritime personal injury and death cases have involved injuries to seamen.[54] Initially, cases concerning injuries to United States citizens or permanent residents can be set aside as implicating no significant choice-of-law issue; traditionally these cases have been treated under United States law.[55] While recent jurisprudential developments[56] may generate defensive arguments to the contrary,[57] this paper assumes that *bona fide* American citizenship or residency of the injury victim at the time of the injury will suffice for the application of United States law.[58]

Another strong tradition holds that United States maritime law applies to injuries sustained by seamen aboard American-flag vessels regardless of the place of injury or the nationality of the victim.[59] Recent decisions and legislation[60] have abrogated that tradition for injuries to foreign nationals sustained in oil and gas operations in the territorial waters or over the continental shelf of nations other than the United States,[61] but for traditional "blue water" seamen it appears that United States law will apply respecting any injury on an American-flag ship.

---

54   The focus here is on suits by seamen against their employers, in which plaintiffs typically invoke the *Jones Act* and the general maritime law doctrines of unseaworthiness and maintenance and cure. Suits by or on behalf of seamen against entities other than the employer may seek recovery under the doctrine of unseaworthiness, but are otherwise unaffected by the doctrines affording special protections to seamen. These cases are therefore treated under "8. Maritime Accidents Injuring Non-Seamen," *infra*. See also note 116, *infra*.

55   See *Uravic v. F. Jarka Co.,* 282 U.S. 234 (1931); *Symonette Shipyards, Ltd. v. Clark,* 365 F. 2d 464 (5th Cir. 1966); Gilmore and Black, *supra* note 37, at pp. 476-77; Tate, *supra* note 44, at p. 204 n. 29; Symeonides, *supra* note 1, at pp. 236-37; Watson, *supra* note 31, at pp. 844-45 n. 93; Albritton, *supra* note 31, at pp. 909-10.

56   See discussion at notes 105-107 and 157-161, *infra*.

57   See, *e.g.,* Albritton, *supra* note 31, at pp. 909-10; Carlson, *supra* note 31, at p. 58.

58   Moving to the U.S. after the injury will generally not "promote" plaintiff into the favored status. See Watson, *supra* note 32, at p. 845 n. 93.

59   See Gilmore and Black, *supra* note 37, at p. 477; Symeonides, *supra* note 1, at p. 237.

60   See "7. Injury and Death Claims by Foreign Offshore Workers", *infra*.

61   Because most of the drilling and other structures involved in these maritime mineral operations are classified as vessels, most of the offshore-oil-and-gas-worker plaintiffs are treated as seamen. See Watson, *supra* note 32, at pp. 832-34, 836, 855-56.

Whether United States law applies to injury and death claims between foreign seamen and foreign shipowners has frequently engaged United States courts. Beginning with the 1953 Supreme Court decision in *Lauritzen v. Larsen*,[62] the courts have used a list of "factors" or "contact points" in analyzing whether there is sufficient American interest in the case to warrant application of United States law.[63] While much relevant litigation and a significant statutory development[64] have occurred since *Lauritzen* was decided, that decision remains the essential starting point.

Plaintiff in *Lauritzen* was a Danish seaman, hurt aboard a Danish-owned, Danish-flag ship in Havana harbor. Suit was brought in the Southern District of New York. The only United States contact – other than the institution of suit in the United States was that the seaman had signed the Danish shipping articles in New York. Holding that American law was not applicable, the Supreme Court announced the methodology to be followed in resolving choice-of-law issues in maritime injury cases, consisting in

> ascertaining and valuing points of contact between the transaction and the states or governments whose competing laws are involved. The criteria, in general, appear to be arrived at from weighing the significance of one or more connecting factors between the shipping transaction regulated and the national interest served by the assertion of authority.[65]

The court then indicated that, historically, seven factors have controlled these choice-of-law determinations and gave direction as to how each of those factors should be weighed in the choice-of-law process:

1. *Place of the wrongful act.* This factor, which would have pointed to Cuban law, was held to be entitled to very minor weight, because ships travel the world's waters and the applicable law should not turn on the fortuity of where the ship happened to be at the time of injury.[66] At the same time, the court recognized that the place of the injury might be important in certain cases in which the public policy of the state where injury occurred is particularly strong.[67]

---

62   345 U.S. 571 (1953).
63   *Lauritzen* involved only the *Jones Act*. Subsequently, *Romero v. Internat. Terminal Operating Co.*, 358 U.S. 354 (1959), held that the same analysis applies to foreign-seaman claims for recovery under the U.S. general maritime law. Later cases have read *Lauritzen* and *Romero* to mean that the same choice-of-law analysis applies to fatal injury litigation invoking the *Death on the High Seas Act*, 46 U.S.C. §§761-68. See Watson, *supra* note 32, at pp. 836-37.
64   See "7. Injury and Death Claims by Foreign Offshore Workers", *infra*.
65   *Supra* note 62, at p. 582.
66   *Ibid.* at 583-84.
67   *Ibid.* at 584.

2. *Law of the flag.* This factor is of "cardinal importance"[68] and should generally prevail "unless some heavy counterweight appears".[69]

3. *Allegiance or domicile of the injured seaman.* This factor could give rise to a strong national interest, as "each nation has a legitimate interest that its nationals and permanent inhabitants be not maimed or disabled from self-support".[70]

4. *Allegiance of defendant shipowner.* This factor was considered significant, because states have an interest in governing the conduct of their citizens on the high seas or in foreign waters. In discussing this factor, the court recognized the practice of registering vessels under flags of convenience, and stated it might be appropriate to go "beyond the formalities of more or less nominal foreign registration to enforce against American shipowners the obligations which our law places upon them".[71]

5. *Place of contract.* This factor was not entitled to significant weight, because the action sounded in tort and because the place of contracting is generally fortuitous; giving significance to this factor would result in different members of the same crew having varied rights.[72]

6. *Inaccessibility of foreign forum.* This factor is of almost no importance with regard to the choice-of-law issue, although it would be relevant in deciding whether to retain jurisdiction or to dismiss on the basis of *forum non conveniens.*[73]

7. *Law of the forum.* This factor was dismissed as of no importance. The court indicated that the due process clause of the Fifth Amendment limits the cases to which United States law can be applied,[74] and stated that the "purpose of a conflict-of-laws doctrine is to assure that a case will be treated in the same way under the appropriate law regardless of the fortuitous circumstances which often determine the forum".[75]

---

68 *Ibid.* at 584.
69 *Ibid.* at 586.
70 *Ibid.* at 586.
71 *Ibid.* at 587. Just before World War II the U.S. government encouraged U.S. shipowners to use foreign flags of convenience to permit trade with allies while technically abiding by neutrality commitments. After the war U.S. shipowners continued the practice, having discovered that it significantly reduced operating and labor costs. See Caskey, "A New Look at Lauritzen v. Larsen, Choice of Law and Forum Non Conveniens" (1978), 38 La. L. Rev. 957 at 961-62 and n. 33.
72 *Supra* note 62, at p. 588.
73 *Ibid.* at 589-90.
74 *Ibid.* at 590-91.
75 *Ibid.* at 591. See, however, the discussion at notes 35-39, *supra.*

Careful reading of *Lauritzen* bears out the general view of the commentators[76] that only the first five factors have any relevance to the choice-of-law determination. Indeed, most of the subsequent cases show that only the first four factors are of much importance. The place where the contract of employment was entered into has not been influential, nor have provisions in such contracts calling for the application of foreign law and/or litigation in a foreign forum.[77] With the exception of plaintiff's having signed the articles of employment in New York, all of the relevant factors in *Lauritzen* pointed to the application of Danish law. On the facts presented to the court, *Lauritzen* was an easy case.[78]

The next Supreme Court consideration of the problem occurred in *Romero v. Internat. Terminal Operating Co.*[79] Plaintiff was a Spanish seaman, hurt aboard a Spanish-owned, Spanish-flag vessel in an American harbor. He sued his Spanish employer and three New York corporations under the *Jones Act* and general maritime law. The court held that *Lauritzen,* which had involved only a *Jones Act* action, controlled the choice-of-law determination as to the general maritime law claims as well.[80] It further held that United States law was inapplicable in the action against the Spanish defendant, indicating that the American locus of the injury made no significant difference:

> To impose on ships the duty of shifting from one standard of compensation to another as the vessel passes the boundaries of territorial waters would be not only an onerous but also an unduly speculative burden, disruptive of international commerce and without basis in the expressed policies of this country. The amount and type of recovery which a foreign seaman may receive from his foreign employer while sailing on a foreign ship should not depend on the wholly fortuitous circumstances of the place of injury.[81]

The court dismissed the action against the Spanish defendant, but held that the claims against the New York defendants should be retained for trial.

Some of the commentators have termed *Romero* another "easy case" for the applicability of non-American law.[82] Others disagree, arguing that the fact that Romero was injured and received treatment in a United States port was entitled to greater weight than afforded by the court because: (i) when a foreign shipowner comes into an American port, thereby deriving substantial revenue from United States com-

---

76   See, *e.g.,* Albritton, *supra* note 31, at p. 883.
77   See Gilmore and Black, *supra* note 37, at pp. 476-77.
78   See *Ibid.* at 472; Albritton, *supra* note 31, at 884; Watson, *supra* note 32, at p. 841.
79   358 U.S. 354 (1959).
80   *Ibid.* at 382.
81   *Ibid.* at 384.
82   See Albritton, *supra* note 31, at p. 884; Watson, *supra* note 31, at p. 841.

merce, he can be held to have assumed the risks of navigation in American waters and cannot claim that the imposition of American standards is unforeseeable; and (ii) the interest in ensuring that local suppliers of medical services do not go unpaid was entitled to consideration.[83] Commentators critical of *Romero* have also argued that there was some risk of unfairness involved in permitting the Spanish shipowner/ employer to sail free of United States courts and United States law while retaining the actions against the three New York defendants.[84]

After *Lauritzen* and *Romero* were decided, the lower federal courts attempted to decide the choice-of-law issue in foreign seamen's cases under the multi-factored analysis of those decisions. However, the decision of the Second Circuit Court of Appeals in *Bartholomew v. Universe Tankships, Inc.,*[85] decided about a month before *Romero*, has been almost equally influential.[86] *Bartholomew* was in truth an "easy case" for the application of United States law. Plaintiff was injured in American waters. He was a permanent resident of the United States, though not a citizen. The vessel was owned by a Liberian corporation and flew the Liberian flag, but all the stock of the Liberian corporation was owned by a Panama corporation which in turn was wholly owned by American citizens. Furthermore, all the corporate officers of the Liberian owner were American citizens, and its principal place of business was New York. Plaintiff had signed articles in the United States, and the voyage on which he was hurt began and ended in the United States. With those American factors, the court had no difficulty concluding that American law should apply.

It was the reasoning, not the result, in *Bartholomew* that guaranteed its importance as a precedent. The court stated that "traditional choice of law techniques may be more misleading than helpful", and rejected a "center of gravity" or "place of most vital connection" approach.[87] Instead, the court indicated that it was inappropriate to "consider and 'weigh' the contacts that do not exist";[88] the only legitimate task of the United States court, given the liberal purposes of the *Jones Act,* was to

---

83 See Symeonides, *supra* note 1, at pp. 249-52. See also B. Currie, "The Silver Oar and All That: A Study of the Romero Case" (1959), 27 U. Chi. L. Rev. 1 at 67, 69-70.

84 See Symeonides, *supra* note 1, at p. 252; Gilmore and Black, *supra* note 37, at pp. 473-74; Caskey, *supra* note 71, at p. 972. Caskey adds the argument that injury in the U.S. often entails investigation of the accident by U.S. authorities as well as the presence of relevant medical records in the United States.

85 263 F. 2d 437 (2d Cir.), cert. denied, 359 U.S. 1000 (1959).

86 Commentators noting (and in these instances deploring) the great influence of *Bartholomew* include Albritton, *supra* note 31, at p. 884; Watson, *supra* note 32, at p. 842.

87 *Supra* note 85, at p. 439-40.

88 *Ibid.* at 441.

determine whether there were "substantial contacts" with the United States:

> [I]t must be said that in a particular case something between minimal and preponderant contacts is necessary if the Jones Act is to be applied. Thus we conclude that the test is that "substantial" contacts are necessary. And while . . . one contact such as the fact that the vessel flies the American flag may alone be sufficient, this is no more than to say that in such a case the contact is so obviously substantial as to render unnecessary a further probing into the facts.[89]

The court also stated that American ownership alone was sufficient to warrant application of the *Jones Act*.[90]

When the Supreme Court returned to the foreign seaman choice-of-law issue in 1970, it gave a strong stamp of approval to the *Bartholomew* approach.[91] Plaintiff in *Hellenic Lines v. Rhoditis*[92] was a Greek seaman hurt aboard a Greek-owned, Greek-flag ship in the port of New Orleans. The Greek corporation that owned the vessel was 95-per cent-owned by a Greek subject who had lived in the United States for 25 years and who managed the corporation from offices in New York and New Orleans. The vessel and her sister ship were frequent visitors to American ports. The entire income of the vessel was derived from voyages which began or ended in the United States. On these facts, the Supreme Court held that the *Jones Act* was applicable:

> The *Lauritzen* test . . . is not a mechanical one. . . . The significance of one or more factors must be considered in light of the national interest served by the assertion of Jones Act jurisdiction.[93] Moreover the list of seven factors in Lauritzen was not intended as exhaustive. . . . [T]he shipowner's *base of operations* is another factor of importance in determining whether the Jones Act is applicable; and there may well be others. . . . We see no reason whatsoever to give the Jones Act a strained construction so that this alien owner, engaged in an extensive business operation in this country, may have an advantage over citizens engaged in the same business by allowing him to escape the obligations and responsibility of a Jones Act "employer".[94]

---

89   *Ibid.* at 440-41.

90   *Ibid.* at 443 n. 4.

91   Defence-oriented commentators have deplored *Bartholomew*. See note 86, *supra*. Carlson, *supra* note 31, at p. 54, suggested that the Second Circuit might have forsaken the *Bartholomew* approach in the interval between that decision and *Rhoditis, infra* note 92, but all the commentators agree that *Rhoditis* approved and in essence adopted *Bartholomew*.

92   398 U.S. 306 (1970).

93   In a footnote at this point in the opinion, the court cited approvingly and quoted from *Bartholomew*.

94   *Supra* note 92, at pp. 308-310 (emphasis in original). It is interesting that something very like the *Rhoditis* court's "competitive edge" argument had been made by plaintiff in *Lauritzen* and rather sternly rejected by the court as properly addressed only to Congress. See *Lauritzen,* 345 U.S. 571 at 593 (1953).

The choice-of-law jurisprudence after *Rhoditis* has been centrally concerned with the criteria for and application of the "base of operations" approach. Two distinct lines of lower court jurisprudence have developed. One group of decisions concerns traditional seamen, employed aboard merchant vessels and the like, sometimes termed "blue water" seamen.[95] The other group of decisions concerns workers engaged in mineral operations in the territorial waters or on the outer continental shelf of countries other than the United States.[96] Because the drilling structures involved in offshore mineral operations are usually classified as vessels, most of these workers would be counted as seamen.[97] In this paper the latter workers will be termed "foreign offshore workers".[98]

In the post-*Rhoditis* jurisprudence the doctrine of *forum non conveniens* began to compete with choice-of-law analysis as a major battleground. Under the next heading, this paper outlines the fundamental elements in *forum non conveniens* analysis and indicates the importance of the *forum non conveniens* doctrine in transnational maritime injury cases.

5. FORUM NON CONVENIENS ISSUES IN TRANSNATIONAL MARITIME INJURY CASES

The discretionary doctrine of *forum non conveniens* permits a court, in which subject-matter jurisdiction, personal jurisdiction and venue are admittedly proper, to decline to hear the case on the view that litigation in another forum would be much more appropriate, both from the standpoint of convenience of trial to the parties and witnesses, and from the standpoint of the court's own interest in maintaining control over its docket and avoiding embroilment with controversies having no significant relationship to the forum.[99] The seminal United States deci-

---

95   See "6. Traditional or 'Blue Water' Seamen: The Post-Rhoditis Choice-of-Law and Forum Non Conveniens Jurisprudence", *infra*.

96   See "7. Injury and Death Claims by Foreign Offshore Workers", *infra*. This paper assumes that injuries in oil and gas operations conducted in the territorial waters and on the outer continental shelf of the United States will continue to be governed by U.S. law. See Watson, *supra* note 32, at p. 827 and n. 3.

97   See note 61, *supra*.

98   It is not always easy to classify a particular case as either "blue water" or "foreign offshore". Certain activities, such as transoceanic towage of drilling rigs, might fit both categories.

99   Among the more useful general references are Barrett, "The Doctrine of Forum Non Conveniens" (1947), 35 Cal. L. Rev. 380; Braucher, "The Inconvenient Federal Forum" (1947), 60 Harv. L. Rev. 908; Bickel, "The Doctrine of Forum Non Conveniens As Applied in the Federal Courts in Matters of Admiralty" (1949), 35 Corn.

sion occurred in 1947 in *Gulf Oil Corp. v. Gilbert*,[100] in which the Supreme Court stated that "[t]he principle of forum non conveniens is simply that a court may resist imposition upon its jurisdiction even when jurisdiction is authorized by the letter of a general venue statute",[101] and that the doctrine "presupposes at least two forums in which the defendant is amenable to process [and] furnishes criteria for choice between them".[102] The court went on to set forth a non-exhaustive list of criteria to be weighed in this essentially discretionary determination. Factors of private interest to be considered include accessibility of proof and witnesses, ease and expense of litigating in the forum, the availability of compulsory process for attendance of witnesses, and the enforceability of a resulting judgment.[103] Factors of public interest to be weighed included the burden on congested local courts and juries imposed by trials having no relation to the forum, and the appropriateness of having the case decided by a court that is at home with the law to be applied.[104]

For a time the United States federal courts were sparing in their use of *forum non conveniens* to remit plaintiffs to trial in a forum abroad, but in recent years the doctrine has taken on exceptional vigor.[105] A major development was the decision of the Second Circuit Court of Appeals in *Alcoa S.S. Co. v. M/V Nordic Regent*,[106] holding that an American corporation's commercial maritime claim against a Liberian vessel should be tried abroad, even though the result would almost certainly be greatly diminished recovery on behalf of plaintiff.[107]

L.Q. 12; Note, "The Convenient Forum Abroad" (1967), 20 Stan. L. Rev. 57; Note, "The Convenient Forum Abroad Revisited" (1977), 17 Va. J. Int. L. 755. See also note 5, *supra*.

100 330 U.S. 501 (1947).

101 *Ibid.* at 507.

102 *Ibid.* at 507.

103 *Ibid.* at 508.

104 *Ibid.* at 508-09.

105 See, *e.g.*, Note, "Forum Non Conveniens and Foreign Plaintiffs in the Federal Courts" (1981), 69 Geo. L.J. 1257 at 1258-59. Courts dismissing cases on the basis of *forum non conveniens* frequently impose conditions designed to mitigate to a degree the harshness of forcing plaintiff to seek his relief abroad. Frequent conditions include requiring defendant to consent to the jurisdiction of the foreign forum, waive any statute of limitations that has accrued during the pendency of the U.S. action, promise to produce documents and witnesses, post security or otherwise guarantee the satisfaction of any judgment rendered in the foreign tribunal, and occasionally to meet part of plaintiff's costs and/or to admit liability. See Watson, *supra* note 4, at pp. 95-96; *Pain v. United Technologies Corp.*, 637 F. 2d 775 (D.C. Cir. 1980), cert. denied, 454 U.S. 1128 (1981).

106 654 F. 2d 147 (2d Cir.) (en banc), cert. denied, 449 U.S. 890 (1980).

107 See Paulsen and Burrick, "Forum Non Conveniens in Admiralty" (1982), 13 J. Mar. L. & Comm. 343.

The Supreme Court's 1981 decision in *Piper Aircraft Co. v. Reyno*[108] greatly magnified the scope of the *forum non conveniens* doctrine. Plaintiff, the representative of the estates of Scottish citizens killed in an aircraft crash in Scotland, sued American manufacturers in the United States. The Court of Appeals for the Third Circuit held that *forum non conveniens* dismissal should not occur when the law of the alternative forum is less favorable to plaintiff than the law of the chosen forum.[109] Reversing, the Supreme Court held that the "possibility of a change in substantive law should ordinarily not be given conclusive or even substantial weight in the forum non conveniens inquiry".[110] The court also held that, while there is some presumption in favor of retaining jurisdiction in the forum chosen by plaintiff, that presumption is not particularly strong when the plaintiffs or real parties in interest are foreign.[111]

As indicated above,[112] the *forum non conveniens* issue interacts with the choice-of-law issue in complex ways in transnational maritime injury cases. Courts often make no effort to separate the two matters.[113] However, in recent transnational maritime injury jurisprudence, the *forum non conveniens* doctrine seems to be emerging as the pre-eminent defensive strategy. In addition to the obvious arguments that the non-United States forum is the more convenient place of trial, it is helpful to defendant to be able to show that an entity from which contribution or indemnity should be sought is not amenable to American jurisdiction. Defensive arguments for *forum non conveniens* dismissal are also greatly aided by defendant suggesting and agreeing to abide by certain conditions, such as submitting to the jurisdiction of the foreign tribunal,

---

108   454 U.S. 235 (1981). See note 36, *supra.*
109   630 F. 2d 149 (1980).
110   *Supra* note 108, at p. 247.
111   *Ibid.* at 255-56.
112   See discussion at notes 36-53, *supra.*
113   In *Anastasiadis v. S.S. Little John,* 346 F. 2d 281 (5th Cir. 1965), cert. denied, 384 U.S 920 (1966), plaintiff, a Greek national, signed articles of employment in Greece and joined the vessel in Texas. Finding work and living conditions wholly unsatisfactory, he left the vessel and was subsequently arrested and incarcerated by U.S. authorities, allegedly because of the vessel master's refusal or failure to extend his visa, and he sued for that injury. The vessel, Liberian-owned and Liberian-flag, was wholly-owned and controlled by a U.S. corporation. Despite the fact of "injury" in the United States and full U.S. ownership of the vessel, the Fifth Circuit Court of Appeals affirmed the trial court's *forum non conveniens* dismissal, stating that *Lauritzen,* while a choice-of-law decision, also furnishes criteria for the *forum non conveniens* determination (at p. 283). Arguably the later decision of that court in *Fisher v. Agios Nicolaos V,* 628 F. 2d 308 (5th Cir. 1980), cert. denied, 454 U.S. 1129 (1981), re-established the distinction between choice-of-law criteria and *forum non conveniens* criteria. See discussion at notes 47-48, *supra.*

waiving any statute of limitations that may have run during the pendency of the United States action, making witnesses and documents available and guaranteeing the satisfaction of the foreign judgment. Whether or not defendant suggests such conditions, they are ordinarily imposed by American courts ordering *forum non conveniens* dismissal, and the availability of this conditional dismissal technique seems to make the American courts a great deal readier to apply the *forum non conveniens* doctrine.

6.   TRADITIONAL OR "BLUE WATER" SEAMEN: THE POST-RHODITIS CHOICE-OF-LAW AND FORUM NON CONVENIENS JURISPRUDENCE

After *Rhoditis,* a dominant theme in the transnational cases involving injuries to traditional seamen has been the criteria for and application of the "base of operations" approach. It has been stated that the jurisprudence is "utterly irreconcilable".[114] The Second Circuit Court of Appeals initially developed a very expansive approach and "came close to holding that American stock ownership alone would be sufficient to justify the application of American maritime laws".[115] At the same time, the Second Circuit has held to the view that injury (and medical treatment) of the injured seaman in the United States is an insufficient basis, standing alone, for invoking American Law.[116] In the 1983 decision in

---

114   Watson, *supra* note 32, at p. 844.

115   Albritton, *supra* note 31, at p. 887. In *Moncada v. Lemuria Shipping Corp.,* 491 F. 2d 470 (2d Cir.), cert. denied, 417 U.S. 947 (1974), plaintiff sued for the death of a Honduran seaman, which occurred in Brazil while he served on a foreign flag vessel owned by a foreign corporation. All the defendant corporation's stock was owned by U.S. citizens, and the court suggested that American ownership alone sufficed for the application of U.S. law (at p. 473). The court also relied on other factors, including the presence of the managing and chartering agent of the vessel in the United States, the fact that all of the corporate officers were U.S. citizens, and that 40 per cent of the vessel's voyages began or ended in U.S. ports. In *Antypas v. Campania Maritima San Basilio, S.A.,* 541 F. 2d 307 (2d Cir. 1976), cert. denied, 429 U.S. 1098 (1977), plaintiff was a Greek seaman hurt on a Greek-flag vessel on the high seas. The vessel was owned by a Panamanian corporation which in turn was owned at least in part by U.S. citizens. The court relied on American ownership, plus the presence of a U.S. agent who seemed to control the ship from the United States, advertisements in the United States, and the handling of earnings and expenses of the vessel from the United States, in support of its conclusion that U.S. law should apply. See also *Mattes v. Nat. Hellenic Amer. Line, S.A.,* 427 F. Supp. 619 (S.D.N.Y. 1977).

116   *Koupetoris v. Konkar Intrepid Corp.,* 535 F. 2d 1392 (2d Cir. 1976). This decision held both that U.S. law was inapplicable and that the trial court correctly dismissed on the basis of *forum non conveniens.*

Albritton, *supra* note 31, at pp. 890-91, also cites *Fitzgerald v. Texaco, Inc.,* 521 F. 2d 448 (2d Cir. 1975), cert. denied, 423 U.S. 1052 (1976), as an example of a more

Cruz v. Maritime Co. of Philippines,[117] the Second Circuit upheld *forum non conveniens* dismissal of a case brought by a Philippine seaman (resident in the United States since the accident) injured in an American port, against a foreign-owned, foreign-flag vessel, finding that the presence of one of defendant's employees and a freight agent in the United States did not establish an American base of operations. The court further stated that *forum non conveniens* was a sound basis for dismissal of the case without any necessity for a detailed inquiry into the choice-of-law issue and that, even if the *Jones Act* were applicable, *forum non conveniens* dismissal might be appropriate.[118] While *Cruz* was a *per curiam* affirmation of the court below, it nevertheless may suggest that the *forum non conveniens* doctrine has taken on enough vigor in the Second Circuit to signal a *de facto* change of direction by that court.[119]

The Third Circuit has been more conservative than the Second, holding that American beneficial ownership of the vessel is insufficient to support the application of United States law, and explicitly rejecting the *Bartholomew/Rhoditis* view that substantial American contacts are enough, without any necessity of comparing or weighing foreign contacts. The Third Circuit Court stated that the *Bartholomew/Rhoditis* approach smacks of "social jingoism".[120] The court used the *Lauritzen* factors in its analysis; the basis of the dismissal, however, was *forum non conveniens.*

The approach of the Court of Appeals for the Fourth Circuit has been similar to the more conservative Third Circuit approach. A 1978 Fourth Circuit decision involved wage claims against a foreign employer on behalf of a foreign seaman.[121] By the great weight of authority,

---

conservative Second Circuit case. However, while the *Fitzgerald* plaintiffs were seamen, they were not suing their employer but rather the owners of a wreck with which the employing vessel collided. The judicial benevolence traditionally afforded seaman plaintiffs relates to actions by seamen against employers. The *Jones Act* and the doctrine of maintenance and cure are confined to actions against employers. The unseaworthiness doctrine has limited application to actions against entities other than plaintiff's employer. Hence, *Fitzgerald* is probably not properly analyzed with the seamen's cases, but rather with the other maritime injury cases treated in "8. Maritime Accidents Injuring Non-Seamen", *infra.* See also note 54, *supra.*

117 702 F. 2d 47 (2d Cir. 1983).
118 *Ibid.* at 48. See also discussion at notes 40-46, *supra.*
119 See also the *Alcoa* decision, discussed at notes 105-107, *supra.*
120 *DeMateos v. Texaco, Inc.,* 562 F. 2d 895 at 902 (3d Cir. 1977), cert denied, 435 U.S. 904 (1978). The *DeMateos* plaintiff was the mother of a Panamanian seaman who got sick on a voyage between Honduras and Costa Rica and died shortly after being hospitalized in Costa Rica. The vessel flew the Liberian flag and was owned by a Panamanian corporation which was a wholly-owned subsidiary of Texaco, Inc. The court held that U.S ownership did not establish a U.S. base of operations when the particular vessel's operations were conducted and directed from abroad.
121 *Fitzgerald v. Liberian S/T Chryssi P. Goulandris,* 582 F. 2d 312 (4th Cir. 1978).

the United States statutes requiring and imposing a penalty for failure to make timely payment of wages apply to foreign vessels in American ports; jurisdiction to hear such claims by foreign seamen is mandatory in the federal courts; and generally a court which retains jurisdiction over a wage claim should retain the "appended" personal injury or death claim as well.[122] (While retaining jurisdiction over the appended personal injury and death claims would not alone mean that American law would govern such claims, there is some indication that a case in this posture has a much improved chance of being governed in its entirety by American law.[123]) The Fourth Circuit Court held that the wage claims were not asserted in good faith, and that the trial court had correctly dismissed plaintiff's remaining (wrongful death) claims on the basis of *forum non conveniens*.[124] A 1983 Fourth Circuit decision upheld choice-of-law and *forum non conveniens* determinations against a Greek plaintiff, hurt in a United States port by the alleged fault of the same defendant sued in the Supreme Court's *Rhoditis* decision. The Fourth Circuit Court held that the *Rhoditis* conclusion, that defendant had an American base of operations, was not entitled to collateral estoppel effect in view of the lapse of a dozen years since the *Rhoditis* injury.[125]

While it is difficult to summarize the rather extensive Fifth Circuit jurisprudence, there is some indication that this Circuit leans toward the more liberal approach associated with the Second Circuit. In 1980 the Fifth Circuit decided *Fisher v. Agios Nicolaos V,*[126] in which a decidedly liberal approach was taken to the choice-of-law issue. Plaintiff decedent was a Greek seaman who joined a Greek-flag ship in Texas and was killled there shortly thereafter. The ship was wholly foreign-owned, but its entire service under its existing ownership was in the United States-Russia grain trade. (It was preparing for its maiden voyage in that trade when the injury occurred.) The court upheld the trial court's decision that American law should apply, and also upheld the trial court's refusal to dismiss the case on the basis of *forum non conveniens. Fisher* is a celebrated case.[127] Whether it is an aberration has provoked vigorous

---

122 See Symeonides, *supra* note 1, at pp. 226-30; Gilmore and Black, *supra* note 37, at pp. 479-80.
123 See Dué, *supra* note 19, at pp. 275-77. *Cf.* Gilmore and Black, *supra* note 37, at pp. 479-80.
124 The *Fitzgerald* plaintiff sued on behalf of a deceased Greek seaman. The ship flew the Liberian flag. Defendant was the Liberian corporate shipowner, owned by Greeks. Injury occurred on the high seas.
125 *Dracos v. Hellenic Lines, Ltd.,* 705 F. 2d 1392 (4th Cir. 1983).
126 628 F. 2d 308 (5th Cir. 1980), rehearing denied, 636 F. 2d 1107 (5th Cir.), cert denied, 454 U.S. 816 (1981).
127 See, *e.g.,* Tate, *supra* note 44.

debate.[128] Subsequent Fifth Circuit decisions have upheld *forum non conveniens* dismissals in cases in which the only American contacts were injury in American waters and occasional visits by the vessel to American ports.[129]

The Ninth Circuit decision in *Rodriguez v. Flota Mercante Grancolombiana, S.A.*[130] upheld *forum non conveniens* dismissal[131] of a case brought by a Colombian seaman, hurt in the United States, against a foreign-owned, foreign-flag ship. The court stated that the existence of some American trade and earnings by the vessel and the presence of an agent in the United States did not suffice for the application of American law or the retention of forum jurisdiction in the United States.[132]

In the Eleventh Circuit, *Szumlicz v. Norwegian Amer. Line, Inc.*[133] upheld the application of United States law to a Polish seaman serving as a musician aboard a Norwegian Caribbean cruise ship, pointing to the fact that the vessel regularly operated cruises out of an American port.

---

128   Commentators regarding *Fisher* as an aberration include Albritton, *supra* note 31, at pp. 893-95, and Watson, *supra* note 32, at pp. 846-48. Judge Tate, on the other hand, points out that there were a number of factors supporting the retention of U.S. jurisdiction and applicability of U.S. law, including injury in a U.S. port, where plaintiff had worked during his entire service with defendants; the vessel's entire service and entire revenue under its present ownership had been from a base of operations in the United States, investigations were conducted by U.S. agencies; substantial adjudication had already been completed in a U.S. forum; and the plaintiff had joined with the maritime tort claims a *bona fide* wage claim arising under U.S. law: Tate, *supra* note 44, at pp. 209-10.

129   *Diaz v. Humboldt*, 722 F. 2d 1216 (5th Cir. 1984); *Volyrakis v. M/V Isabelle*, 668 F. 2d 863 (5th Cir. 1982).

But see *Abraham v. Universal Glow, Inc.*, 681 F. 2d 451 (5th Cir. 1982), where it was held that the existence of a good-faith wage claim by a foreign seaman against a foreign vessel established mandatory jurisdiction, and that the remaining personal injury claims should ordinarily be retained when joined with a good-faith wage claim.

It should be noted that another seaman injured in the same accident that gave rise to *Volyrakis, supra,* sought and secured a recovery in state court. The state court denied defendant's *forum non conveniens* and other defensive motions: *Symeonides v. Cosmar Compania Naviera, S.A.*, 433 So. 2d 281 (La. App. 1st. Cir.), writ ref., 440 So. 2d 731 (La. 1983), cert. denied, 104 S. Ct. 1442 (1984). See discussion of this litigation in Dué, *supra* note 19, at pp. 277-80.

130   703 F. 2d 1069 (9th Cir.), cert. denied, 104 S. Ct. 84 (1983). One U.S. contact urged without success by plaintiffs was that defendant was a plaintiff in unrelated litigation pending in a U.S. court. While the argument did not succeed, defendants should be aware that the institution of litigation within the United States is likely to generate the argument that this is a factor suggestive of significant operations being conducted in the United States.

131   The court also held that there was no subject-matter jurisdiction, with a concurring judge pointing out the flaw in that approach. See discussion at notes 30-34, *supra*.

132   But see *Dalla v. Atlas Maritime Co.*, 562 F. Supp. 752 (C.D. Cal. 1983).

133   698 F. 2d 1192 (11th Cir. 1983).

While it would be difficult to reconcile and rationalize all of the above-discussed jurisprudence, it seems clear from very recent decisions that the courts have become more reluctant to entertain foreign-seaman claims under United States law. One explanation may be the influence of the foreign offshore-worker decisions, treated below. The key factor is probably the recent invigoration of the *forum non conveniens* doctrine, which seems to reflect an increasing concern of American courts for their own crowded dockets.[134]

7. INJURY AND DEATH CLAIMS BY FOREIGN OFFSHORE WORKERS[135]

The early United States cases involving claims by workers hurt while engaged in offshore-oil-and-gas operations in the territorial waters or over the continental shelf of foreign nations seem to have proceeded on the assumption that the choice-of-law principles developed in the *Lauritzen* line of cases were applicable without modification.[136] (These principles would sustain the application of American law in many of these cases because the defendant was owned and controlled by American interests.) However, it has been pointed out that there are clear distinctions between these cases and "blue water" cases, arguably warranting diferent choice-of-law treatment. Unlike traditional shipping, offshore operations remain in one spot for a significant period of time, and are always conducted within an area claimed by some sovereign state.[137]

These differences soon produced a different judicial approach to the availability of American relief.[138] As of this writing, there is a

---

134   The Supreme Court's expansion of the *forum non conveniens* doctrine in *Piper Aircraft Co. v. Reyno*, 454 U.S. 235 (1981), was based on part on crowded docket concerns: "The American courts, which are already extremely attractive to foreign plaintiffs, would become even more attractive. The flow of litigation into the United States would increase and further congest already crowded courts" (at 252). Many other recent *forum non conveniens* cases reflect the docket congestion concern.

135   This paper uses the term "foreign offshore workers" to refer to workers other than U.S. citizens or residents who sustain injury while engaged in mineral operations in the territorial waters or over the continental shelf of nations other than the United States. As is explained at note 61, *supra,* most of the plaintiffs in this category are treated as seamen. See also note 98, *supra.*

136   See *Farmer v. Standard Dredging Corp.*, 167 F. Supp. 381 (D. Del. 1958); *Rode v. Sedco, Inc.*, 394 F. Supp. 206 (E.D. Tex. 1975).

137   Watson, *supra* note 32, at p. 849, points out that the 1958 Geneva Convention on the Territorial Sea and the Contiguous Zone, 450 U.N.T.S. 206, has "internationalized the position taken earlier by the United States and other countries in asserting jurisdiction over the Outer Continental Shelf."

138   In the "blue-water" cases, there had been confusion as to whether the "base of

sizeable body of jurisprudence refusing American relief in injury cases brought by foreign offshore workers against American shipowners and employers, in some cases involving American-flag vessels. The most recent of these decisions are articulated as *forum non conveniens* dismissals.[139]

The result of the foregoing decisions has been codified and expanded by legislation. Effective December 29, 1982 and applicable to injuries occurring on or after that date,[140] the *Jones Act*[141] has been amended by the addition of a new paragraph (b) as follows:

> (1) No action may be maintained under subsection (a) of this section [the original *Jones Act*] or under any other maritime law of the United States for maintenance and cure [or] for damages for the injury or death of a person who was not a citizen or permanent resident alien of the United States at the time of the incident giving rise to the action if the incident occurred–
>
>> (A) while that person was in the employ of an enterprise engaged in the exploration, development, or production of off-shore mineral or energy resources – including but not limited to drilling, mapping, surveying, diving, pipelaying, maintaining, repairing, constructing, or transporting supplies, equipment or personnel, but not including transporting those resources by a vessel constructed or adapted primarily to carry oil in bulk in the cargo spaces; and

---

operations" inquiry properly focussed on defendant's operations in general or on the particular vessel or venture involved in the accident. See Albritton, *supra* note 31, at pp. 891-93. In the foreign offshore cases, it has become clear that the focus is on the particular venture. The recent foreign offshore cases have also reversed the *Lauritzen* hierarchy, in which the place of the injury is ordinarily not very important and the law of the flag ordinarily paramount, by holding that the place of the injury is virtually paramount and the law of the flag relatively unimportant.

139 See *Koke v. Phillips Petroleum Co.*, 730 F. 2d 211 (5th Cir. 1984) (U.S. flag) (*forum non conveniens*); *Needham v. Phillips Petroleum Co. of Norway*, 719 F. 2d 1481 (10th Cir. 1983) (*forum non conveniens*); *Fajardo v. Tidewater, Inc.*, 707 F. 2d 858 (5th Cir. 1983) (*forum non conveniens*); *De Oliveira v. Delta Marine Drilling Co.*, 707 F. 2d 843 (5th Cir. 1983) (*forum non conveniens*); *Chick Kam Choo v. Exxon Corp.*, 699 F. 2d 693 (5th Cir. 1983), cert. denied, 104 S. Ct. 98 (*forum non conveniens*); *Bailey v. Dolphin Internat., Inc.*, 697 F. 2d 1268 (5th Cir. 1983) (*forum non conveniens*); *Vaz Borralho v. Keydril Co., infra*, note 142 (*forum non conveniens*); *Zekic v. Reading & Bates Drilling Co.*, 680 F. 2d 1107 (5th Cir. 1982) (*forum non conveniens*); *Alvestad v. Monsanto Co.*, 671 F. 2d 908 (5th Cir.), cert. denied, 103 S. Ct. 489 (U.S. 1982) (*forum non conveniens*); *Chiazor v. Transworld Drilling Co.*, 648 F. 2d 1015 (5th Cir. 1981), cert. denied, 455 U.S. 1019 (1982), (*forum non conveniens*); *Phillips v. Amoco Trinidad Oil Co.*, 632 F. 2d 82 (9th Cir. 1980), cert. denied, 451 U.S. 920 (1981) (U.S. flag) (failure to state a claim under U.S. law); *Chirinos de Alvarez v. Creole Petroleum Corp.*, 613 F. 2d 1240 (3d Cir. 1980) (failure to state a claim under U.S. law); *House v. Santa Fe Internat. Corp.*, 1978 A.M.C. 1899 (S.D. Tex.) (U.S. flag) (failure to state a claim under U.S. law), modified, 1978 A.M.C. 2348 (S.D. Tex.).

140 The legislation, s. 503 of *Public Law* 97-389, contained a "saving clause" providing: "The amendment made by this section does not apply to any action arising out of an incident that occurred before the date of enactment of this section."

141 46 U.S.C. §688.

(B) in the territorial waters or waters overlaying the continental shelf of a nation other than the United States, its territories, or possessions. As used in this paragraph, the term "continental shelf" has the meaning stated in Article I of the 1958 Convention on the Continental Shelf.

(2) The provisions of paragraph (1) of this subsection shall not be applicable if the person bringing the action establishes that no remedy was available to that person—

(A) under the laws of the nation asserting jurisdiction over the area in which the incident occurred; or

(B) under the laws of the nation in which, at the time of the incident, the person for whose injury or death a remedy is sought maintained citizenship or residency.

This legislation codifies the choice-of-law result reached in the foreign offshore-worker cases discussed above, but arguably goes beyond the reasoning process in those cases. It deprives the foreign offshore mineral worker of a cause of action regardless of the vessel's special nature and relatively long-term, fixed location in foreign waters, and regardless of whether any of the relevant operations are of a fixed or long-term nature.[142]

Presumably this legislation will prevent litigation of foreign off-shore-oil-worker injury claims in American courts in most cases. However, two matters will provoke litigation. First, there is an apparent ambiguity in the provisions of paragraph (2) of the new subsection (b) of the *Jones Act* which states that the exclusion from American remedies is not applicable if plaintiff shows no remedy to be available to him under the laws of the nation with jurisdiction over the accident site *or* under the laws of the nation of his citizenship or residency. As worded, the legislation would arguably permit the assertion of United States rights if the plaintiff's home country denied a remedy, even if the country with jurisdiction over the accident site did provide a remedy, or vice versa. The legislative history is not fully revealing with respect to this ambiguity, which has not been discussed in any reported decision. Explaining the Bill in the Senate, Senator Long said:

[A] foreign worker engaged in mineral extraction activities in waters over the continental shelf of a foreign nation may not seek a remedy for his work-related injury in U.S. courts if he has a remedy in his home country, or in the country with jurisdiction over the accident site, if different. Should there be no remedy overseas, the foreign worker would then, and only then, be able to adjudicate his claim in U.S. courts.[143]

This statement assumes that paragraph (2) of the new legislation means that United States remedies are precluded if there is a remedy in either

---

142   See discussion in *Vaz Borralho v. Keydril Co.,* 710 F. 2d 207 at 209-10 (5th Cir. 1983), denying rehearing of panel decision at 696 F. 2d 379 (5th Cir. 1983).

143   Cong. Rec., December 10, 1982, p. S 14364.

the accident-site country or the plaintiff's home country; in effect, Senator Long reads the word "or" in that paragraph to mean "and". Similar statements were made by Congressmen Breaux[144] and Pritchard,[145] explaining the legislation on the House of Representatives side. Such legislative history, while sparse, suggests that the ambiguity will probably not avail the plaintiff who raises it.

Second, it is arguable that the 1982 legislation is in conflict with certain treaties of friendship, commerce and navigation between the United States and other nations. These treaties generally include "access" provisions assuring that foreign nationals will have "free and open access" to the courts of the United States.[146] The report of the House of Representatives Committee states that the legislation will not offend against such treaties:

> The Supreme Court has found that, while this type of provision grants procedural rights, it "does not define substantive rights but leaves them to be ascertained by the law governing the courts and administered and enforced in them." Majorano v. Baltimore and Ohio Railroad, 213 U.S. 268. The courts have generally found that the substantive rights granted by the Jones Act do not extend to foreign nationals who lack sufficient contacts with the United States. These court decisions are not a denial of equal access but rather a determination of lack of standing. The decisions generally hold that the litigant has no right which can be enforced in a U.S. court. [The legislation] codifies this case law and clarifies that the substantive rights granted by the Jones Act do not extend to foreign offshore workers.
>
> The legislation is in accord with customary international law and international agreements in that it recognizes the rights of a nation to regulate activity within its territorial waters and in the Outer Continental Shelf adjacent to the coast of that nation. The present situation whereby domestic United States law is applied to actions and occurrences with the jurisdiction of a sovereign foreign nation is an unwarranted application and extraterritorial extension of U.S. law and not in accord with our treaties of friendship and navigation.[147]

Despite those assurances, however, the State Department originally advised that it "cannot support" the legislation because the Bill "could . . . give rise to claims by U.S. Treaty partners that the United States is not providing the national treatment in terms of access to U.S. courts generally required by our treaties of friendship, commerce, and naviga-

---

144 Cong. Rec., December 10, 1982, p. H 9452: "If no remedy exists in either [accident-site or plaintiff's home] forum, they may pursue Jones Act actions in U.S. courts."

145 Cong. Rec., December 10, 1982, p. H 9453: "If there is a remedy available to him through a foreign jurisdiction, then he is precluded from instituting an action in the U.S. courts. However, if the injured party can show that there is no remedy available to him in either the country where the accident occurred, or his place of citizenship or residence, then he would be permitted to pursue his legal action in U.S. courts."

146 This matter was discussed but not resolved in *Vaz Borralho v. Keydril Co., supra* note 142, at pp. 210-11 (and n. 2), 212-14.

147 H.R. Rep. No. 97-863, 97th Cong., 2d Sess., p. 7 (1982).

tion".[148] The Court of Appeals for the Fifth Circuit – discussing but not resolving the treaty argument – stated that "[t]he Executive Department apparently changed its mind, as the bill was signed by the President", and expressed doubt that "access" treaty provisions should be read to require the availability of United States relief to foreign offshore workers.[149]

It is uncertain whether either the suggested ambiguity in the *Jones Act* amendment or its uncertain impact upon "access rights" in treaties will be persuasive on plaintiffs' behalf in many cases. The likelihood is that foreign offshore injury cases have largely been foreclosed from the applicability of United States law.

8. MARITIME ACCIDENTS INJURING NON-SEAMEN

(a) Aviation Cases

Many aviation cases give rise to admiralty jurisdiction and are hence potentially susceptible to the maritime choice-of-law analysis developed from *Lauritzen* in the seamen's cases.[150] Commentators[151] and some decisions[152] have indicated that the Lauritzen-derived principles govern. On the other hand, some of the maritime aviation decisions betray significant confusion as to the appropriate choice-of-law analysis. In two recent Court of Appeals decisions, courts treating the choice-of-law issue as but one of the factors involved in the *forum non conveniens* analysis made a provisional determination on the choice-of-law point without apparent attention to the *Lauritzen* principles.[153] Several earlier district court opinions managed to resolve the choice-of-law issue without revealing anything about the source or content of the principles employed.[154]

---

148   H.R. Rep. 97-863, 97th Cong., 2d Sess., pp. 13-14 (1982).
149   *Vaz Borralho v. Keydril Co., supra* note 142, at p. 213 and n. 5.
150   See note 1, *supra.*
151   See Symeonides, *supra* note 1, at p. 235 n. 51; Thomas, *supra* note 1, at p. 75.
152   See *Re Air Crash Disaster Near Bombay,* 531 F. Supp. 1175 at 188-91 (W.D. Wash. 1982); *Noel v. United Aircraft Corp.,* 202 F. Supp. 556 at 557-58 (D. Del. 1962); *Bergeron v. Koninklijke Luchtvaart Maatschappij, N.V.,* 188 F. Supp. 594 at 596-97 (S.D.N.Y. 1960); *Noel v. Airponents, Inc.,* 169 F. Supp. 348 at 351 (D.N.J. 1958).
153   *Pain v. United Technologies Corp.,* 637 F. 2d 775 at 793 (D.C. Cir. 1980), cert. denied, 454 U.S. 1128 (1981); *Dahl v. United Technologies Corp.,* 632 F. 2d 1027 at 1032 (3d Cir. 1980).
154   *Hammill v. Olympic Airways, S.A.,* 398 F. Supp. 829 (D.D.C. 1975); *Noel v. Linea Aeropostal Venezolana,* 260 F. Supp. 1002 (S.D.N.Y. 1966). One court held that U.S. law was applicable by analogy to early decisions preferring the law of the forum in maritime collision cases: *Fernandez v. Linea Aeropostal Venezolana,* 156 F. Supp. 94 at 96-98 (S.D.N.Y. 1957).

In the aviation cases brought by United States citizens or residents in which choice of law was the central issue, the earlier decisions showed some preference for American law.[155] One decision applied American law on behalf of a non-American decedent killed on the high seas in a crash of a Venezuelan airliner bound from New York to Venezuela, relying on early maritime collision cases preferring forum law.[156]

The *forum non conveniens* doctrine is fully applicable in maritime aviation cases.[157] More recent decisions have tended to focus on that defence, and may suggest a change of attitude on the part of the courts. In *Pain v. United Technologies Corp.*,[158] one of the five victims of a North Sea helicopter crash was an American citizen, resident of Norway. Defendants were the American manufacturer and the Norwegian operator of the helicopter. Upholding *forum non conveniens* dismissal, the District of Columbia Circuit Court treated the choice-of-law issue as a relatively minor factor in the *forum non conveniens* analysis, and suggested that Norwegian law would probably dominate in the trial of the action.[159] The same approach was taken by the Third Circuit in *Dahl v. United Technologies Corp.*,[160] in which the crash had occurred in Nor-

---

Most maritime aviation cases involve fatalities and thus bring into play the *Death on the High Seas Act (DHSA)*, 46 U.S.C. §§761-68. One additional source of complexity in *DHSA* cases is presented by the fact that §761 establishes a U.S. cause of action and §764 additionally provides for a cause of action in U.S. courts under applicable foreign law. Some courts hold that a choice must be made, under applicable choice-of-law principles, between the two provisions. See *Re Air Crash Disaster Near Bombay, supra* note 152, at pp. 1184-88; Thomas, *supra* note 1, at pp. 73-79. Other courts have held that §§761 and 764 are cumulative in effect, affording plaintiff access in appropriate cases to both U.S. and foreign law. See, *e.g., Fernandez v. Linea Aeropostal Venezolana, supra.*

155 See Symeonides, *supra* note 1, at p. 235 n. 51. In *Hammill v. Olympic Airways, S.A., supra* note 154, decedent was a U.S. tourist killed in a crash of a Greek domestic flight in Greek territorial waters, and the court held U.S. law applicable without engaging in any choice-of-law analysis. In two cases arising from the high seas crash of a Venezuelan airliner bound from New York to Venezuela, the courts applied U.S. law on behalf of U.S. decedents: *Noel v. United Aircraft Corp., supra* note 152 (defendant a U.S. corporation); *Noel v. Airponents, Inc., supra* note 152 (defendant a U.S. corporation). *Cf. Noel v. Linea Aeropostal Venezolana, supra* note 154 (at plaintiff's behest, Venezuelan law held applicable). But see *Bergeron v. Koninklijke Luchtvaart Maatschappij, supra* note 152, refusing to apply U.S. law to claims on behalf of a U.S. citizen killed on the high seas in the crash of a Dutch airliner bound from Shannon to New York.

156 *Fernandez v. Linea Aeropostal Venezolana, supra* note 154, at pp. 96-98 (defendant was the Venezuelan carrier).

157 See Paulsen and Burrick, *supra* note 107.

158 637 F. 2d 775 (D.C. Cir. 1980), cert. denied, 454 U.S. 1128 (1981).

159 *Ibid.* at 793. It should be noted that one of the conditions of the dismissal was that the U.S. defendant admit liability.

160 632 F. 2d 1027 (3d Cir. 1980).

wegian territorial waters and none of the decedents were American citizens or residents. In *Re Air Crash Disaster Near Bombay,*[161] a district court held that Indian law applied to litigation on behalf of 188 Indian and two American decedents against American manufacturers, but denied defendants' *forum non conveniens* motion solely because it appeared that the Indian courts would hold the actions to be irrevocably time-barred.

While there are too few reported maritime aviation decisions to permit confident speculation, probably the *forum non conveniens* defence is at least as potent here as in the seamen's cases, and the courts seem inclined to give sympathetic attention to motions to dismiss on that basis. *Pain* and *Dahl* were cited approvingly in *Piper Aircraft Co. v. Reyno,*[162] in which the Supreme Court held that the prospect that plaintiff would be governed by less favorable law in the foreign forum is not a significant factor weighing against *forum non conveniens* dismissal, and that a foreign plaintiff's choice of a United States forum is not entitled to much deference or presumptive weight in the *forum non conveniens* analysis.

(b) Miscellaneous Maritime Injury Cases

Two actions on behalf of deceased seamen against entities other than the employers of the deceased[163] focussed on the *forum non conveniens* defence and discussed the choice-of-law issue as one of the factors involved in the *forum non conveniens* analysis.

In *Fitzgerald v. Texaco, Inc.,*[164] plaintiffs represented the estates of twelve German seamen killed when the vessel on which they were serving struck the submerged wreck of defendants' vessel twelve miles off the English coast. The wrecked vessel was owned by a Panamanian corporation which was a wholly-owned subsidiary of Texaco, Inc., and flew the Panamanian flag. Upholding *forum non conveniens* dismissal, the court stated that "[l]iability for a collision on the high seas between vessels flying different flags is determined according to the general maritime law as interpreted by the courts of the forum in which the action proceeds".[165] The court correctly anticipated the *Piper Aircraft*[166] holding, that *forum non conveniens* dismissal is appropriate even

---

161   531 F. Supp. 1175 (W.D. Wash. 1982).
162   454 U.S. 235 (1981).
163   See notes 54 and 116 *supra,* explaining why these cases are arguably subject to different principles than seamen's litigation against employers.
164   521 F. 2d 448 (2d Cir. 1975), cert. denied, 423 U.S. 1052 (1976).
165   *Ibid.* at 452. *Cf. Fernandez v. Linea Aeropostal Venezolana,* discussed *supra* note 154.
166   *Supra* note 162.

though the law of the alternative forum is less favorable to plaintiffs' chances of recovery.[167] The court concluded that the private and public factors set forth in *Gulf Oil Corp. v. Gilbert*[168] pointed to *forum non conveniens* dismissal. Dissenting, Judge Oakes urged the applicability of the seamen's cases; indicated that the true ownership of the vessel by Texaco, Inc. and Texaco's base of operations in the United States supported the application of United States law; and stated that the entire doctrine of *forum non conveniens* should "be re-examined in the light of the transportation revolution that has occurred since [*Gilbert* was decided in 1947] . . . and in the light of the dispersion of corporate authority, as here, by the use of multinational subsidiaries to conduct international business."[169]

Plaintiffs in *Alegria v. Grand Bassa Tankers, Inc.,*[170] represented the estates of two seamen, whose nationality does not appear in the report of the case, injured in a collision between their ship and defendants' Liberian-flag ship in the Straits of Singapore. Defendants were the vessel owner, a Liberian corporation, and Cities Service Tankers Corporation, its American parent. Refusing to dismiss the case on the basis of *forum non conveniens,* the court indicated that defendants' arguments, derived from the *Lauritzen* line of cases, were irrelevant, stating: "We are not dealing here with a choice of law but with a choice of forum, and *Gulf Oil Corp. v. Gilbert* is the applicable authority rather than *Lauritzen v. Larsen.*"[171] The court refused to dismiss, taking the view that defendants with a principal place of business in the forum must show that retaining jurisdiction would work clear prejudice.

Given the special solicitude traditionally shown by the courts on behalf of seamen victims, it is likely that the perceived recent tendency to deny American relief to foreign seamen will obtain with at least equal force in the maritime injury cases involving victims other than seamen. It is worthy of note that, in litigation based on injuries occurring in vessel collisions, the older jurisprudence preferring forum law apparently retains some current persuasiveness.[172] Whether that principle will prevail against *forum non conveniens* defences remains to be seen, but in light of the *Piper Aircraft*[173] holding that a change in applicable law

---

167 The *Piper* court, *supra* note 162, at pp. 250-51, cited *Fitzgerald* with approval.
168 330 U.S. 501 (1947).
169 *Supra* note 164, at p. 456 and n. 3. See also Judge Friendly's article, "Indiscretion About Discretion" (1982), 31 Emory L.J. 747 at pp. 749-54, 758 and n. 35, suggesting the need for re-examination of the *forum non conveniens* doctrine.
170 337 F. Supp. 401 (S.D.N.Y. 1971).
171 *Ibid.* at 403.
172 See *Fitzgerald, supra* note 164, and *Fernandez, supra* note 154.
173 *Infra* note 174.

unfavorable to plaintiff is not a factor to be weighed against *forum non conveniens* dismissal, it appears somewhat unlikely.   .

9. CONCLUSION

While the foregoing survey of jurisprudence on the availability of United States relief to victims of transnational maritime accidents reveals a considerable amount of doctrinal confusion, the overall tendency of the law seems clear. The *Rhoditis* era of relative liberality is in the process of being succeeded by a period of retrenchment. The 1982 amendment to the *Jones Act* has largely foreclosed United States relief to foreign offshore workers. With increasing frequency, other maritime accident victims are thwarted by the *forum non conveniens* defence.

Several factors probably explain this trend. Courts dismissing cases on the basis of *forum non conveniens* often refer to the congested dockets of United States federal courts.[174] Courts concluding that American law should not apply discuss international comity and the desirability of American ownership of international business ventures.[175] Congress amended the *Jones Act* to protect American businesses and their foreign subsidiaries from "billions" in injury claims and from being placed at a competitive disadvantage with foreign venturers.[176] And perhaps the

---

174   *Piper Aircraft Co. v. Reyno,* 454 U.S. 235 at 252 (1981): "The American courts, which are already extremely attractive to foreign plaintiffs, would become even more attractive. The flow of litigation into the United States would increase and further congest already crowded courts."

175   *De Mateos v. Texaco, Inc.,* 562 F. 2d 895 at 902 (3d Cir. 1977), cert. denied, 435 U.S. 904 (1978): "It would be an extreme suggestion, we think, that American law could govern relations between Texpan [a wholly-owned Panamanian subsidiary of Texaco] and the employees in its Panamanian gasoline stations because its stock was owned by a multinational business enterprise incorporated in Delaware. It is no less extreme to suggest that American law should govern the relations between Texpan and its employees on vessels it uses in the transportation of petroleum between Central American countries. Either suggestion is a variety of social jingoism, which presumes that the 'liberal purposes' of American law must be exported to wherever our multinational corporations are permitted to do business. Some of our laws, to other nations, may not appear as liberal as the Jones Act appears to us, and extreme applications of such an effort might well result in those nations closing their door to such corporations, to their and our competitive disadvantage."

176   Cong. Rec., December 10, 1982, p. S14364, remarks of Senator Long: "American offshore service companies and their foreign subsidiaries are being severely impacted by a multitude of lawsuits, aggregating claims over a billion dollars, brought by foreign offshore oil and gasfield workers. ... The United States should not continue to export its remedies for foreign workers' work-related injury claims which arose in foreign waters. Since no other country allows its judicial system to be used by foreign citizens for incidents occurring within the jurisdiction of foreign nations, U.S. offshore service companies and their foreign subsidiaries are at a competitive disadvantage with their many foreign competitors."

"international ambulance-chasing" controversy[177] has had its influence.

In any event, the message to litigators is clear. Diligent defence counsel will emphasize the recent *forum non conveniens* decisions. Plaintiffs' counsel may be required to demonstrate that trial in the United States forum would be equally or more convenient than elsewhere, and that there were significant day-to-day contacts between a *bona fide* American base of operations and the particular voyage or venture that produced the injury.

---

177   See discussion at notes 5-18, *supra.*

CONFLICT OF LAWS AND PERSONAL INJURY IN THE EASTERN CANADIAN OFFSHORE: THE AFTERMATH OF THE *ARCTIC EXPLORER* AND *OCEAN RANGER* SINKINGS

Michael F. Harrington*

As a moth is drawn to the light, so is a litigant drawn to the United States. If he can only get his case into their courts, he stands to win a fortune. At no cost to himself, and at no risk of having to pay anything to the other side. The lawyers there will conduct the case 'on spec' as we say – or on a 'contingency fee' as they say. The lawyers will charge the litigant nothing for their services but instead they will take 40% of the damages, if they win the case in court, or out of court on a settlement. If they lose, the litigant will have nothing to pay to the other side. The courts in the United States have no such costs deterrent as we have. There is also in the United States a right to trial by jury. These are prone to award fabulous damages. They are notoriously sympathetic and know that the lawyers will take their 40% before the plaintiff gets anything. All this means that the defendant can be readily forced into a settlement. The plaintiff holds all the cards.[1]

Such cynical protestations are contained in the opening sentences of Lord Denning in a judgment upholding an injunction order issued by a deputy judge of the High Court against "forum shopping" in the United States by an English doctor in pursuit of damages in contract and

---

*The author is with the firm of Stirling, Ryan, St. John's Newfoundland.

1 *Smith Kline & French Laboratories Ltd. v. Bloch,* [1983] 2 All E.R. 72 at 74 (C.A.).

tort against an English pharmaceutical company and its American parent. At the same time, Lord Denning expressed his unhappiness with the House of Lords decision in *Castanho v. Brown & Root (U.K.) Ltd.*[2]

These English injunction cases and others dealing with stay of proceedings constitute one important ingredient of a complex mixture of conflict of laws problems in the maritime law field connected with oil and gas exploration and production on the Eastern Canadian offshore.

1. INTRODUCTION

The sinkings of the seismic vessel *Arctic Explorer* and MODU *Ocean Ranger* have brought many of the above issues into focus. The purpose of this paper is to explore from a Canadian perspective the scope of the conflict of laws problems emerging in the field of injury and wrongful death claims.

This paper will discuss: (1) the potential remedies available to oil rig workers, both industrial and marine, and their dependants in Canadian courts; (2) the effect of Canadian federal and provincial workers' compensation schemes; (3) the choice of law dilemma; and (4) defence strategies available to combat "forum shopping" by Canadian and foreign claimants in jurisdictions outside Canada in respect of incidents occurring in Eastern Canadian waters considered to be the high seas.

The complexity of the *Arctic Explorer* and *Ocean Ranger* litigation was compounded by potential U.S. remedies available to Canadian and other foreign claimants (absent the issue of "forum non conveniens") including recovery for conscious pain and suffering and punitive damages. While discussing some of these complexities, the regime which may exist in future in light of the post *Ocean Ranger* U.S. Jones Act amendment[3] will be dealt with in greater detail.

Lord Denning's desire to keep litigation with a substantial English connection in an English court to the exclusion of foreign proceedings

---

2   [1981] 1 All E.R. 143, [1981] A.C. 557 (H.L.). The House of Lords affirmed a Court of Appeal judgment, Denning M.R. dissenting, [1980] 3 All E.R. 72 allowing an injured Portuguese seaman to discontinue English proceedings and pursue Texas State Court proceedings. The U.S. proceedings had been enjoined at first instance by the English Court.

3   Jones Act, 46 U.S.C. S 688, as amended, H.R. 3942-7. This amendment prohibits legal action by foreign citizens or residents for maintenance and cure or for damages for "injury or death" arising out of foreign energy and mineral exploration and production operations where a remedy is available in the place of the foreigner's citizenship or residency. The fact that the remedy might be workers' compensation benefits would seem to be irrelevant – see *In re M.V. Arctic Explorer* No. 81-3381 (U.S. Fed. Dist. Ct., Houston Division, May 8, 1984) pp. 28, 29.

can be traced back to his speech in the case of *The Atlantic Star*[4] in which
he said:

> No one who comes to these courts asking for justice should come in vain . . . This right
> to come here is not confined to Englishmen. It extends to any friendly foreigner. He
> can seek the aid of our courts if he desires to do so. You may call this 'forum shopping'
> if you please, but if the forum is England, it is a good place to shop in, both for the
> quality of the goods and the speed of service.

Lord Denning was, in fact, criticizing forum shopping unless its aim
was to keep litigation in England.

The House of Lords concurred with Denning M.R.'s disdain for
"forum shopping" but overturned his decision. Lord Reid stated:[5]

> My Lords, with all respect, that seems to me to recall the good old days, the passing of
> which many may regret, when inhabitants of this island felt an innate superiority over
> those unfortunate enough to belong to other races.

It is against this backdrop that the *Arctic Explorer*[6] and *Ocean
Ranger*[7] litigation can be evaluated. The claimants in those cases sought
to maximize their recovery potential by commencing U.S. proceedings.
In this way, they would avoid the effect of Newfoundland workers'
compensation legislation. The defendants, on the other hand, pleaded
the existence of adequate Canadian remedies and criticized the claimants' efforts to avoid Canadian jurisdiction by "forum shipping" in the
United States.

2. ARCTIC EXPLORER LITIGATION

The *Arctic Explorer* sinking resulted in Canada in a limitation of
liability proceeding[8] together with actions by some Canadian claimants

---

4   [1972] 3 All E.R. 705 at 709, [1972] 3 W.L.R. 746 at 757 (C.A.). Dutch owners of a
barge had initiated actions both in England and in Belgium against the Dutch owners
of the *Atlantic Star* in respect of a collision in the River Schelde near Antwerp. The
owners of the *Atlantic Star* applied for a stay of the English proceedings. This was
refused at first instance and in the Court of Appeal.

5   [1974] A.C. 436, [1973] 2 All E.R. 175 at 181 (H.L.).

6   On July 3, 1981, this Canadian flagged and owned seismic vessel, time chartered to a
U.S. company, sank in Canadian territorial waters 5 miles off the northeast coast of
Newfoundland causing the loss of 10 Canadians, 2 Australians and 1 American.
There were Canadian and foreign survivors.

7   On February 15, 1982, this U.S. designed, flagged and owned self-propelled semi-
submersible offshore drilling unit, built in Japan, operating under a drilling agreement between two Canadian companies as operator and contractor (a Canadian
affiliate of the U.S. owner) sank on the high seas 175 nautical miles from St. John's,
Newfoundland, killing 84 men including 15 Americans. The drilling agreement was
governed by the laws of Alberta. The operator held drilling permits from the
Governments of Canada and Newfoundland.

8   *Carino Co. and Geophysical Service Inc. v. All Persons or Parties Claiming . . . in*

in the Newfoundland Supreme Court against the Canadian owner and the U.S. charterer. U.S. litigation was also commenced against the U.S. time charterer and its parent company. The latter litigation was consolidated in the United States Federal District Court (Southern District of Texas) through the institution of a U.S. limitation of liability proceeding.

A U.S. federal district judge, apparently paying particular attention to the Canadian limitation action, the right of a time charterer to limit liability as a matter of substantive Canadian law and the many Canadian connecting factors associated with the casualty, granted a *forum non conveniens* motion by the U.S. defendants. The result of this motion was to send all actions including the claim of the dependants of the one American decedent,[9] to Canada for adjudication in the Canadian limitation proceeding.

It is clear that claims against registered employers, *i.e.* the Canadian owner and U.S. charterer, in Canadian courts by *Arctic Explorer* claimants were barred by virtue of the Newfoundland Workers' Compensation Act[10] or the Federal Merchant Seaman Compensation Act.[11] In the absence of such legislation the personal representative and the dependants of the deceased crew members could have made tort claims in the Newfoundland Supreme Court under provincial fatal accidents legislation even if the place of the casualty was outside Newfoundland provincial boundaries on the high seas.[12] At the same time, claims in tort based on negligence against the charterer and unseaworthiness against the

---

connection with the sinking of the Canadian ship Arctic Explorer F.C. No. T-4480-81. The Statement of Claim filed also sought an injunction to restrain Canadian claimants from pursuing remedies in U.S. courts.

9 *Supra,* note 3, judgment filed May 8th, 1984 (not yet reported). See the Canada Shipping Act, R.S.C. 1970, c. S-9, s. 649(1)(a). See *Bethlemen Steel Corp. v. St. Lawrence Seaway,* [1978] 1 F.C. 464. These matters relating to limitation of liability are discussed in other papers in this collection.

10 *Workers' Compensation Act,* R.S. Nfld. 1970, c. 403, s. 11.

11 *Merchant Seamen Compensation Act,* R.S.C. 1970, c. M-11, ss. 12, 13 and 14. The question of whether provincial or federal legislation should apply was discussed but not resolved in *Paré v. Rail & Water Terminal (Que.) Inc.,* [1978] 1 F.C. 23. Even if the place of accident was out of Newfoundland, the Newfoundland Act would likely apply. *Ibid.,* s. 10(4).

12 If these claims were characterized as "admiralty" matters, problems could arise in the Newfoundland Supreme Court. See *Cull v. Rose and A.G. Nfld.* (1982), 37 Nfld. & P.E.I.R. 476. Goodridge J. held that the Newfoundland Supreme Court had no jurisdiction in admiralty by virtue of the 1949 Terms of Union with Canada which repealed s. 4 of the Newfoundland Judicature Act originally enacted in 1889 which declared that court to be a court of admiralty. This decision has been questioned by 1983 obiter dicta in *Gould v. Cornhill Ins. Co.* (1982), Nfld. C.A. No. 191 (unreported).

owner could have been made in the Federal Court of Canada by virtue of the Canada Shipping Act[13] and the Federal Court Act.[14]

In reality, however, Canadian claimants would be confronted with the application of the Newfoundland Workers' Compensation Act or the Merchant Seamen Compensation Act. The latter Act only applies to seamen not covered by provincial workers' compensation schemes, provided they are engaged on a foreign or home-trade voyage.[15] The question of which legislation would apply is not entirely clear.[16] If the casualty occurred within the territory of Newfoundland up to its three mile limit, the Newfoundland compensation legislation would clearly apply to the exclusion of the federal legislation.[17] On the other hand, if the casualty involved a vessel outside Newfoundland and in Canadian territorial waters or on the high seas then the following points would arise:

1. Is Newfoundland the place of employment so that the Newfoundland legislation may apply?[18]
2. If the Newfoundland Act does not apply, was the vessel engaged in a foreign or home-trade voyage so as to make the federal legislation applicable?
3. Were all of the crew "seamen" within the meaning of the Canada Shipping Act definition?

In comparison to the *Ocean Ranger* litigation, the Canadian side of the *Arctic Explorer* litigation was relatively straightforward. The only potential defendants in Canada in the latter case were registered employers under the Newfoundland Workers' Compensation scheme against whom civil action in the Federal and Newfoundland Courts was barred as the Workers' Compensation Board of Newfoundland would have exclusive jurisdiction over the claims arising from injury or death of members of the crew.[19]

---

13   *Supra* note 9, s. 719.
14   *Canada Shipping Act*, R.S.C. 1970, c. S-9, s. 719. *Federal Court Act*, R.S.C. 1970 (2nd Supp.), c. 10, ss. 2, 22(1), 22(2)(*d*) and (*g*), and 22(3). See also *Paré v. Rail & Water Terminal (Que.) Inc.*, [1978] 1 F.C. 23 at 25, 26.
15   *Merchant Seamen Compensation Act*, R.S.C. 1970, c. M-11, s. 4.
16   *Paré v. Rail & Water Terminal (Que.) Inc., supra* note 14.
17   *Supra* note 15.
18   *Workers' Compensation Act*, R.S.N. 1970, c. 403, s. 10.
19   All outstanding claims are near final settlement. See also Newfoundland Workers' Compensation Act, ss. 11, 12, *supra* note 10, without the 1982 amendment which was enacted after the *Ocean Ranger* disaster. The effect of this amendment will be discussed *infra*.

3. OCEAN RANGER LITIGATION

(a) General Applications

The *Ocean Ranger* litigation is anything but straightforward on both sides of the U.S. – Canadian border and the Canadian conflict of laws problems will assume even greater future prominence in relation to the Eastern Canadian offshore in the light of the new U.S. Congressional bar against foreign lawsuits arising from foreign offshore accidents.[20]

The major portion of offshore oil and gas exploration and production activity in Eastern Canada will occur on the continental shelf offshore Nova Scotia and Newfoundland, *i.e.* on the high seas. It is important to note that most operators and contractors working in Eastern Canada are registered employers under the Nova Scotia and Newfoundland workers' compensation schemes. However, the operation of offshore drilling units present many more legal complications than do the operations of seismic or supply/standby vessels.

First, there arises the question of whether all offshore drilling units are considered to be ships. Recent Canadian decisions particularly related to drill ships and semi-submersibles, tend to confirm that they are.[21] There is a lingering question of whether jack-rigs would also be in this category, although the broad approach taken in *Queen v. St. John Shipbuilding & Dry Dock Co.*[22] indicates that even they might be considered ships while on location.

Secondly, besides the apparent applicability of Canadian maritime law to accidents involving offshore drilling units is the fact that The Canada Oil and Gas Drilling Regulations impose specific statutory duties on the oil companies as operators as well as on contractors to ensure safe operations particularly of the drilling units, notwithstanding that in reality the oil companies contract out their drilling obligations to major drilling companies and ancillary contractors.[23]

Thirdly, the question of the appliction of the Nova Scotia and Newfoundland workers' compensation scheme becomes a difficult question when the casualty clearly occurs outside provincial boundaries, but where the claimant was hired in a particular province, main-

---

20   *Supra* note 3.
21   *R. v. St. John Shipbuilding & Dry Dock Co.* (1981), 126 D.L.R. (3d) 353 (F.C.A.); *S.I.U. v. Crosbie Offshore Services Ltd.* (1982), 135 D.L.R. (3d) 485 (F.C.A.) at 495: "The rigs are also ships," *per* the Chief Justice. See also *Spicer*, "Some Admiralty Issues in Offshore Oil and Gas Development" (1982), 20 Alta. L. Rev. 153 at 157-160.
22   *Ibid.* at 362.
23   SOR/79-82 and SOR/80-641. See discussion of the establishment of duties and standard of care against operators by *Hayashi,* "Offshore Casualties in Canadian Waters" (1983), 20 Alta. L. Rev. 165 at 190-193.

tains a residence in the province and was out of the province as part of his hiring and employment within the province at the time of the accident.[24]

(b) Forum Shopping

The "Ocean Ranger" sinking created a spectacle of "forum shopping". Actions were first commenced on behalf of dependants of U.S. and Canadian decedents in the U.S. Federal District in both New Orleans, Louisiana and Beaumont, Texas. Other U.S. federal and state actions were commenced in Kentucky, California and South Carolina. Principal defendants named initially were the parties to the drilling contract, Mobil Oil Canada Ltd. (operator), and Odeco Drilling of Canada Ltd. (contractor) and their parent and certain affiliate companies. Later the U.S. designer and Japanese builder were joined.

Actions were also commenced in the trial divisions of the Federal Court of Canada and the Supreme Court of Newfoundland pleading that the rig was a "ship" and relying upon the fatal accidents provisions in the Canada Shipping Act[25] and the Newfoundland Fatal Accidents Act[26] and Survival of Actions Act.[27]

The Canadian counsel for Canadian claimants took the position that the Canadian litigation commencing after the U.S. litigation was only initiated to protect the claimants from the one-year limitation of action provision applicable to Canadian death claims on vessels or otherwise under the Canada Shipping Act[28] and the Newfoundland Fatal Accidents Act[29] and Survival of Actions Act.[30]

The named defendants were not limited to registered employers under the Newfoundland workers' compensation scheme but clearly involved viable third party tortfeasors such as the U.S. rig designer, an Odeco affiliate, the Japanese builder, and the American Bureau of Shipping which classed the rig and inspected construction at the Japanese shipyard.

There were no survivors, but many of the persons having any knowledge of what occurred are Canadian residents. The Canada Oil

---

24 For discussion of likely application of Newfoundland Workers' Compensation Act to rig accidents on the high seas off Newfoundland, see Mendes "Newfoundland Workers' Compensation Legislation: Constitutional and Conflict of Laws Issues Arising from Offshore Oil and Gas Exploration" (1983), 21 Alta. L. Rev. 1 at 5-11.

25 *Supra* note 9, s. 714.

26 R.S.N. 1970, c. 126.

27 R.S.N. 1970, c. 365.

28 *Supra* note 9, s. 722.

29 *Supra* note 26, s. 5.

30 *Supra* note 27, s. 5.

and Gas Lands Administration (COGLA), as well as other Canadian regulatory authorities had been involved in rig inspections and a Canadian Royal Commission was established to investigate the cause.

The jurisdictional battle was waged on two fronts. After consolidation of the U.S. cases under the multi-district litigation rules and transfer to New Orleans, a U.S. Federal District Court issued a minute entry in June, 1983, granting a *forum non conveniens* motion to the Mobil and Odeco defendants effectively retaining the claims of U.S. citizens and sending the Canadian claimants to Canada to pursue their remedies there.

Prior to the *forum non conveniens* dismissal, Mobil and Odeco defendants also unconditionally appeared in the Newfoundland court proceedings without having been served, demanded copies of the Statements of Claim and requested an order for the commencement of discovery. The Newfoundland Court ordered the Statements of Claim to be delivered but did not order the commencement of discovery.[31]

After the dismissal to Canada, the U.S. attorneys for the Canadian claimants commenced a joint action in the Texas State Court which subsequently reverted into the hands of Judge Robert Collins' court in New Orleans where the original dismissal to Canada occurred.[32] Judge Collins' original dismissal has been reargued and the written reasons for his original dismissal have not yet been filed.

The Fifth Circuit Court of Appeals, (the Court before which any appeals will come) while recognizing the general trend towards prohibiting foreigners from suing in U.S. courts as the result of foreign offshore casualties involving U.S. flagged rigs, will have to deal with the apparently unprecedented instance, in the Ocean Ranger case, of a U.S. court keeping the U.S. claims and sending the foreigners to their home forum.

The heads of damages in U.S. maritime death claims are broader than those permitted in Canada.[33] The U.S. and Canadian claimants are seeking punitive in addition to pecuniary damages in the U.S. Courts. A claim for conscious pain and suffering will also be asserted on the facts of the case.

The heads of damages to which surviving dependants suing in Canadian courts arising out of death cases from an offshore accident

---

31 *Foley v. Ocean Drilling & Exploration Co.* (1983), 40 Nfld. & P.E.I.R. 427 (Nfld. S.C.).

32 The route was circuitous. The state action was removed to Federal Court at Galveston, Texas, referred to the multi-district litigation panel in Atlanta and transferred to New Orleans. A plaintiffs' motion to remand to state court was rejected by the federal District Judge at Galveston.

33 See Zurolo and Berry, "Wrongful Death Damages in Offshore Accidents" (1983), V. 19 No. 1 The Forum 92.

would be entitled have been clearly spelled out in recent judgments of the Supreme Court of Canada[34] and include loss of support to dependants and loss of guidance to children. No recovery would appear to be available to the estate for conscious pain and suffering as such is excluded by provincial survival of actions statutes.[35] Also, recovery for punitive damages seems highly unlikely, given the current state of Canadian tort jurisprudence.[36]

This analysis of Canadian remedies in particular is important especially for the Newfoundland offshore since the provincial workers' compensation legislation was amended retroactively in 1982 after the "Ocean Ranger" sinking.[37] The amendments replaced a claimant's election either to claim compensation or sue third party tortfeasors (other than registered employers associated with the incident) with the right to claim compensation *and* sue third party tortfeasors.[38] The Board is given a right to claim reimbursement against a compensation recipient for benefits paid, where the claimant receives settlement or judgment funds by virtue of the commencement of any action.[39]

Assuming the Newfoundland workers' compensation legislation would apply to offshore exploration areas such as Hibernia, this legislation would only provide immunity from lawsuits in Canada against registered employers. Compensation claimants could initiate their own tort actions in Canadian courts against third party tortfeasors. If the legislation does not apply, compensation claimants would be in a position to sue for the negligence of the employers as well as third party tortfeasors.

---

34   *Keizer v. Hanna,* [1978] 2 S.C.R. 342; *Lewis v. Todd,* [1980] 2 S.C.R. 694. The governing principles for assessment of damages in personal injury claims in Canada have been enunciated in the so-called Supreme Court of Canada trilogy: *Andrews v. Grand & Toy Alta. Ltd.,* [1978] 2 S.C.R. 229; *Thornton v. Board of School District No. 57 (Prince George),* [1978] 2 S.C.R. 267; *Teno v. Arnold,* [1978] 2 S.C.R. 287.

35   Newfoundland Survival of Actions Act, *supra* note 27, s. 11(*g*). In Nova Scotia, see Survival of Actions Act, R.S.N.S. 1967, c. 298; Fatal Accidents Act, R.S.N.S. 1967, c. 100.

36   In *Nichols v. Guiel* (1983), 145 D.L.R. (3d) 186 (B.C. S.C.), Esson J. noted the absence of any Canadian or Commonwealth case in which exemplary damages have been awarded in a wrongful death action or in any action arising out of a motor vehicle accident. Not only were such damages not contemplated under provincial fatal accidents legislation intended and interpreted to allow damages for pecuniary loss only but also there must be proof that the tortious conduct, though deliberately reckless it may have been, was directed against the plaintiff or her late husband. Clearly the latter factor would also apply to claims for exemplary damages arising out of bodily injury.
       See also *Castanho v. Brown & Root,* [1981] A.C. 557 at 571 (H.L.).

37   S.N. 1982, c. 11.

38   *Ibid.,* s. 11(1).

39   *Ibid.,* s. 11(5).

The inevitable question would be: what are the applicable laws which might apply to the incident?

In a wrongful death case involving vessels, it would appear that surviving dependants could sue in the Federal Court of Canada relying on the fatal accident provisions of the Canada Shipping Act and general Canadian maritime law,[40] and in the Newfoundland Supreme Court (with or without admiralty jurisdiction) relying on the provincial fatal accidents legislation.[41]

Assuming an offshore drilling unit is a "ship", then there seems little doubt that the Federal Court would have jurisdiction to entertain the claim.[42] Since most operators and contractors have bases of operations onshore Newfoundland, and agents resident in Newfoundland who are subject to service of process, it is likely that the Newfoundland court would also be a proper and convenient forum for such litigation.[43]

4. CHOICE OF LAW

Assuming a Canadian court has jurisdiction and is willing to exercise it based on *forum conveniens* considerations, the next difficult question for the court is the proper choice of law to govern the determination of the issues between the parties. The matter is particularly troublesome with regard to accidents on the "high seas", *i.e.* drilling areas like Hibernia.

Canadian courts continue to rely on the conflict of laws rules formulated in *Phillips v. Eyre*[44] to determine choice of law. To ground a suit in Canada, two conditions must be met, *i.e.* (1) the wrong must be of such a character that it would be actionable if committed in Canada, and (2) the act must not have been "justifiable"[45] by the law of the place where it was done.

Using these criteria and the application of the Newfoundland compensation legislation to the offshore, an action arising from an accident at Hibernia could not be taken in Canadian courts against registered

---

40   *Supra* note 9, s. 714. See also *Stein v. The Kathy K,* [1976] 2 S.C.R. 802.

41   *Supra* notes 26 and 27.

42   *Tropwood A.G. v. Sivaco Wire & Nail Co. et al,* [1979] 2 S.C.R. 157; *Wire Rope Indust. of Can. (1966) Ltd. v. B.C. Marine Shipbldrs. Ltd.,* [1981] 1 S.C.R. 363.

43   See Mendes' discussion, *supra* note 24, at p. 11 *et seq.*

44   (1870) L.R. 6 Q.B. 1, as followed in *McLean v. Peddigrew,* [1945] S.C.R. 62.

45   "Justifiable" has been viewed in the context that an act or neglect which is neither actionable nor punishable cannot be said to be other than "justifiable" – see *Walpole v. Can. Nor. Ry.* (1922), 70 D.L.R. 201 at 205 (P.C.). English courts adopted a double actionability test in *Chaplin v. Boys,* [1971] A.C. 356 (H.L.). For a thorough review of English and Canadian rules, see *Going v. Reid Bros. Motor Sales* (1982), 35 O.R. (2d) 201 (H.C.).

employers because the Newfoundland Workers' Compensation Act would constitute a bar to such suits by workers or their dependants for tortious conduct committed within the province.[46] This would not affect the right to sue third party tortfeasors.

If the Newfoundland legislation does not apply, then the first condition of *Phillips v. Eyre* could easily be met by a potential claimant. The existence of the Canadian oil and gas drilling regulations which impose statutory duties for safe offshore drilling operations would greatly assist a tort claimant in meeting the second condition, *i.e.* that the alleged tortious act is not "justifiable".[47]

The choice of law decision-making process is further complicated in the maritime setting by section 274 of the Canada Shipping Act[48] which states:

> Where in any matter relating to a ship or to a person belonging to a ship there appears to be a conflict of laws, then, if there is in this Part any provision on the subject that is hereby expressly made to extend to that ship, the case shall be governed by that provision; but if there is no such provision the case shall be governed by the law of the port at which the ship is registered.

The important issue is whether in any "high seas" accident offshore Eastern Canada there will always be a conflict of laws question in wrongful death and injury cases which by virtue of section 274 of the Canada Shipping Act may require the law of the vessel's port of registry to apply. This would be particularly important when one considers that many foreign flagged rigs and support vessels have worked and will continue to work off Eastern Canada.

The most careful consideration of this important question in Canada is contained in *Gronlund v. Hansen.*[49] The British Columbia Court of Appeal had before it a wrongful death claim involving a Canadian vessel registered at Vancouver. The death was due to a collision on the high seas approximately ten miles off the British Columbia coast, *i.e.* the high seas. Alternative pleas of the provincial Families' Compensation Act[50] and the Canada Shipping Act[51] were contained in the statement of claim.

The grounds of appeal against the trial judgment allowing the action under the provincial fatal accidents legislation were:

---

46   See full discussion by Mendes, *supra* note 24, at pp. 11-14.
47   *Supra* note 23 including Hayashi discussion. Consider also the Canada Shipping Act, *supra* note 9, s. 714, as well as rules of international maritime law including the SOLAS (Safety of Life at Sea) conventions.
48   *Supra* note 9.
49   (1969), 4 D.L.R. (3d) 435 at 438-444 (B.C. C.A.).
50   R.S.B.C. 1960, c. 138 (now R.S.B.C. 1979, c. 120).
51   *Supra* note 9, s. 719.

1.   The Families' Compensation Act of British Columbia does not operate extra-
     territorially. It does not confer and, by reason of the limited legislative jurisdiction of
     the Provincial Legislature, it cannot confer on the dependants of one whose death is
     caused by negligence committed on the high seas a right of action for damages for
     such death.

2.   The Appellant submits that the Learned Trial Judge erred in finding that the
     Families' Compensation Act applied when if the drowning had occurred at the same
     location as the result of damage occasioned by the propeller of the "ALEUTIAN
     QUEEN", the Canada Shipping Act, Part XVII, Sections 725 to 733 would have
     applied. The Appellant submits that the Learned Trial Judge should have found that
     the existence of the provisions of the Canada Shipping Act left no area of legislation
     open to the Province of British Columbia in these circumstances and that accord-
     ingly the Families' Compensation Act could not be applied in the case of a death on
     the high seas involving a Canadian registered vessel.

The appeal was dismissed. The court placed great reliance upon and
applied the choice of law principles set forth by the Supreme Court of
Canada in *Canadian National Steamships Co. v. Watson*.[52] That case
involved a negligence action tried in the Quebec Queen's Bench involving a British vessel registered at Vancouver. A Quebec crewman who
lived in Montreal was injured off Bermuda while the vessel was enroute
to Prince Edward Island from the West Indies. Negligence was proven
against the master. The Supreme Court of Canada adopted the choice of
law approach of *Phillips v. Eyre*.[53] It said the Quebec claimant was
required to prove an act or default actionable by the law of Quebec, the
lex fori, and to establish that the alleged tort was non-justifiable[54] by the
lex loci delicti. In addition the court said that the claimant was entitled
to the presumption that general law of the place where the alleged
wrongful act occurred is the same as the *lex fori* unless the defendant can
prove otherwise.[55]

   The defendants in *Watson* argued the application of section 274 of
the Canada Shipping Act.[56] The Supreme Court held that the section
would apply to give effect to the law of British Columbia where the
vessel was registered, but confirmed the lower court entitlement to
consider the law of that province to be the same as that of the province of
Quebec unless the contrary was proven.[57]

   Applying these principles, the British Columbia Court of Appeal in
Gronlund[58] held that the defendant's act would have been actionable in

52   [1939] S.C.R. 11.
53   *Supra* note 44.
54   *Supra* note 45.
55   *Supra* note 52 at 14.
56   *Supra* note 9. This section is equivalent to the Merchant Shipping Act, 1894 (Imp.), c.
     60, s. 265.
57   *Supra* note 52, at 15. See also *McLean v. Pettigrew, supra* note 44.
58   *Supra* note 49, at 443-4.

British Columbia and that the defendant had failed to prove that the act or neglect would be justifiable on the high seas. In this latter respect, the court suggested that act could not be "justifiable" because it would be actionable under the Canada Shipping Act[59] and general maritime law.[60]

The important question posed by the decision in *Canadian National Steamships Co. v. Watson* is whether a tort action relating to an offshore accident will automatically be considered to create a conflict of laws not expressly covered by Part III of the Canada Shipping Act and, therefore, dictate the application of the law of port of registry.[61]

This could lead claimants to argue the application of U.S. or Norwegian law to an action proceeding in Canadian courts where U.S. or Norwegian drilling rigs are involved. The British Columbia Court of Appeal attempted to finesse this issue by two approaches:

1. Resting its judgment on the presumption that the general law of the place where the wrongful act occurred is the same as the law of British Columbia so as to remove a potential conflict of laws.[62]
2. If a conflict of laws existed, then the fact that vessel was registered at Vancouver, British Columbia, meant that the law of that province applied in any event pursuant to section 274 of the Canada Shipping Act.[63]

The lingering question is whether the presumption enunciated in the *Canadian National Steamships* case will offset the potential application of section 274 of the Canada Shipping Act.[64]

5.   INJUNCTIVE RELIEF AS A DEFENCE TO FORUM SHOPPING

Finally, it is important to outline potential defence strategies which may counteract forum shopping by Canadian or foreign claimants injured or killed on the Canadian offshore where substantial Canadian connections exist.

Of course, the rig owner or charterer (on the assumption the rig is a "vessel") or seismic or supply/standby vessel owners have the right to

---

59   S. 726, now s. 719, *supra* note 9.
60   See *Davidson v. Hill,* [1901] 2 K.B. 606 at 616.
61   *Supra* note 9, s. 274. This would effectively oust the application of the *Phillips v. Eyre* criteria.
62   *Gronlund v. Hansen, supra* note 49, at 443.
63   *Ibid.* at 444.
64   See also discussion by Mendes, *supra* note 24, at p. 13, footnote 50. Plaintiffs' U.S. attorneys in the *Ocean Ranger* litigation argued in their supplemental brief on their rehearing motion before the Federal District Court in New Orleans on the *forum non conveniens* issue that section 274 would oblige Canadian courts to apply U.S. law.

commence a limitation of liability proceeding in Canada. Also defendants have the right to appear voluntarily in Canadian courts where
protective actions have been commenced following the commencement
of foreign proceedings and to attempt to activate the Canadian proceedings by moving for discovery.[65] There is also the possible merit of
consenting to judgment in Canada in an attempt to limit the financial
exposure of the defendants if American proceedings are pending. It is
interesting to speculate whether a Canadian court, clearly the natural
forum for litigation based on the facts, would be prepared to enjoin
Canadian claimants or foreign citizens residing in Newfoundland or
Nova Scotia from pursuing claims for injury or wrongful death in
foreign courts.[66] This speculation brings us back to the line of English
stay of proceedings and injunction cases referred to at the outset.[67]

In both the *Arctic Explorer*[68] and *Ocean Ranger*[69] Canadian litigation, the defendants made claims for injunctive relief against Canadian
residents pursuing U.S. litigation. These applications have not been
heard in either case.

Walsh J. of the Federal Court in the *Ocean Ranger* litigation has
however voiced doubts about the court's jurisdiction to grant such a
remedy by way of *obiter dicta* in an application by the claimants as
defendants for leave to file a conditional appearance[70] when he said:

> While the merits of Plaintiffs' Statements of Claim are not before the Court in the
> present proceedings, but merely the question of the Court's jurisdiction . . . I have no
> hesitation in finding that while it may eventually be found that this Court is a *forum
> conveniens* for the hearing of the Defendants' claims, no injunction can or would be
> issued to restrain Defendants from instituting proceedings as they have in the United
> States. This Court cannot and should not tell foreign Courts what cases they may hear
> nor can it exercise jurisdiction in personam over Canadian citizens nor tell them in
> what extra-territorial jurisdictions they may bring proceedings.

---

65   *Foley v. Ocean Drilling, supra* note 31.
66   The matter of which court is the natural and proper forum is tied to the doctrine of
     forum conveniens. This doctrine is discussed generally in *Castel,* "Jurisdiction and
     the Exercise of Discretion by the Court – *Forum Conveniens*" (1971), 49 Can. Bar
     Rev. 466. See also *McLean,* "Jurisdiction and Judicial Discretion" (1969), 18 Int.
     and Comp. L.Q. 931; Spence, "Conflict of Laws in Automobile Negligence Cases"
     (1949), 27 Can. Bar Rev. 661; *Antares Shipping Corp. v. The Capricorn* (1976), 65
     D.L.R. (3d) 105 (S.C.C.) – "the overriding consideration must be whether some
     other forum is more convenient and more appropriate for the pursuit of the action
     and for securing the ends of justice".
67   *The Atlantic Star, supra.* note 4; *Castanho v. Brown & Root (U.K.) Ltd., supra.* note 2;
     Smith, Kline Laboratories Ltd., supra. note 1.
68   *Supra* note 8.
69   F.C. T-533-83.
70   Page 13 of unreported reasons.

It is significant that the English injunction cases were not before the court on that occasion but the judge's comments reflect the need for defendants to clearly demonstrate that a Canadian court is the proper and natural forum for offshore Canadian accident claims. These English cases are also important on the matter of the staying of Canadian proceedings where Canada is not the proper forum.

On a more practical level, to justify the grant of an injunction, the defendants must show: (1) that the Canadian court is a forum to whose jurisdiction they are amenable, and in which justice can be done at substantially less inconvenience and expense, and (2) the injunction does not deprive the plaintiff of a legitimate personal or juridical advantage which would be available to him if he invoked the foreign jurisdiction.[71]

In the *Castanho* case, the House of Lords upheld a Court of Appeal judgment (Denning M.R. dissenting) setting aside an injunction order issued against a Portuguese subject, resident in Portugal, employed by a Panamanian company and injured on an American ship while lying in an English port. The Portuguese seaman had initially commenced English proceedings to which defendants had attorned and made interim payments to the plaintiff. The plaintiff later sought to discontinue proceedings to pursue an action in Texas. The House of Lords appeared to be significantly influenced in this case by the fact (1) that the claimant was a Portuguese citizen and resident and not an English citizen or resident; (2) that the only connection between England and the incident was that it was the place of the accident (although a U.K. subsidiary of Brown & Root Inc. was a defendant); (3) that the only outstanding issue in the case was the issue of damages, since liability had already been admitted in England, and finally (4) that Texas appeared to be as natural and proper a forum as England for suing a group of Texas-based companies.[72]

In assessing the two prerequisites established for the possible granting of an injunction, it is clear that the important determination will turn on the question of the disadvantage to which the injured claimant might be put by being restrained from pursuing further proceedings. Obviously, no attempt would be made to bring an injunction application in any litigation arising out of an injury or wrongful death case unless there were substantial connections with Canada, thereby making it clear that a Canadian court would be the proper and convenient forum for the litigation. The principles involved in the doctrine of *forum conveniens* would be applicable. The first test would likely be met,

---

71   *Castanho v. Brown Root (U.K.) Ltd.,* [1981] A.C. 557 at 575 (H.L.) *per* Lord Scarman.
72   *Ibid.* at 575-577.

particularly if it is clear that "justice could be done at substantially less inconvenience and expense" by virtue of the fact that the incident had occurred offshore Eastern Canada over which the Canadian government has a significant regulatory regime in place, and most of the potential witnesses together with the claimant would likely be resident in Canada.[73] Where the offshore accidents involve Canadian registered oil rigs or supply vessels subject to a drilling agreement or charter party between two Canadian companies which have received operating approvals from the Canada Oil and Gas Lands Administration, and most potential witnesses are residing in Eastern Canada, the application of the *forum conveniens* doctrine should lead to the conclusion that a Canadian court is the proper and natural forum for any resulting litigation. The trend of the *forum conveniens* dismissal cases in the United States, especially those decisions which emphasize the fact that U.S. flagged drilling units often remain in foreign exploration areas and subject to foreign governmental regulatory regimes for extended periods of time, would support this conclusion.[74]

Parker J. at first instance in the *Castanho* case[75] had acknowledged that the prospect of higher damages in the United States could be a legitimate advantage to a claimant but then discarded this factor on the grounds that it would be unjust that one of two claimants suffering identical injuries suing in Texas as well as England would be in a position to recover greater compensation. The House of Lords felt that this was an irrelevant consideration and felt that in light of the initial finding of the trial judge, the granting of an injunction clearly violated the second test in that an injunction must not deprive the injured claimant of a legitimate personal or juridical advantage which would have been available to him if he invoked the American jurisdiction.

Against this background, it is important to analyze the unanimous decision of the English Court of Appeal in *Smith, Kline & French Laboratories Ltd., et al v. Bloch*[76] in which a lower court injunction enjoining U.S. proceedings was upheld against an English doctor who was party to a contract with the English subsidiary of an American pharmaceutical company. There was no evidence of any U.S. connec-

---

73   This analysis would more easily apply to claims brought by Canadian citizens and residents as opposed to those by foreign workers who may have been living in Eastern Canada for a short time as part of their employment contract for oil companies, drilling contractors or ancillary contractors.

74   *Phillips v. Amoco Trinidad Oil Co.,* 632 F. 2d 82 (9th Cir. 1980); *Chiazor v. Transworld Drilling Co.,* 648 F. 2d 1015 (5th Cir. 1981); *Vaz Borralho v. Keydril Co.,* 696 F. 2d 379 (5th Cir. 1983); *Koke and O'Sullivan v. Phillips Petroleum Co.,* Nos. 82-2388 and 82-2389 (5th Cir. April 5, 1984).

75   [1980] 1 All E.R. 689 (Q.B.D.).

76   [1983] 2 All E.R. 72 (C.A.).

tion to the litigation except for the fact that the U.S. parent had been sued. It was evident that England was the proper forum. The court disapproved of the notion that the claimant could take advantage of contingency fee arrangements with American attorneys to pursue U.S. litigation when England appeared to be the most convenient forum for the litigation.[77] Lord Denning cited with approval the United States Supreme Court decision in *Piper Aircraft Company v. Reyno*[78] as upholding the principle that:

> The Plaintiff has no longer an inborn right to choose his own forum. He no longer wins the toss on every throw. The decision rests with the courts. No matter which jurisdiction is invoked, the court must hold the balance between the plaintiff and the defendant. It must take into account the relative advantages and disadvantages to each of them: Not only the juridical advantages and disadvantages, but also the personal conveniences and inconveniences: Not only the private interests of the parties but also the public interests involved.[79]

Lord Denning attempted to distinguish *Smith Kline* from *Castanho* by noting that in the latter case, the plaintiff had an undisputed claim for damages against a Texas-based group of companies. The only outstanding issue was quantum.[80]

However, it is clear that evidence that a Canadian claimant in the United States or any other foreign jurisdiction would obtain higher damages could severely militate against the prospects of obtaining an injunction.[81]

Evidence was led by affidavit in *Smith Kline* that even if the U.S. court allowed the English doctor's action to proceed in Pennsylvania, the Pennsylvania courts would likely apply English law to determine the quantum of damages.

The English Court of Appeal in *Smith Kline* relied upon the following factors in concluding that the plaintiff should be restrained from proceeding in the United States:

1. England was the natural and proper forum for the proceedings. The potential witnesses were mostly in England.
2. The proper law of the contract was English law.
3. It was likely that the amount of damages recoverable in Pennsylvania courts would be based on English law both in contract and in tort.
4. The American parent company was willing to submit to the juris-

---

77   *Ibid.*, p. 78 (Denning, M.R.); p. 86 (O'Connor, L.J.).
78   102 S. Ct. 252 (1982).
79   *Supra* note 76, at 78.
80   *Ibid.*
81   *Supra* note 2, p. 152.

diction of the English court, even though the court felt that it was an unnecessary party in the circumstances of the case.

5.   The fact that a Pennsylvania court might award exemplary damages was considered to be a highly speculative possible advantage as opposed to a real advantage.
6.   The fact that the case could have been prosecuted in the U.S. with minimum risks of costs because of contingency fee arrangements should not be regarded as a juridical advantage.
7.   The fact that the case would be tried by a jury in Pennsylvania and that damages, if recovered, would be much higher than in England was not considered a juridical advantage particularly given the type of case under consideration by the court and also given the fact that the plaintiff would have to pay perhaps 40% of what he recovered to his attorney.
8.   Prior commencement of litigation in the United States was not a relevant factor.

The result of the application of these principles to wrongful death and injury claims arising out of offshore accidents is not entirely clear. For example, American courts particularly in maritime cases generally apply American law both as to liability and damages once they have assumed jurisdiction. Since American law grants compensation for conscious pain and suffering as well as punitive damages both under the Jones Act and under the general maritime law (remedies under the Death on the High Seas Act are limited to pecuniary damages), claimants would argue that an injunction by a Canadian court restraining them from pursuing American litigation would be depriving them of a legitimate personal or juridical advantage. However, the factual circumstances might be such as to suggest to a Canadian court that the remote likelihood of conscious pain and suffering or punitive damages being awarded in the circumstances of the case would cause it to fall within the criteria set forth in *Smith Kline*.[82]

The Jones Act amendment[83] prohibiting claims by foreigners injured in offshore oil and gas related accidents in American courts will be the main protection available to the oil industry. The injunction remedy may well be an important defence mechanism with respect to incidents occurring on drilling units of other foreign flag states.

---

82   The prospects for establishing a case for injunctive relief would appear to have been particularly strong in the "Arctic Explorer" litigation as the facts are applied to the *Smith Kline* principles. See *Supra,* note 6, for factual summary.

83   *Supra,* note 3.

6. CONCLUSION

Whether in future the light can be turned off by defendant's counsel for Lord Denning's moth-like plaintiffs drawn to the U.S. courts is a difficult question to answer. However, it must be clear by now that in future the complexity of conflict of laws problems surrounding Canadian offshore wrongful death and injury claims will be no less unrelenting, despite recent changes to the Jones Act and the general maritime law of the United States. As the exploration phase moves to the production phase, the potential presence 200 miles off Newfoundland of enormous concrete gravity-based production platforms (which would certainly not be classed as "vessels") will add to the legal intricacies that plaintiffs' and defendants' counsel will be required to litigate.

THE RESOLUTION OF
CONFLICT OF LAWS
ISSUES IN MARITIME LIMITATION
OF LIABILITY CLAIMS

LIMITATION OF SHIPOWNERS' LIABILITY UNDER U.S. LAW – DOES ANY OTHER LAW APPLY?

*Elliott B. Nixon**

1. INTRODUCTION

In the United States the right of shipowner under federal law to limit his liability arising out of a maritime catastrophe originated 133 years ago in the Limitation of Liability Act, 1851. The principle had been recognized much earlier in European maritime jurisprudence; the French Ordonnance de la Marine, promulgated in 1681 during the reign of Louis XIV to codify many customs and practices of an earlier era, provided in Title 4, Art. II:

> The owners of the ship shall be answerable for the deeds of the master; but shall be discharged, abandoning their ship and freight.[1]

In England shipowners were first protected against theft of cargo by the ship's personnel in a statute enacted in 1733,[2] intended to "promote the increase of the number of ships and vessels and to prevent any discouragement to merchants and others from being interested and concerned therein". Eighty years later this protection was extended to

---

*Of the New York Bar. Partner, Burlingham Underwood & Lord. Editor, *American Maritime Cases*.

1 Translation from the text reprinted at 30 Fed. Cas. 1206. The early *fortune de mer* concept in continental jurisprudence is reviewed in Alex. Rein, "International Variations on Concepts of Limitation of Liability", 53 Tulane L. Rev. 1259 at 1261-63 (1979).
2 Responsibility of Shipowners Act, 7 Geo. 2, c. 15.

loss or damage arising from collision,[3] but the shipowner could only limit to the value of the ship and freight *before* the casualty.

The American statute of 1851 was enacted with a similar promotional purpose – to encourage investment in shipping at a time when the primitive marine steam engines with their regrettable tendency to set ships afire,[4] were adding a new dimension to the traditional perils of the sea. In the middle of the nineteenth century marine liability insurance was in its infancy and corporate form of organization was little used by shipowners. It is therefore scarcely surprising that American shipowners should have welcomed a specialized kind of maritime bankruptcy procedure capable of co-ordinating all claims arising out of a particular disaster.

Reduced to essentials, the 1851 statute[5] provided:

the liability of the owner . . . of any . . . vessel for any embezzlement, loss or destruction . . . of any property, goods, or merchandise, shipped or put on board of such . . . vessel,

or

for any loss, damage or injury by collision,

or

for any act, matter or thing, loss, damage or forfeiture, done, occasioned, or incurred without the privity or knowledge of such owner . . . shall in no case exceed the amount or value of the interest of such owner . . . in such . . . vessel, and her freight then pending.

Obviously the statutory phraseology left room for considerable interpretation: Who qualifies as "owner"? What constitutes "the amount or value" of his interest in the vessel? Does the statute's protection extend to liability arising out of events occurring prior to the voyage on which the casualty occurred? During the next three decades the

---

3   Responsibility of Shipowners Act, 1813, 53 Geo. 3, c. 159. Protection was not extended to cover claims for loss of life and personal injury until passage of the Merchant Shipping Act, 1854, 17 & 18 Vict., c. 104, which established a special fund of £15 per ton for sea-going vessels. The history of limitation of liability in England is discussed in Michael Thomas, "British Concepts of Limitation of Liability", 53 Tulane L. Rev. at 1205-1209 (1979).

4   *The Lexington,* 47 U.S. (6 How.) 344, 12 L. Ed. 465 (1848).

5   Act of March 3, 1851, c. 43, § 3 (the present text is at 46 U.S. Code s. 183). The Limitations Act was substantially amended in 1935 and 1936 following the disastrous fire and stranding of passenger ship *Morro Castle:* Act of August 29, 1935, ch. 804, 49 Stat. 960; Act of June 5, 1936, ch. 521, 49 Stat. 1479. Among other changes, 46 U.C. Code § 183 was amended to require the shipowner to establish an additional fund of $60 per ton for the satisfaction of personal injury and death claims if the limitation fund would otherwise be insufficient to pay all losses in full. See James J. Donovan, "The Origins and Development of Limitation of Shipowner's Liability", 53 Tulane L. Rev. at 999-1034 (1979). In 1984 an amendment to increase the $60 figure to $420 per ton passed the House of Representatives but was not acted upon by the Senate. H.R. 3486, 98th Cong., 2d Sess.

answers to many of these questions were supplied by court decisions: "Owner" included both the registered owner and a bareboat charterer, whether domestic or foreign;[6] the limitation fund was the vessel's value *after* the casualty plus the prepaid freight,[7] excluding hull insurance payable to the owner;[8] the privilege of limitation extended only to claims arising out of the voyage on which the vessel was engaged.[9]

Two other even more fundamental questions are still with us today: (1) what is meant by "privity or knowledge", and (2) may foreign law affect the amount of the shipowner's limitation fund? Neither question has been definitely resolved in terms of every possible factual situation. This paper addresses the latter question.

2. DECISIONS AS TO APPLICABLE LAW

The Scotland,[10] involved the right of a British shipowner to invoke the American limitation statute following the sinking of its vessel in a high seas collision with an American ship. The Supreme Court in 1881 held that the statute did apply to foreign shipowners; it also took the opportunity to comment on the applicability of foreign law in collision cases:

> [I]f a collision occurs on the high seas, where the law of no particular state has exclusive force, but all are equal, any forum called upon to settle the rights of the parties would *prima facie* determine them by its own law as presumptively expressing the rules of justice; but if the contesting vessels belonged to the same foreign nation, the court would assume that they were subject to the law of their nation . . . and would determine the controversy accordingly. If they belonged to different nations, having different laws, since it would be unjust to apply the laws of either to the exclusion of the other, the law of the forum; that is, the maritime law as received and practised therein, would properly furnish the rule of decision.[11]

Thirty-one years later, in 1912, the British-flag liner *Titanic* sank in the North Atlantic after colliding with an iceberg. Her English owner filed a proceeding to limit its liability under American law in the New York federal court. Numerous claimants, many of them English, intervened, asserting that any right to limitation should be determined under English law, which would have resulted in a larger limitation fund. The district judge concluded that the American statute was inapplicable,

---

6 *Dyer v. Nat. Steam Navigation Co. (The Scotland),* 105 U.S. 24 (1881). Addition of the words "whether American or foreign" to modify "owner" was accomplished by the 1935 amendment, 49 Stat. 960.
7 *Norwich & New York Transp. Co. v. Wright,* 80 U.S. 104 (1871).
8 *The City of Norwich,* 118 U.S. 468 (1886), decided by a 5-4 majority.
9 *The Rose Culkin,* 52 Fed. 328 (SDNY 1882).
10 105 U.S. 24 (1881).
11 *Ibid.* at 29-30.

based on his reading of *The Scotland:* no nation's law has extraterritorial effect; a ship on the high seas is part of the country to which she belongs; and liability for torts is governed by the *lex loci delicti.*[12] The Second Circuit Court of Appeal declined to rule on the thorny issues before it but, instead, certified them for decision by the Supreme Court.[13] In an opinion by Justice Holmes the Supreme Court reversed.[14] While conceding that "the foundation for recovery upon a British tort is an obligation created by British law", Justice Holmes ruled that the forum court may "decline to enforce that obligation except within such limits as it may impose".[15] The concomitant of this doctrine is, of course, that neither an injunction restraining the prosecution of claims against the shipowner nor a judgment in a limitation proceeding in a U.S. court has any extraterritorial effect.

This pronouncement from on high dominated subsequent rulings on the applicability of the Limitation Statute. Indeed, s. 411 of the American Law Institute's *Restatement of Conflict of Laws,* published in 1934, laid down as hornbook law that "the limitation of liability in a maritime cause of action is determined by the law of the forum, irrespective of the law which created the cause of action".[16]

This somewhat simplistic principle, which at least had the merit of clarity of application, was cast into doubt by Justice Frankfurter's 1949 opinion for the Supreme Court in *The Norwalk Victory.*[17] The American shipowner wanted Belgium law applied in its proceeding to limit its liability for cargo claims arising out of a collision with a British flag vessel in Belgian waters. The reason for this attempt was plain enough: under American law the post-collision value of the American vessel was $1 million, but under the law of Belgium the shipowner could limit liability to only $325,000. The lower courts dismissed the shipowner's application, citing *The Titanic.* The Supreme Court remanded for a determination as to whether, under Belgian law, the limitation "attache[d] to the right," in which case an American court could apply such a "substantive" provision, or was merely intended "to cut down the amount recoverable by a claimant" as a matter of procedure, in which case an American court should apply its own Limitation Act.[18]

---

12   *The Titanic,* 209 Fed. 501 (SDNY 1913).
13   *Ibid.* at 513 (2d Cir. 1913).
14   *Oceanic Steam Nav. Co. v. Mellor,* 233 U.S. 718 (1914).
15   *Ibid.* at 732.
16   The Reporter, with commendable caution, deleted this section from the Second Edition published in 1971.
17   *Black Diamond S.S. Co. v. Robert Stewart & Sons Ltd.,* 336 U.S. 386, 1949 AMC 393 (1949).
18   336 U.S. at 395-96, 1949 AMC at 400.

Whether the Supreme Court's decision in *The Norwalk Victory* is consistent with the doctrine laid down in *The Titanic* has been the subject of much judicial and scholarly comment. In 1954 the Second Circuit Court of Appeals held that the earlier decision had not been overruled. *The Western Farmer*[19] was a suit in New York by German cargo owners against a non-carrying Norwegian-flag vessel for damages sustained in a high seas collision. The district judge dismissed the action, concluding that English law (including the English limitation of liability act) should govern because other litigation against the shipowner was pending in England. The Court of Appeals reversed, relying on *The Titanic* for the proposition that "such statutes are part of the remedy and the law of the forum applies".[20]

Lower court decisions on the issue are conflicting. In *The Yarmouth Castle*[21] the owner of a Panamanian flag vessel invoked the American Limitation Act after its vessel had been destroyed by fire on the high seas. The Florida district court, following the lead of the Supreme Court in *The Norwalk Victory,* heard extensive testimony on the law of Panama. Based on this evidence it concluded that the Panamanian requirement that the shipowner include its hull insurance proceeds in the limitation fund was "substantive" and should therefore be made a prerequisite to any grant of limitation of liability.

Nine years later a New York federal court declined to follow this reasoning. In *The Eurypylos*[22] Panamanian law was held not to govern the amount of the fund to be surrendered by a foreign shipowner seeking to limit liability arising out of an explosion aboard a Panamanian-flag vessel on the high seas. The Court noted that foreign law could apply only if it provided for a *lower* limitation fund than that required by the American Act.[23]

Perhaps the most thorough analysis of the "substantive/procedural" distinction is found in the district and circuit court opinions in *The Steelton.*[24] There an American shipowner had petitioned in a Canadian court to limit liability following its vessel's collision with a bridge over the Welland Canal. It deposited a sum in Canadian dollars equiv-

---

19   *Kloeckner Reederei v. A/S Hakedal,* 210 F. 2d 754, 1954 AMC 643 (2 Cir. 1954), appeal dismissed 348 U.S. 801 (1954).
20   210 F. 2d at 757, 1954 AMC at 647.
21   *In re Chadade S.S. Co.,* 266 F. Supp. 517, 1967 AMC 1843 (S.C. Fla. 1967).
22   *In re Tai Chi Navigation (Panama),* 416 F. Supp. 371, 1976 AMC 1895 (SDNY 1976). The *Yarmouth Castle* decision was distinguished in *Petition of Lidoriki Maritime Corp.,* 410 F. Supp. 919 (E.D. Pa. 1976) which declined to apply Panamanian law requiring surrender of hull insurance proceeds as part of the limitation fund.
23   416 F. Supp. at 379, 1976 AMC at 1907.
24   *Bethlehem Steel Corp. v. St. Lawrence Seaway Authority,* [1978] 1 F.C. 464, 79 D.L.R. (3d) 522, 1977 AMC 2240 (1977).

alent to U.S. $691,000 and the Canadian court ordered all claimants to file in that proceeding. However, when sued by some of the claimants in Ohio, the shipowner petitioned to limit its liability under the American Act, while asserting the benefit of s. 647 of the Canada Shipping Act. After considering expert testimony as to whether the Canadian statute was substantive or procedural, the U.S. district court concluded that it was procedural since it merely provided a means of scaling down claims to a proportionate share of a limited fund. As a consequence, the shipowner was ordered to establish a limitation fund of $850,000 as required by American law.[25] The Court of Appeals for the Sixth Circuit endorsed this result[26] and the Supreme Court denied review.[27]

In a very recent decision in *The Cimadevilla,*[28] a New York federal court held that a Spanish shipowner, seeking to limit liability arising out of a collision with a Panamanian vessel in Spanish waters, would be required to deposit a limitation fund of $1.8 million as required by law. The shipowner had contended that, since Spain was a signatory to the 1956 Brussels Convention, the Convention constituted the substantive law of Spain which the American court should apply in determining the amount of the fund. After considering expert testimony as to Spanish law and reviewing American decisions, the court followed *The Steelton* and concluded that "the Brussels Convention, if applicable, is procedural in nature" and that the law of the American forum applied. It specifically disagreed with the contention that "when the foreign limitation of liability is lower than that of the forum, it is therefore substantive".

3.   APPLICABILITY OF OTHER CHOICE OF LAW CRITERIA

So far as jurisdiction is concerned, the Limitation of Liability Act's mandate is extremely broad: it authorizes a United States court in admiralty to entertain an action by an American or foreign shipowner (or bareboat charterer) to limit liability in respect of any vessel casualty occurring anywhere in the world. Yet there are indications in decisions rendered during the past three decades that, even though an American

---

25   In *re Bethlehem Steel Corp.,* 435 F. Supp. 944, 1977 AMC 2252 (N.D. Ohio, 1976). The Court of Appeals later affirmed the district court's conclusion that it would give effect to one aspect of Canadian law found to be "substantive", *i.e.,* the principle that no recovery could be had for purely economic losses claimed by other shipowners whose vessels' movements had been delayed by the blocking of the Welland Canal.

26   631 F. 2d 441, 1980 AMC 2122 (6th Cir. 1980).

27   Cert. denied 450 U.S. 921 (1980).

28   SDNY July 17, 1984, No. 83-Civ. 5039 (Canella, D.J.).

court has jurisdiction over a dispute, other facts should be taken into account in determining how that jurisdiction should be exercised. In its seminal 1953 decision in *Lauritzen v. Larsen*,[29] the Supreme Court provided a list of "contacts" to be weighed in deciding whether to take jurisdiction of a Danish seaman's personal injury action in an American court against a Danish shipowner. The most important were (1) the place of the wrongful act, (2) the law of the ship's flag, and (3) the allegiance or domicile of the plaintiff and of the shipowner. These criteria have since been applied in determining the law applicable to other categories of cases.

Even if an American court concludes that foreign law applies, it may nevertheless retain jurisdiction and decide the issues on the basis of that law as developed by expert testimony. Alternatively, it can conclude that a weighing of public and private interest factors (including the availability of witnesses and resort to compulsory process to compel their attendance) justifies dismissal of the action on the basis of *forum non conveniens*. In such instances, dismissal is frequently made subject to conditions designed to ensure that proceedings in a foreign court will not be subject to time bar defences, and that security posted in the American action will be available for the satisfaction of any eventual foreign judgment.

A recent federal district court decision[30] in Texas illustrates how these considerations apply in the context of a limitation proceeding. It involved claims for the deaths of one American and twelve Canadian citizens arising out of the total loss of a Canadian-flag vessel in Canadian waters. The *Arctic Explorer* was an oceanographic research vessel under time charter to an American corporation which, since it could not qualify as an "owner," was not entitled to invoke the American Limitation of Liability Act. However, when suits were brought against it in Texas, the charterer filed for limitation both under the American statute and under s. 649(1) of the Canada Shipping Act which does allow a time charterer to limit. After hearing expert testimony as to whether under Canadian law this right on the part of a time charterer was substantive or procedural, the court concluded that it was substantive because it attached to a right created by the statute. Weighing the relevant public and private interest factors, the court held that the balance of convenience favored trial in a Canadian forum, rejecting claimant's argument that their workmen's compensation remedy in Canada was "so inadequate in amount as to be no remedy at all".

---

29   345 U.S. 571, 1953 AMC 1210 (1953).
30   *In re Geophysical Service, Inc.* SD Tex, May 8, 1984, C.A. No. 81-3381 (McDonald, D.J.).

How much weight should be given to the likelihood that remitting an American plaintiff to a foreign forum may result in the application of a lesser limit of shipowner liability? This question vexed the Second Circuit Court of Appeals in *The Nordic Regent*,[31] an action by an American corporation against a Liberian-flag vessel which had collided with the plaintiff's pier in Trinidad. The claim was for some $8 million but under Trinidad law the shipowner's liability was susceptible of being limited to only $570,000. After reargument *en banc* the Court held (7-2) that the district judge had not abused his discretion in dismissing the American plaintiff's New York action on condition that the shipowner submit to Trinidad jurisdiction and guarantee payment of any Trinidad judgment. In concluding that the plaintiff's American citizenship did not create any special rule of *forum non conveniens,* the majority of the court disagreed with the dissenting judges' conclusion that a citizen's choice of forum should not be disturbed unless the defendant can establish vexation, harassment, and manifest injustice.

No decided case has gone so far as to hold that an *American* shipowner's limitation proceeding should be dismissed when the owner claims the protection of American law. Unless and until *The Titanic* is overruled by the Supreme Court, it would appear that an American court can go no further than to apply foreign law to issues deemed to be "substantive", and that it is likely to do so only in instances where the shipowner's limitation fund under that law is *less* than under foreign law.

4. INTERNATIONAL CONVENTIONS

In a 1970 decision, *Petition of Bloomfield Steamship Co.,*[32] the Second Circuit Court of Appeals, noting that ships engaged in international trade should expect to be involved in legal proceedings in more than one country, commented:

> Forum shopping... is not a term of opprobrium but a way of life and each party seeks what appears to be the best legal haven. Additionally, the absence of an international concursus which can be obtained only through the treaty making processes of the United States leaves a decree in a limitation proceeding clothed with domestic, not international, recognition.[33]

The problems involved in achieving such international recognition for limitation proceedings were addressed by the Comité Maritime International from the very year of its foundation in 1897. During the

---

31   *Alcoa S.S. Co. v. M/V Nordic Regent,* 654 F. 2d 147, 1980 AMC 309, cert. den. 449 U.S. 890, 1981 AMC 2098 (1980).

32   422 F. 2d 728, 1970 AMC 521.

33   422 F. 2d at 736, 1970 AMC at 533.

succeeding decades, attempts were made to reach international agreement on a convention obligating the signatory nations to recognize limitation of liability proceedings in the courts of other signatories.[34] After an abortive convention in 1924 which never entered into force,[35] the Comité achieved some success with the 1956 "International Convention Relating to the Limitation of the Liability of Owners of Sea-Going Ships",[36] which did achieve a sufficient number of ratifications to go into effect in 1968. However, the ravages of worldwide inflation during succeeding years made it plain that that Convention's liability limits, based on a hypothetical Poincaré gold franc, were too low. In 1976, under the aegis of the International Maritime Consultative Organization, a new "International Convention on Limitation of Liability for Maritime Claims"[37] was agreed upon and is currently in the ratification process. It adopts higher limits for calculating the shipowner's liability, based on the fluctuating value of the special drawing right as defined by the International Monetary Fund.

The failure of the United States to ratify any of these Conventions enhances the likelihood of forum shopping in the limitation of liability context. However, the same is true of many other areas of American maritime law. Notably, the United States stands alone among the major maritime nations in its failure to ratify the Brussels Collision Liability Convention of 1910,[38] under which the navigational faults of the carrying vessel are imputed to the cargo on board. The effort to accomplish the same result by incorporation of a so-called "both to blame" clause in bills of lading was scotched by the Supreme Court,[39] with the result that "innocent cargo" will always attempt to bring suit in the United States, regardless of the locale of the collision, thus making it prudent for the shipowner to file for limitation. By the same token, shipowners are inclined to seek the benefits of the archaically low "fund" under the limitation statute, although this inclination may be tempered by the fact that American judges are more likely than not to deny limitation.[40]

---

34   The CMI'S role in drafting the Conventions is reviewed in Edgar Gold, *Maritime Transport: The Evolution of International Marine Policy and Shipping Law* (Lexington Books, 1981) at pp. 152-53; 207-08; 292-93; 359.

35   6 *Benedict on Admiralty* (Cohen ed. 1984), at p. 5-2.

36   *Ibid.* at p. 5-11.

37   *Ibid.* at p. 5-32.

38   *Ibid.* at p. 3-11.

39   *United States v. Atlantic Mutual Ins. Co.*, 343 U.S. 236, 1952 AMC 659 (1952).

40   In *Olympic Towing Corp. v. Nebel Towing Co.*, 419 F. 2d at 235, 1969 AMC at 1578, the Fifth Circuit commented that "in the vast majority of cases limitation is denied for one reason or another". A *Statistical Analysis of Limitation of Liability Cases, 1953-1981*, prepared by Donald C. Greenman, Esq. of Baltimore for the Maritime Law Association of the United States, indicates that during this period limitation

The applicability of another type of international convention could have been raised, but was not, in the *Amoco Cadiz* litigation. The owner of a Liberian supertanker commenced a proceeding in the Northern District of Illinois federal court to limit its liability arising out of the total loss of the *Amoco Cadiz* and her crude oil cargo following a 1978 stranding off the coast of Brittany. Claims were filed by the insurers of the cargo, and also by various French private and governmental interests seeking recovery of pollution clean-up costs. In its April 18, 1984 decision, dealing only with the question of liability, not damages,[41] the district court held that French substantive law would have applied "if it had been proved different from that of the United States. However, it was not proved different ... [and] [t]he claims will be decided in accordance with U.S. law."[42] The reason for the claimants' reluctance to sue in France or to have French law applied in the American action was that both France and Liberia, but not the United States, were parties to the International Convention on Civil Liability for Oil Pollution, Brussels, 1969,[43] which could have limited their recovery. The shipowner, on the other hand, was hoping (in vain, as it turned out) to limit liability to the relatively modest fund prescribed by the American statute.

5.   FUTURE LEGISLATION

At this time it is impossible to predict whether new legislation will be enacted by the U.S. Congress to bring the American limitation procedures more in line with those under the 1976 International Convention.[44] There are those who take the position that the whole concept is outdated and should be abolished altogether. In this era of government subsidies to shipping, it is difficult to argue that limitation is still necessary to fulfill the Limitation Act's original purpose of putting American shipowners on an equal footing with their foreign com-

---

was denied in 83 cases and granted in only 46, although "the statistics show a gradually increasing trend allowing the right to limit". MLA Document No. 640, June 15, 1982, pp. 7435-37.

41   Re Oil Spill by the Amoco Cadiz off the coast of France on March 16, 1978, 1984 AMC 2123.

42   *Ibid.* at 2189.

43   6 *Benedict on Admiralty* (Cohen Ed., 1984) p. 6-62.20.

44   On March 21, 1984 proposed legislation entitled "Limitation of Liability Act of 1984", H.R. 5007 was introduced in the House of Representatives. Its provisions follow closely those of the 1976 Convention (see note 36, *supra*) but they express higher tonnage limits in U.S. dollars. No action has been taken on this Bill, which is supported by the Maritime Law Association of the United States; it will presumably be reintroduced after the next Congress convenes in January, 1985.

petitors. Perhaps a more plausible argument is that continuation of the limitation concept enables shipowners' liability insurers to estimate more accurately their likely exposure in the event of a catastrophe, thus keeping down insurance costs which must ultimately be passed along to shippers, passengers, and other "consumers" of ocean shipping services. In the final analysis an "everybody's doing it" justification, based on a widespread international acceptance of the 1976 Convention, may prove as effective as any other in persuading Congress to preserve the limitation concept.

One thing seems clear. Even if the American Congress should enact some form of new legislation, the American limits of shipowner liability will probably be higher than elsewhere, with the result that the doors to the forum shopping emporium may be expected to remain open for business as heretofore.

6. CONCLUSION

The answer to the question posed in the title of this paper must remain a qualified one: In shipowners' limitation of liability proceedings, courts will apply foreign law, but only where there are important contacts with a foreign jurisdiction whose law provides a substantive right. However, when foreign law is asserted by claimants merely to require the shipowner to put a limitation fund higher than that prescribed by the United States Limitation of Liability Act, the United States statute will probably prevail.

SHIPOWNERS' LIMITATION OF LIABILITY AND THE CANADIAN CONFLICT OF LAWS

*Sean Harrington**

Although Canada is not a party to the 1957 International Convention relating to the Limitation of the Liability of Owners of Sea-going ships, many of its provisions are found in sections 647 to 655 of the Canada Shipping Act,[1] appended hereto.

Briefly put, Canadian and foreign shipowners and charterers, even if not by demise, may limit their liability for wrongful death, personal injury and property damage claims caused by shipboard personnel or attributable to ship navigation or management if they establish they are without "actual fault or privity".[2] Property damage liability is always limited to 1,000 gold francs per limitation ton, which is the greater of the ship's net register tonnage plus engine room space or 300 tons. In case of personal injury or wrongful death the liability is extended to 3,100 gold francs per ton, with such claimants having priority over 21/31sts of the fund and entitlement to the residue, if any, after property claims have been paid out of the other 10/31sts. Gold francs are converted into Canadian dollars through the medium of the International Monetary Fund's Special Drawing Rights (SDR). 15.075 gold francs equals one SDR,[3] the Canadian dollar equivalent of which on March 31st, 1984 was $1.35845. On that basis 1,000 gold francs equals $90.11.

Not all foreign law is similar. Under the provisions of the United States Limitation of Shipowners' Liability Act,[4] liability is limited to

---

* Partner, McMaster Meighen, Montreal and Toronto. Mr. Harrington is a member of the Executive Committee, Canadian Maritime Law Association.

1   R.S.C. 1970, c. S-9.

2   In the case of a corporation, a fault personal to its directing mind or alter ego. The authorities are set out in a Canadian context in *B.C. Telephone Co. v. Marpole Towing Ltd.,* [1971] S.C.R. 321, [1973] 2 Lloyd's R. 159, and refer to *Lennard's Carrying Co. v. Asiatic Petroleum Co.,* [1915] A.C. 705 (H.L.). Oil pollution liability and limitations thereof such as found in Part XX of the *Canada Shipping Act,* R.S.C. 1970, c. S-9 and the *Arctic Waters Prevention Pollution Act,* R.S.C. 1970 (1st supp.) c. 2 are beyond the scope of this paper.

3   Canada Shipping Act Gold Franc Conversion Regulations S.O.R./78-73.

4   U.S.C.A. Title 46.

the value of the ship, and pending freight, with a deemed minimum value of U.S. $60.00 per gross ton, less crew space, available by priority to wrongful death and personal injury claimants. A charterer, not by demise, is not entitled to limit liability.

Under the 1976 Convention on Limitation of Liability for Maritime Claims (not yet in force), owners and charterers may limit their liability, even for wreck removal claims, unless "it is proved that the loss resulted from his personal act or omission, committed with the intent to cause such loss, or recklessly and with knowledge that such loss would probably result". The monetary limits are much higher. For instance, a property damage fund based on 10,000 limitation tons, which is $901,100. under Canadian law, would be 1,754,000 SDR's or $2,382,721.30. As under Canadian law the fund is dramatically increased for the benefit of wrongful death and personal injury claimants.

Under Canadian law an owner cannot limit his statutory debts for the removal of his own wreck[5] or for personal injury and wrongful death claims of his Canadian crew,[6] which are governed by no-fault Workmen's Compensation plans. Section 647(4) provides that liability to foreign crews cannot be limited in accordance with our law if the employment contract is governed by a foreign law which sets either a higher limit or no limit at all.

The courts have recognized the underlying overt philosophy behind statutory limitation of liability. In *British Columbia Telephone Co. v. Marpole Towing Ltd.*[7] Mr. Justice Ritchie said:

> the limitation of liability provisions ... are expressly designed for the purpose of encouraging shipping and affording protection to shipowners against bearing the full impact of heavy and perhaps crippling pecuniary damage sustained by reason of the negligent navigation of their ships on the part of their servants or agents

In *The Bramley Moore,*[8] Lord Denning said:

> One final word ... the principle underlying limitation of liability was that the wrongdoer should be liable according to the potentiality of damage. Thus a small tug towing a great liner can do immense damage. It should, therefore, have a high measure of liability. I do not think that that is the right approach. The principle underlying limitation of liability is that the wrongdoer should be liable according to the value of his ship and no more. A small tug has comparatively small value and it should have a correspondingly low measure of liability, even though it is towing a great liner and

---

5   *Margrande Compania Naviera S.A. v. The Leecliffe Hall's Owners,* [1970] Ex. C.R. 870, distinguishing *Marwell Equipment Ltd. v. Vancouver Tug Boat Co.,* [1961] S.C.R. 43, which dealt with an earlier version of the statute.

6   *The Leecliffe Hall, ibid,* and *Bonavista Cold Storage Co. Ltd. v. Walter* (1959), 20 D.L.R. (2d) 744.

7   [1971] S.C.R. 321 at 338.

8   [1964] P. 200, [1964] 1 All E.R. 105 at 109 (C.A.).

does great damage. I agree that there is not much room for justice in this rule; but limitation of liability is not a matter of justice. It is a rule of public policy which has its origin in history and its justification in convenience.

In addition to the proviso that foreign crews are not to be adversely affected by our limitation of liability laws, other specific mention is made of foreign claims and foreign courts. In distributing the Canadian limitation fund, the court may take account of claims that may be established before foreign courts and postpone distribution to permit a claim against the Canadian fund. In releasing a ship or other maritime property arrested in Canada the court may take cognizance of security in place elsewhere, as long as overall security is not less than the limitation fund set by Canadian law. Tonnage of foreign ships is calculated in the Canadian mode.

Although the Federal Court of Canada by virtue of section 22(3)(c) of the Federal Court Act[9] has jurisdiction over maritime claims whether arising in Canadian or foreign waters or the high seas, section 43 provides that no action may be commenced in Canada by the same person against the same defendant in a collision if a foreign action on the same cause of action is pending, and no action *in personam* may be commenced in Canada on a collision unless the defendant resides or has a place of business here, the cause of action arose here or the parties submitted to our jurisdiction. Since collisions often give rise to limitation actions, the court, on a practical level, has no jurisdiction over many causes which could give rise to limitation.

Although Canada has had its share of limitation cases, only a few have made mention of the conflict of laws. They must be read with care as the Act, and its inspiration, the various United Kingdom Merchant Shipping Acts, have been frequently amended. The early history of limitation statutes was set out in *The Stoomvaart Maatschappy Nederland v. The Peninsular and Oriental Steam Navigation Company*,[10] which can be up-dated by reference to Marsden, *The Law of Collisions at Sea*,[11] and Temperley, *Merchant Shipping Acts*.[12] The earlier statutes were read as construing benefits on certain flag ships only.

It is submitted that both the right to limit and the measure of the resulting fund are matters of substance and should be governed by the *lex causae.*

In *The A.L. Smith and The Chinook v. Ontario Gravel Freighting*

---

9   R.S.C. 1970 (2nd Supp.), c. 10.
10   (1882), 7 App. Cas. 795 (H.L.).
11   11th ed., ed. K. McGuffie (London, Stevens & Sons Ltd., 1961).
12   7th ed., ed. M. Thomas and D. Steel (London, Stevens & Sons, 1976).

Company,[13] the Supreme Court, on appeal from the Exchequer Court, Toronto Admiralty Division, dealt with a collision between the American tug *A.L. Smith* and her tow the American dumb barge *Chinook* in U.S. waters with the plaintiff's Canadian barge. The plaintiff ignored a U.S. limitation action instituted by the tug A.L. SMITH and arrested both tug and tow in Canada. A bailbond was given. The U.S. limitation proceedings were only mentioned in the context of an unsuccessful attempt to have the Canadian action dismissed on the grounds of *forum non conveniens.* On the particular facts, the tug and tow were both found to blame so that no measure of limitation, be it American, Canadian or Imperial, worked to the defendants' advantage.

In his dissent, Mr. Justice Anglin found the *A.L. Smith* alone to blame and exonerated the *Chinook.* He went on to say that the *A.L. Smith's* liability, should it be subsequently found that the collision occurred without her owners' privity and knowledge, was limited to her value and pending freight in accordance with American law, because:

> The statutory limitation of a shipowner's liability is not *lex fori. . . .* and, where the collision occurs in the domestic waters of the foreign ship held to be at fault, the *lex loci commissi delicti* determines the extent of her liability.

He also said that the relevant provisions of the Canada Shipping Act could not be invoked as their application was on their own terms confined to "the navigation of Canadian waters" and that the Imperial Merchant Shipping Act only:

> . . . applies to foreign vessels when before British courts in respect of collisions which occur either in British territorial waters or on the high seas, it does not determine the liability of a foreign vessel for a wrong commited by her within the territorial limits of the country to which she belongs.

Cope v. Doherty[14] held that the provisions of the Merchant Shipping Act,[15] limiting liability did not apply to a collision on the high seas between foreign ships. By the time of the *A.L. Smith* case the wording of the Imperial statute had been changed, and now that Canada has evolved into a fully independent state the reference to navigation of Canadian waters has been deleted from our Act.

The Supreme Court next dealt with the collision between the Norwegian flag *Storstad* and the British flag *Empress of Ireland* in the St. Lawrence River in *Canadian Pacific Railway Company v. The S.S. Storstad*[16] on appeal from the Exchequer Court, Quebec Admiralty

---

13   (1915), 51 S.C.R. 39.
14   (1858), 2 De G. & J. 614, 44 E.R. 1127, referred to by Anglin J. in *Smith and Chinook, ibid.* at 72.
15   1854, 17 & 18 Vict., c. 104.
16   (1917), 56 S.C.R. 324, varying 16 Ex. C.R. 472.

District. The *Storstad* had been found alone to blame in first instance and did not appeal. The ship had been sold and the proceeds were in court. As the claims greatly exceeded the fund, the wrongful death and personal injury claimants alleged a priority over a portion of the fund in accordance with the applicable law, be it British or Canadian. The Supreme Court held that the Imperial Merchant Shipping Act[17] applied as it had been explicitly extended to Canada, which was still a colony, and that the Canadian Act only applied to Canadian flag ships. The court gave the wrongful death and personal injury claimants priority on the grounds that the collision had occurred without the actual fault or privity of the *Storstad* owners, even though they had not taken a limitation action.

On appeal to the Privy Council,[18] it was held that the proceeds of the sale should be divided amongst all claimants *pro rata*. According to Lord Sumner:[19]

> Limitation of liability is the creation of statute. It is a provision in favour of the shipowner, and operates to restrict the rights of those to whom he is liable. Incidentally the sections furnish the rule by which to determine the rights of parties interested in the fund created by the operation of the sections themselves, but if the shipowner, for whatsoever reason, does not bring the sections into operation, no one else can do so, and they do not in such case have effect. This is the result of the enactment itself, for it expressly provides for procedure to limit the shipowner's liability, and sets up no principle or rule as to the rights of different classes of claimants apart from such limitation.

The latest decision in Canada specifically dealing with limitation of liability and the conflict of laws is the decision of Mr. Justice Addy in *Bethlehem Steel Corporation v. The St. Lawrence Seaway Authority et al.*[20] Plaintiff's ship the *Steelton* struck a bridge in the Welland Canal, inflicting considerable damage to the bridge and bringing on the closure of both the bridge and the canal. Bethlehem admitted liability, sued for limitation and deposited a fund into court measured in accordance with Canadian law. As it was also being sued in the U.S., it took a similar limitation action there.

The issue before the court was whether bridge and canal users who only suffered economic loss had a claim in tort against the owners and through them to the fund. It was held that they had not. After noting that Bethlehem could claim against its own Canadian fund with respect to liabilities honoured elsewhere, the court added:[21]

---

17   *Supra* note 15.
18   [1920] A.C. 397 (P.C.), reversing 56 S.C.R. 324 (note 16 *supra*).
19   *Ibid.* at 401.
20   [1978] 1 F.C. 464.
21   *Ibid.* at 475-476.

The right of recovery of the claimants in the U.S. action has not yet been determined. It appears that the very great majority of those claims, if not all of them, will fall within the same category as the claims – which I have disallowed. It appears also, following a ruling by Krupanski J., who heard the application dealing with the limitation fund to be deposited in the U.S. action, that, following the same principles recognized by Canadian courts and most nations of the Western World, United States courts, in order to determine liability in tort cases, apply the *lex loci delicti commissi.*

It is nevertheless of prime importance to bear in mind that where the tort on which the claims are founded has been committed in Canada, this Court must not allow any credit against the limitation fund here for a claim declared valid by a foreign court unless that claim would have been recognized as valid at law in Canada; it would be nothing short of ludicrous to hold otherwise, for Canadian claimants would then be obliged to suffer a reduction in the amount to which they would otherwise have been entitled to receive from the fund merely because a claimant has chosen to appeal to a foreign jurisdiction rather than to a Canadian court where his claim would have failed.

Since the *Steelton,* it has been held by another judge of the Federal Court, Trial Division, Mr. Justice Dubé in *Interocean Shipping Company v. M.V. Atlantic Splendor,*[22] that pure economic losses are recoverable in tort if the losses flowed directly, and were reasonably foreseeable. The case is under appeal.

Although the facts giving rise to the *Atlantic Splendour* case arose in Quebec, and the *Steelton's* in Ontario, Mr. Justice Dubé made no reference to Quebec civil law principles. While neither Quebec civil law nor the common law ever stands still, articles 1053 to 1075 of the Quebec Civil Code have been interpreted as establishing liability in tort for direct and immediate damages caused to "another" by one's fault. "Another" includes persons who would not have lived in Lord Atkin's neighbourhood. Foreseeability is not really an issue and economic-loss claims have never been automatically excluded as they used to be at common law. The *Steelton* could have struck a bridge in Quebec, and economic-loss claimants could have taken action in the Federal Court or in the Quebec Superior Court. While we know that the essential *lex non scripta* portions of the Canadian maritime law administered by the Federal Court derive from English maritime law[23] and that the Federal Court only administers federal law[24] we know neither the extent of Canadian maritime law[25] nor the extent that law referentially adopts

---

22   (1983), 26 C.C.L.T. 189 (Fed. T.D.).

23   *Tropwood A.G. v. Sivaco Wire & Nail Co.,* [1979] 2 S.C.R. 157; *Wirerope Indust. Canada, (1966) Ltd. v. B.C. Marine Shipbldrs. Ltd.,* [1981] 1 S.C.R. 363.

24   *Que. North Shore Paper Co. v. Can. Pac. Ltd.,* [1977] 2 S.C.R. 1054; *McNamara Const. (Western) Ltd. v. R.,* [1977] 2 S.C.R. 654.

25   *Tropwood* and *Wire Rope Indust.,* supra, note 23.

provincial law, which of course may vary from province to province.[26] Furthermore although only the Federal Court can administer and distribute a limitation fund against which there are several claimants, the provincial courts which have concurrent jurisdiction in admiralty matters generally must entertain a defence based on limited liability.[27] In *Associated Metals and Minerals Corp. v. Aris Steamship Co. (The Evie W)*,[28] Chief Justice Jackett of the Federal Court of Appeal said:[29]

> Admiralty law and the various bodies of "provincial" law concerning property and civil rights co-exist and overlap and, in some cases at least, the result of litigation concerning a dispute will differ depending on whether the one body of law or the other is invoked.[30]

Since the *lex loci delicti commissi* is, at one and the same time, Canadian maritime law, or the law of the province in which the tort was committed, the limitation of liability provisions of the Canada Shipping Act should not be construed as denying a valid provincial cause of action, nor as depriving the shipowner of his right to limit liability. This issue, of course, was not before Mr. Justice Addy in the *Steelton* as it was implicit that the *lex loci delicti commissi,* be it Ontario law or Canadian maritime law, was one and the same.

Meanwhile, across the border, the owners of the *Steelton* were endeavouring to have the economic-loss claims dismissed outright on the ground that there was no cause of action under the *lex loci delicti commissi,* and to have the limitation fund measured in accordance with Canadian law which was less than the value of the *Steelton* and her pending freight. They succeeded in the former, but not the latter. Dealing first with the limitation fund,[31] Judge Krupansky stated the following U.S. conflict of law rule:[32]

> It is a well-settled principle that "in the absence of some overriding domestic policy translated into law, the right to recover for a tort depends upon and is measured by the law of the place where the tort occurred," the lex loci delicti commissi. Black Diamond S.S. Corporation v. Robert Stewart & Sons (Norwalk Victory), 336 U.S. 386, 396, 1949 AMC 393.

---

26   *Bensol Customs Brokers Ltd. v. Air Canada,* [1979] 2 F.C. 575, especially LeDain J. at 583; *R. v. Montreal Urban Community Transit Comm.,* [1980] 2 F.C. 151 *per* Pratte J. at 153. See also *Kellogg Co. v. Kellogg,* [1941] S.C.R. 242 *per* Rinfret J. at 249-250; and *Stein v. The Kathy K.,* [1976] 2 S.C.R. 802.

27   *Fort William v. McNamara Const. Co.* (1957), 10 D.L.R. (2d) 625 (Ont. S.C.); and *Walithy Charters Ltd. v. Doig* (1979), 15 B.C.L.R. 45 (S.C.).

28   [1978] 2 F.C. 710. Leave to appeal to S.C.C. granted 20 N.R. 50n (C.A.)

29   *Ibid.* at 717.

30   Noted, but neither specifically approved nor disapproved on appeal to the Supreme Court [1980] 2 S.C.R. 322, and in *Zavarovalna Skupnost Triglav v. Terrasses Jewellers Inc. and Bank of Montreal,* S.C.C., March 1, 1983.

31   [1977] A.M.C. 2203, [1977] 1 Lloyd's R. 310.

32   *Ibid.* at 2205.

He went on to say that the forum would apply foreign substantive law and its own rules of procedure. However, unlike in Canada, characterization into substance or procedure falls to be decided by the *lex loci delicti commissi* and not by the forum.[33] After hearing conflicting evidence from Canadian lawyers as to how we would characterize the limitation provisions of the Canada Shipping Act, and noting the dearth of Canadian jurisprudence, he held that under Canadian law the right to limit was substantive but that the measurement provisions were procedural. He therefore ordered that the owners establish a fund in the amount required by U.S. law rather than the lesser amount under Canadian law.

The learned judge then[34] dismissed the economic-loss claims on the ground that they were unfounded under the *lex loci delicti commissi,* and that there was no overriding domestic policy requiring him to ignore the *lex causae.* Both decisions were maintained on appeal[35] and a petition by economic-loss claimants to the Supreme Court for a writ of certiorari was dismissed.

Due to evolving Canadian jurisprudence, tort claims arising in Canada for economic loss would probably not be as readily dismissed by a United States court today. Suppose a U.S. court was dealing with an application by a time charterer to limit liability. On the basis that the Canadian law providing the right to limit is substantive, the charterer should be permited to limit liability in a U.S. action even if he would not be permitted to do so under U.S. domestic law. Since the time charterer has no interest in the ship, and if no freight was pending, liability would not just be limited but would be excluded outright unless he was equated to a shipowner, and subject to the quantification provisions applying to shipowners. In many cases, and certainly when the ship has sunk, the Canadian limits are higher.

There are two other Canadian admiralty cases which should be considered even though they do not deal with limitation of liability *per se.* Both cases were handed down the same day: *Todd Shipyards Corporation v. Altema Compania Maritima S.A. (The Ioannis Daskalelis),*[36] and *Drew Brown v. The Ship Orient Trader et al.*[37]

---

33 J. Castel, *Canadian Conflict of Laws* (Toronto: Butterworths, 1975) at p. 44: "The rule is quite clear and free from controversy that in interpreting its own conflict rules, a court must apply its own characterization. The connecting factor is part of the conflict of law rules of the *lex fori* and must be interpreted by that law". But see Dicey & Morris, *The Conflict of Laws,* 9th ed., ed. J. Morris (London: Stevens & Sons, Ltd., 1973) pp. 19-33.

34 Note 31 *supra* at 2252.

35 [1980] A.M.C. 2122.

36 [1974] S.C.R. 1248, [1974] 1 Lloyd's R. 174.

37 [1974] S.C.R. 1286, [1973] 2 Lloyd's R. 174.

Todd Shipyards had effected necessary repairs to the Greek flag *Ioannis Daskalelis* while she was in the United States. The ship was subject to a Greek mortgage. The ship was arrested and sold in Canada, but the fund generated by the proceeds was not sufficient to satisfy the claims. Under Canadian domestic law, a mortgage outranks a necessaries claim. In fact, a necessaries claim does not even give rise to an action *in rem* unless there is personal liability on the part of the owner of the *res*.[38] It was proven as a fact, however, that Todd Shipyards had a maritime lien under the laws of the United States. The court held that a foreign maritime lien would be enforced here, but according to the priority which a right of that nature has under our own procedure. Since under our own ranking, a maritime lien outranks a mortgage, Todd Shipyard was given priority. Mr. Justice Ritchie, speaking for the court, referred to Mr. Justice Newcombe's words in the *Strandhill*,[39] "it must – be remembered that it is the right and not the remedy which is regulated by the *lex loci*."

The *Orient Trader*[40] contracted by way of Bills of Lading to carry tin slabs from Malaysia to Hamilton. The Bills of Lading, with the usual liberty clauses, specifically provided that the contracts were subject to U.S. law. The ship proceeded to Toronto rather than to Hamilton, under agreement that the tin would be trucked to Hamilton. However, following a dispute with the stevedores, the carrier decided to proceed to Ashtabula, Ohio where the tin, together with other cargo, would be discharged. A fire broke out prior to sailing from Toronto. The cargo owners took action for damage to the cargo and the carrier counterclaimed for general average contribution. While all five judges agreed that all questions of substantive law were to be governed by U.S. law, the majority held that the carrier was not liable because an unreasonable deviation did not deprive it of the protection of the U.S. Fire Statute, and that the owners' G.A. claim was recoverable.

The three judges in the majority gave separate speeches.

Although agreeing with Mr. Justice Pigeon, Mr. Justice Ritchie in a short concurring opinion stated:[41]

As the parties gave legal force to their agreement in accordance with the law of the United States of America, that is the proper law of the contract and the law by which,

---

38 *Westcan Stevedoring Ltd. v. The Armar,* [1973] F.C. 1232; *Saab Inc. v. Shipping Ltd.,* [1976] 2 F.C. 175, affirmed [1979] 1 F.C. 461 (C.A.); *McCain Produce Co. v. The Rea,* [1978] 1 F.C. 686; *Logistec Corp. v. The Sneland,* [1979] 1 F.C. 497; and *Marlex Petroleum, Inc. v. The Har Rai,* [1982] 2 F.C. 617, reversed 4 D.L.R. (4th) 739 (Fed. C.A.).

39 [1926] S.C.R. 680.

40 *Supra* note 37.

41 *Ibid.* at 1288.

in accordance with their own choice, the legal rights and remedies of the parties, in relation to the carriage of the appellant's cargo, are to be determined.

Mr. Justice Pigeon said:[42]

On the basis that under the proper law of the contract the deviation is to be treated as a breach, the further question whether such a breach gives a right of recovery irrespective of the defence afforded by the U.S. Fire Statute is, in my view, a question that must be considered under U.S. law because it has to do with the substance of the remedies available under the contract and, therefore, must be decided according to the proper law of the contract. We are not dealing here with a tort committed in Canada but with a breach of contract. There is conclusive authority to show that all questions of substantive law pertaining to a breach of contract are governed by the law of the contract. In *Livesley v. Horst,* [1924] S.C.R. 605, Duff J. speaking for this Court said (at pp. 607, 608):

> In principle, it is difficult to discover a solid ground for refusing to classify the rights to damages for breach of contract with other rights arising under the proper law of the contract, and recognizable and enforceable as such.

In a separate concurring speech, Mr. Justice Laskin, as he then was, said:[43]

Parties to a contract are entitled, subject to limitations which it is unnecessary to spell out in this case, to choose the law that will govern the interpretation and application of the terms of their bargain. . . . Although this is a matter which does not call for decision here, I do not think that it automatically follows that if a contract, originally subject to or governed by foreign law, is held to have lost its force because of fundamental breach, the law of the forum becomes the applicable law to determine the ensuing rights and liabilities of the contracting parties. The attendant circumstances may point to another conclusion.

As Oliver Wendell Holmes, Jr., once said, "The prophecies of what the courts will do in fact, and nothing more pretentious, are what I mean by the law." Considering that our courts have had such little occasion in the past to consider the conflict of laws in the context of limitation actions, any surmise on my part may be no more than free-flight fancy. Assume the following Canadian maritime conflict of law rules:

1.   Our courts will not enforce a right arising under foreign law which is inconsistent with our fundamental public policy;[44]
2.   To found an action on a tort committed in another jurisdiction the wrong must be of such a character that it would have been actionable if committed here and it must not have been justifiable by the *lex loci delicti commissi;*[45]

---

42   *Ibid.* at 1313.
43   *Ibid.* at 1318.
44   Dicey & Morris, *supra* note 33, p. 70.
45   The leading case in Canada is still *McLean v. Pettigrew,* [1945] S.C.R. 62 which followed *Phillips v. Eyre* (1870), L.R. 6 Q.B. 1 and *Machado v. Fontes,* [1897] 2 Q.B. 231. The Ontario Supreme Court declined to apply the "proper law of the tort" test in *Going v. Reid Brothers Motor Sales Ltd.* (1982), 35 O.R. (2d) 201 (H.C.).

3. Torts committed on the high seas are governed by Canadian maritime law because:
    but here the loss occurred on the high seas, which are within the common jurisdiction of all countries. From time immemorial actions for such a tort have been maintained, even against foreigners who could be served in this country, and they are tried according to maritime law as administered in this country . . .;[46]
4. Contractual rights and liabilities are governed by the proper law of the contract, the *lex causae.*
5. Remoteness and heads of damage are matters of substance governed by the *lex causae.* The *lex causae* is the law of the contract but in cases of tort is still somewhat an open question;[47]
6. The right to limit liability is a matter of substance;[48]
7. Procedure, including the quantification of damages, is governed by the *lex fori;*[49]
8. The assumption of both Castel and Dicey and Morris that all aspects of limitation of liability are governed by the statute prevailing in the *lex fori* should be tested.[50]

---

46   *The Chartered Mercantile Bank of India v. Netherlands India Steam Navigation* (1883), 10 Q.B.D. 521 (C.A.). This is an over-simplification. Where only one ship is involved, the law of the flag may be applied. See Dicey & Morris, *supra* note 33, 971 and ff.

47   *Boys v. Chaplin,* [1971] A.C. 356, [1969] 2 All E.R. 1085 (H.L.).

48   See *The Storstad, supra* note 16.

49   Dicey & Morris, supra, note 33, p. 1099 and ff. The question remains what is substance and what is procedure. In *Nat. Gypsum Co. v. Nor. Sales Ltd.,* [1964] S.C.R. 144, on appeal from the Exchequer Court of Canada, Quebec Admiralty District, the three majority judges, all from Quebec, held that the enforceability of an arbitration clause was a matter of procedure to be governed by the *lex fori.* At the time, absent a specific Exchequer Court Rule, matters of procedure were to be governed by the laws of the province. The court refused to give effect to the arbitration clause because it was "clause compromissoire" which was contrary to Quebec public policy. Such clauses are no longer invalid. The two dissenting judges, both from common law provinces, held that the substantive law administered by the Exchequer Court was English maritime law and that under that law the enforceability of an arbitration clause was a matter of substance to be governed by the proper law of the contract, in the case at bar the law of the United States. Since the clause was valid under that law, and the laws of England for that matter, the proper course was to stay the Canadian action.

50   Castel, *supra* note 33 only cites the text of the statute itself at p. 660. See also Dicey & Morris, *supra,* note 33 at p. 975. Although English courts have routinely applied the English limitation statute to matters occurring elsewhere there has been no discussion of foreign law, or whether that law differed from English law (*The Athelvictor,* [1946] P. 42, 78 Lloyd's R. 529; *The Abadesa,* [1968] P. 656, [1968] 1 Lloyd's R. 496 and *The Mecca,* [1968] P. 665, [1968] 2 Lloyd's R. 17). The latter two cases held that the conversion of gold francs into pound sterling was procedural.

Let us run through a few examples which demonstrate that the limitation of liability provisions of the Canada Shipping Act do not fall easily into conflict of law categories. The *lex causae* of one claim may differ from the *lex causae* of another; one arises from breach of contract, the other sounds in tort; one arose in Canada, another on the high seas and yet another in the territorial waters of another state; and weaving in and out is a somewhat illusive sense of public policy.

To avoid any discussion as to the effects of deviation, suppose the *Orient Trader* had proceeded directly to Hamilton and that due to a miscue during off-loading stevedores and crew were injured and cargo damaged. No proof was made of U.S. law except the package or unit limitation under COGSA and the limitation of liability statute. It was further established that under the crew contract the shipowner could limit his liability in the same manner and to the same extent as the limitation provisions under the Canada Shipping Act.

The crew and stevedores (in all likelihood the Ontario Workmen's Compensation Board plus the individual stevedores for the excess claim, if any, after statutory compensation) would share *pari passu* in 21/31sts of the fund. If the miscue was attributable to, say, error in the management of the ship which did not revert back to failure to exercise due diligence to make the ship seaworthy prior to and at the commencement of the voyage, the cargo would have no claim whatever against the shipowner under the Bill of Lading and hence no claim against the fund. The remaining 10/31sts would also go to the personal injury claimants.

If the miscue arose from mismanagement of cargo then the owner would be liable but "in any event" could invoke the per package or unit limitations of the contract and COGSA. Our courts would limit liability to the Canadian equivalent of U.S. $500.00 per package or in the case of goods not shipped in packages $500.00 per customary freight unit, even though under our own law the limitation is Canadian $500.00 per package or shipping unit.[51] There is no customary freight unit limitation. Having assessed liability subject to per package limitation, the cargo would be paid out of 10/31sts of the fund, with the residue, if any, going to satisfy any unpaid damages of the personal injury claimants.

What if the crew contract was subject to U.S. law? If the value of the *Orient Trader* and her pending freight was less than the Canadian fund, section 647(4) of the Canada Shipping Act apparently directs that security is obtainable in Canada even if security measured in accordance with U.S. law had already been given by the owners in the U.S.[52] Even if the value of the *Orient Trader* and her pending freight was higher, it does

---

51   *The Doroty v. Atl. Consol. Foods Ltd.*, [1981] 1 F.C. 783 (C.A.).
52   Canada Shipping Act, R.S.C. 1970, c. S-9, s. 654(1).

not follow that the personal injury claimants would be better off, as they only have priority on the first $60.00 per ton. However to make it easy we shall attribute the cargo damage to the excepted peril of mismanagement of the ship.

At first glance, it appears that the crew has no claim at all to the Canadian fund because the owner's liability was not limited by section 647. The stevedores and crew both benefit. However, if the owners established a fund for the crew in the U.S. the court should take account of the foreign claim and allow the owner to claim against his own fund. If the ship was worth $4,000,000.00, her Canadian limitation fund $2,000,000.00 and the crew and stevedore claims each $2,500,000.00 then the shipowner's liability for personal injury and wrongful death claims should be limited to $3,000,000.00: $1,000,000.00 with respect to the stevedores (one-half of the Canadian fund) and $2,000,000.00 for the crew (one-half of the American fund). If the Federal Court can recognize foreign claims, certainly it has sufficient control over its own process to assess the owner's limited liability with respect to the crew directly.

Add a time charterer to the brew who, as the Bill of Lading carrier, even after package limitation, has incurred considerable liability to cargo owners. If we follow Castel and Dicey and Morris, the time charterer would be entitled to limit in accordance with Canadian law, even though he was not entitled to limit at all under U.S. law. It seems rather peculiar that we would give effect to a foreign law exempting a time charterer from liability (*i.e.,* error of management of the ship) and to a package limitation measured according to the proper law of the contract but would determine that he was entitled to global limitation simply because the ship was arrested and the case proceeded here. The section has not been held to be of such public order to prevent owners from either contracting out of all liability or from contracting to limits higher than the statute.[53] Since under the proper law of the contract the time charterer is not entitled to limit liability, effect should be given to that bargain the same time as it was to exonerate the owners of the *Orient Trader* in the actual case before the courts.

To vary the theme still again, make the crew and cargo contracts subject to a law similar to the 1976 Limitation Convention, except with the specific proviso that the owner could limit his liability towards the crew. The stevedore claim arising in tort would still be governed by Canadian law, the *lex loci delicti commissi.* The crew would be subject to the more beneficial limitation figures. If we were to apply our own Act to the cargo it would be subject to a lesser global limitation than under the

---

53   Temperley, *Merchant Shipping Acts, supra* note 12 at p. 178.

law of the contract. If we gave full effect to the contract, cargo's rights would not be cut down as much.

Suppose however there was "actual fault or privity" but no personal intentional or reckless act or omission. By applying the law of the forum, crew and cargo would benefit. Then again there may not have been sufficient evidence to allow the court to make a finding. Under our law the burden of proof is upon the shipowner claiming limitation while under the Convention the burden is upon the claimant attempting to break limitation. Evidence is normally considered a matter of procedure governed by the *lex fori*.

All the above claims arise from breach of contract except the stevedores' claim. As the relationship between the shipowner and the stevedores giving rise to a duty of care rests on the stevedores attending on board the ship in Canada there should be no reason whatever to consider any other law. The ship, in coming to Canada, submitted herself to our laws.[54]

As Mr. Justice Laskin, as he then was, said in *Jordan House v. Menow:*[55]

> The common law assesses liability for negligence on the basis of a breach of a duty of care arising from a foreseeable and unreasonable risk of harm to one person created by the act or omission of another.

Canadian and U.S. ships travel each other's waters freely. Some of the locks in the St. Lawrence Seaway are in Canada, others are in the U.S., and in the Great Lakes and connecting rivers the border often runs right down the middle of the navigable channel.

We cannot consider global limitation of liability on tort claims without first looking at our conflict of law rules. The duty of care owed to one's neighbour may not be fleeting but long-standing, such as the duty of care owed to a supernumerary upon a ship. It is forseeable that a Canadian ship en route from one Canadian port to another might run aground in either Canadian or U.S. waters in circumstances that would give rise to a claim in tort by a Canadian person on board.

Dicey and Morris[56] state that the normal conflict of law rule must be satisfied. Assuming the act was done in the U.S. and was not justifiable according to U.S. law everything else would be decided by Canadian law and relative justice between the parties would be done. But what if the act was justifiable under U.S. law and gave rise to no cause of action?

---

54   *Laane and Baltser v. Estonian State Cargo & Passenger S.S. Line,* [1949] S.C.R. 530 *per* Rand J. at 544.
55   [1974] S.C.R. 239 at 247.
56   *Supra* note 33 at pp. 974-975.

In *Boys v. Chaplin,*[57] the House of Lords was concerned with a road accident in Malta involving two Englishmen, who were going their separate ways on the Maltese roads. Under Maltese domestic law the damages would have been £53 for expenses and monetary loss. There would have been no recovery for pain and suffering and loss of amenities fixed in English law at £2,500. As Lord Pearson noted, without the monetary loss there would have been no cause of action whatever under Maltese law.

However, since there was civil liability, the rest of the case proceeded as if the tort had been committed in England. The separate speeches by the Law Lords, and in the Court of Appeal below, differ in many respects. Most indicated that heads of damage were a matter of substance but to be governed by *lex fori.* Lord Guest held that compensation for pain and suffering should not be considered as a head of damage apart from patrimonial loss as a whole. It was merely an element in the quantification of the total compensation and, as a matter of remedy, rather than of right, must be determined by the *lex fori.*

Lord Denning, whose decision in the Court of Appeal,[58] was referred to favourably by Lord Hodson, made the most telling remark of all, which was that both vehicles were fully insured against liability by the same English company.

Lord Denning agreed with the principles set out in *Babcock v. Jackson,*[59] a U.S. decision, and said:[60]

> After considering the authorities, I am of opinion that we should apply the proper law of the tort, that is, the law of the country with which the parties and the act done have the most significant connexion. And once we have decided which is the correct law to apply, I think that law should be applied, not only to ascertaining whether there is a cause of action, but also to ascertaining the heads of damage that are recoverable and also the measure of damages; for these are matters of substantive law. They are quite distinct from the mere quantification of damages, which is a matter of procedure for the lex fori.

The application of any hard and fast rule may work an injustice in particular cases. As Lord Hodson said:[61]

> The search for justice in the individual case must often clash with fixed legal principles especially perhaps when choice of law is concerned.

Lord Pearson added:[62]

---

57   *Supra* note 47.
58   [1968] 1 All E.R. 283 (C.A.).
59   [1963] 2 Lloyd's R. 286.
60   *Supra* note 58 at 286-287.
61   *Supra* note 47 at 378.
62   *Ibid.* at 395.

I do not think there is any exact and authoritative definition of the boundary between substantive law and procedural (or adjectival or non-substantive) law, and the boundary remains to be settled by further decision in particular cases. In the present case I think it would be artificial and incorrect to treat the difference between the English law and the Maltese law, which materially affects the determination of the rights and liabilities of parties, as a matter only of procedural law.

The duty of care in an ongoing relationship, even *ex contractu,* should not vary with the bends in the river.

Lord Denning's distinction in *Boys v. Chaplin* between the measure of damages and the quantification of damages is apt. In limitation of liability the measure is the unit of account, such as the gold franc, and the number of tons. The quantification would be the conversion of that measure, be it calculated in special drawing rights or in foreign currency, to Canadian currency.

Furthermore a distinction should be drawn between the quantification of damages on the one hand and the quantification of a limit of liability on the other. The 1976 Convention clearly shows that the right to limit is inexorably linked with the amount of liability. The trade-off was an increased measure of liability against a more unbreakable limit.

Limitation in all respects should be considered a matter of substance. The right should not be divorced from the law giving rise to the liability. Both should be decided according to the *lex causae.* Since different claims may be governed by different *lex causae,* claims of the same class may recover in full or in different lesser percentages. A multi-cameral fund may give rise to administrative difficulties but they are not insurmountable. To quote Lord Diplock in the *Halcyon Isle:*[63]

> In distributing a limited fund that is insufficient to pay in full all creditors of a debtor whose claims against him have already been quantified and proved, the court is not any longer concerned with enforcing against the debtor himself the individual creditors' original rights against him. It is primarily concerned in doing even handed justice between competing creditors whose respective claims to be a creditor may have arisen under a whole variety of different and, it may be, conflicting systems of national law.

However, limitation of liability limits recovery not because of the impecuniosity of the defendant but as a matter of public policy. The court should therefore show more concern with the relationship of each and every creditor to the debtor. It is not unjust in the light of such policy that some claims be not limited, or that others of the same class be limited to a greater or lesser extent. Unless limitation is abolished outright[64] we should not be concerned that one of the toilers in the vineyard received more.

---

63   [1981] A.C. 221 at 230-231, [1980] 2 Lloyd's R. 325 (H.L.).
64   Global limitation of liability is at the heart of many international conventions. It is a

The limitation of liability provisions of the Canada Shipping Act can be reconciled with general conflict of law principles. Foreign and Canadian shipowners alike may limit their liability in accordance with Canadian law if their liability arose under Canadian law or a law taken to be the same as ours, *i.e.*, liability on the high seas or liability under foreign law, not proved as a fact to be different. The reference to the calculation of a foreign ship's tonnage would be taken as a matter of substance only to apply when the *lex causae* is Canadian. Public policy would be limited to not giving full credit to a smaller fund established elsewhere if under Canadian conflict of law rules the court considered that the foreign court was not establishing the fund in accordance with the proper *lex causae*.

There is a further safeguard in the court's administration of its own process. It may stay or dismiss an action based on blatant forum-shopping.[65]

---

fiction to say that the right to limit is an aberration from general principles of law. The law implicitly limits liability through the medium of such concepts as foreseeability, unreasonable risk, remoteness, economic loss and neighborliness. Even when liability is not limited, recovery may be limited by such creatures of the state as corporations limited by share capital, and by bankruptcy and insolvency statutes.

65   *Forum non conveniens* plays an important role in the determination of whether leave to serve *ex juris* should be granted and whether an action should be stayed or dismissed. If a valid action *in rem* is in place the court is likely prepared to hear all connexed actions *in personam* even if leave to serve *ex juris* must be given (*Antares Shipping Corp. v. The Capricorn*, [1977] 2 S.C.R. 422). Absent the action *in rem*, the court will not give leave to serve *ex juris* unless there is a proper connection between Canada and the facts giving rise to the dispute (*Elesguro Inc. v. SSangyong Shipping Co.*, [1981] 2 F.C. 326). The court will not likely dismiss an action unless it is really vexatious (*Magnolia Ocean Shipping Corp. v. Soladad Maria*, unreported decision of the Fed. Ct. (Can.) T.D., Marceau J. April 30th, 1981, No. T-744-81). "In order to justify a stay, two conditions must be satisfied, one positive and the other negative: (a) the defendant must satisfy the Court that there is another forum to whose jurisdiction he is amenable in which justice can be done between the parties at substantially less inconvenience or expense, and (b) the stay must not deprive the plaintiff of a legitimate personal or juridical advantage which would be available to him if he invoked the jurisdiction of the English Court". (*MacShannon v. Rockware Glass Ltd.*, [1978] 1 All E.R. 625 *per* Lord Diplock at 630, applied by the Federal Court of Appeal in *Yasuda Fire & Marine Ins. Co. v. Nosira Lin* (1984), 52 N.R. 303 (Fed. C.A.). Since limitation actions are related to interpleader the decision of Rouleau J. in *China National Trade Transportation Corp. v. Matthew Ship Chartering Ltd. et al*, No. T-2574-83, February 13th, 1984, may be pertinent. Various parties were interested in freight money in the hands of the sub-charterer. The sub-charterer wished to interplead in Canada, but an *ex parte* application to serve one of the interested parties was set aside on the grounds that Canada was not a convenient forum. The case is under appeal. The touchstones of the law in this area are s. 50 of the Federal Court Act, R.S.C. 1970, c. 10 (2nd Supp.) and Rule 307 of the General Rules and Orders of the Federal Court of Canada.

APPENDIX

Canada Shipping Act, ss. 647-655 as amended:

647. (1) For the purpose of this section and sections 648 to 653

"gold franc" means a unit consisting of sixty-five and one half milligrams of gold of millessimal fineness 900;

"ship" includes any structure launched and intended for use in navigation as a ship or as a part of a ship.

(2) The owner of a ship, whether registered in Canada or not, is not, where any of the following events occur without his actual fault or privity, namely,

(a) where any loss of life or personal injury is caused to any person on board that ship;

(b) where any damage or loss is caused to any goods, merchandise or other things whatever on board that ship;

(c) where any loss of life or personal injury is caused to any person not on board that ship through

(i) the act or omission of any person, whether on board the ship or not, in the navigation or management of the ship, in the loading, carriage or discharge of its cargo or in the embarkation, carriage or disembarkation of its passengers, or

(ii) any other act or omission of any person on board that ship; or

(d) where any loss or damage is caused to any property, other than property described in paragraph (b), or any rights are infringed through

(i) the act or omission of any person, whether on board that ship or not, in the navigation or management of the ship, in the loading, carriage or discharge of its cargo or in the embarkation, carriage or disembarkation of its passengers, or

(ii) any other act or omission of any person on board that ship;

liable for damages beyond the following amounts, namely,

(e) in respect of any loss of life or personal injury, either alone or together with any loss or damage to property or any infringement of any rights mentioned in paragraph (d), an aggregate amount equivalent to 3,100 gold francs for each ton of that ship's tonnage; and

(f) in respect of any loss or damage to property or any infringement of any rights mentioned in paragraph (d), an aggregate amount equivalent to 1,000 gold francs for each ton of that ship's tonnage.

(3) The limits on the liability of an owner of a ship set by this section apply in respect of each distinct occasion on which any of the events mentioned in paragraphs (2)(a) to (d) occur without that owner's actual fault or privity, and without regard to any liability incurred by that owner in respect of that ship on any other occasion.

(4) This section does not apply to limit the liability of an owner of a ship in respect of any loss of life or personal injury caused to, any loss of or damage to property or any infringement of any right of, a person who is employed on board or in connection with a ship under a contract of service if that contract is governed by the law of any country other than Canada and that law does not set any limit to that liability or sets a limit exceeding that set by this section.

648. (1) Where any liability is alleged to have been incurred by the owner of a ship in respect of any loss of life or personal injury, any loss or damage to property or any infringement of any right in respect of which his liability is limited by section 647 and several claims are made or apprehended in respect of that liability, the Admiralty Court may, on the application of that owner, determine the amount of his liability and distribute that amount rateably among the several claimants; and such court may stay any proceedings pending in any court in relation to the same matter, and it may proceed in such manner and subject to such regulations as to making persons interested parties to the proceedings, and as to the exclusion of any claimants who do not come in within a certain time, and as to requiring security from the owner, and as to payment of any costs, as the court thinks just. [Re-en. R.S.C. 1970, c. 10 (2nd Supp.), s. 65.]

(2) A judge of the Court in making a distribution under subsection (1) where there are claims in respect of loss of life or personal injury, and of loss of or damage to property or the infringement of any right, shall distribute rateably among the several claimants the amount at which the liability has been determined, as follows:

(a) twenty-one thirty-firsts of the amount shall be applied in payment of claims in respect of loss of life and personal injury; and

(b) ten thirty-firsts of the amount shall be applied in payment of claims in respect of loss of or damage to property or infringement of any right, and to the satisfaction of the balance of any claims in respect of loss of life and personal injury remaining unpaid after distribution of the amount applied pursuant to paragraph (a).

(3) [Repealed R.S.C. 1970, c. 10 (2nd Supp.), s. 65.]

(4) In making a distribution under this section of the amount determined to be the liability of the owner of a ship, the Court may, having regard to any claim that may subsequently be established before a court outside Canada in respect of that liability, postpone the distribution of such part of the amount as it deems appropriate.

(5) No lien or other right in respect of any ship or property shall affect the proportions in which any amount is distributed by the Court under this section among the several claimants.

649. (1) Sections 647 and 648 extend and apply to

(a) the charterer of a ship;

(b) any person having an interest in or possession of a ship from and including the launching thereof; and

(c) the manager or operator of a ship and any agent of a ship made liable by law for damage caused by the ship

where any of the events mentioned in paragraphs 647(2)(a) to (d) occur without their actual fault or privity, and to any person acting in the capacity of master or member of the crew of a ship and to any servant of the owner or of any person described in paragraphs (a) to (c) where any of the events mentioned in paragraphs 647(2)(a) to (d) occur, whether with or without his actual fault or privity.

(2) The limits set by section 647 to the liabilities of all persons whose liability is limited by section 647 and subsection (1) of this section arising out of a distinct occasion on which any of the events mentioned in paragraphs 647(2)(a) to (d) occurred apply to the aggregate of such liabilities incurred on that occasion.

650. (1) The owners of any dock or canal, or a harbour commission, are not, where without their actual fault or privity any loss or damage is caused to any vessel or vessels, or to any goods, merchandise, or other things whatever on board any vessel or vessels, liable to damages beyond an aggregate amount equivalent to one thousand gold francs for each ton of the tonnage of the largest registered British ship that, at the time of such loss or damage occurring is, or within a period of five years previous thereto has been, within the area over which such dock, or canal owner, or harbour commission performs any duty or exercises any power; and a ship shall not be deemed to have been within the area over which a harbour commission performs any duty or exercises any power by reason only that it has been built or fitted out within such area, or that it has taken shelter within or passed through such area on a voyage between two places both situated outside that area, or that it has loaded or unloaded mails or passengers within that area.

(2) For the purposes of this section the term "dock" includes wet-docks and basins, tidal-docks and basins, locks, cuts, entrances, dry docks, graving-docks, gridirons, slips, quays, wharfs, piers, stages, landing places, and jetties.

(3) For the purposes of this section the term "owners of a dock or canal" includes any person, or authority, having the control and management of any dock or canal, and any ship repairer using the same, as the case may be.

(4) Nothing in this section imposes any liability in respect of any such loss or damage on any such owners, or commission, in any case where no such liability would have existed if this Act had not passed.

651. (1) For the purposes of sections 647 and 650 the tonnage of any ship that is less than three hundred tons shall be deemed to be three hundred tons. [Re-en. 1976-77, c. 38, s. 6(2).]

(2) Where money has been paid into court in respect of any liability to which a limit is set by section 647 or 650, the ascertainment of that limit shall not be affected by a subsequent variation of the amounts deemed to be equivalent to 3,100 gold francs and 1,000 gold francs respectively pursuant to

(a) an order of the Governor in Council made under this Act prior to September 20, 1977, or

(b) a regulation of the Governor in Council made pursuant to the *Currency and Exchange Act* on or after September 20, 1977

unless the amount of the money so paid in was less than the limit as ascertained in accordance with the order or regulation that was in force under paragraph (a) or (b) at the time such money was paid in. [Re-en. 1981, c. 47, s. 40(2).]

652. (1) For the purposes of sections 647 to 650, the tonnage of a steamship shall be its register tonnage with the addition of any engine-room space deducted for the purpose of ascertaining that tonnage; and the tonnage of a sailing ship shall be its register tonnage.

(2) There shall not be included in such tonnage any space occupied by seamen or apprentices and appropriated to their use that is certified under the regulations made pursuant to section 231.

(3) The measurement of such tonnage shall be,

(a) in the case of a British ship registered elsewhere than in Canada, according to the law of that Commonwealth country where the ship is registered;

(b) in the case of a Canadian ship or a ship recognized as a British ship, according to the law of Canada; and

(c) in the case of a foreign ship, according to the law of Canada, if capable of being so measured.

(4) In the case of any ship that is incapable of being measured under the law of Canada, the Minister shall, on receiving from or by direction of the court hearing the case such evidence concerning the dimensions of the ship as it is found practicable to furnish, give a certificate under his hand stating what would, in his opinion, have been the tonnage of such ship if it had been duly measured according to the law of Canada; and the tonnage so stated in such certificate shall, for the purposes of sections 647 and 650, be deemed to be the tonnage of such ship.

653. The limitation of liability under sections 649 and 650 relates to the whole of any losses and damages that may arise upon any one distinct occasion, although such losses and damages may be sustained by more than one person, and applies whether the liability arises at common law or under any Act of Parliament and notwithstanding anything contained in such Act.

654. (1) Where a ship or other property is arrested in connection with a claim that appears to the Court to be founded on a liability to which a limit is set by section 647, or security is given to prevent such arrest or to obtain release therefrom, the Court may order the release of the ship, property or security if

(a) security that, in the opinion of the Court, is satisfactory (in this section referred to as a "guarantee") has previously been given in Canada or elsewhere in respect of such liability or any other liability incurred on the occasion giving rise to such claim, and the Court is satisfied that if the claim is established the amount for which the guarantee was given or such part thereof as corresponds to the claim will be actually available to the claimant; and

(b) the guarantee is for an amount not less than the limit set by section 647 or in the event that the guarantee is less than such limit additional security is given which together with the guarantee is for an amount not less than such limit.

(2) The Court shall order the release of the ship, property or security in the circumstances mentioned in subsection (1) where the guarantee referred to in that subsection was given in a port of a country that is declared, pursuant to subsection (3), to be a Convention country, and the port

(a) is the port where the event giving rise to the claim in respect of which the ship or property was arrested or the security was given, as the case may be, occurred or if the event did not occur in a port, the first port of call after such event occurred; or

(b) where the claim is for loss of life, personal injury or damage to cargo, is the port of disembarkation or discharge.

(3) The Governor in Council may by order declare any country in respect of which the International Convention relating to the Limitation of the Liability of Owners of Seagoing Ships signed at Brussels on the 10th day of October 1957, is in force, to be a Convention country.

(4) Where the release of a ship or other property or security is ordered by the Court pursuant to subsection (1) or (2), the person on whose application such order is made shall be deemed to have submitted to the jurisdiction of the Court to adjudicate on the claim in respect of which the ship or property was arrested or the security was given, as the case may be.

(5) For the purposes of this section

(a) a guarantee that consists of security given in more than one country shall be deemed to have been given in the country in which any such security was last given;

(b) any question as to whether the amount of any security is by itself or together with any other amount not less than the limit set by section 647 shall be determined as of the time at which such security is given; and

(c) where only part of the amount for which a guarantee is given in respect of a liability is available to a claimant, that part shall not be taken to correspond to his claim if any other part of the amount may be available to any other claimant in respect of a liability to which no limit is set by section 647.

655. (1) No judgment or decree for a claim founded on a liability to which a limit is set by section 647 shall be enforced by the Court, except so far as it is for costs, if security for an amount not less than such limit has been given in Canada or elsewhere in respect of that liability or any other liability arising on the same occasion and the Court is of the opinion that the security is satisfactory and is satisfied that the amount for which it was given or such part thereof as corresponds to the claim will be actually available to the person in whose favour the judgment or decree was given or made.

(2) For the purposes of this section

(*a*) any question as to whether the amount of any security is not less than the limit set by section 647 shall be determined as of the time at which such security is given; and

(*b*) where only part of the amount for which security has been given is available to the person in whose favour the judgment or decree was given or made, that part shall not be taken to correspond to his claim if any other part of the amount may be available to any other claimant in respect of a liability to which no limit is set by section 647.

THE RESOLUTION OF CONFLICT OF LAWS ISSUES IN CLAIMS INVOLVING MARITIME LIENS AND RIGHTS *IN REM*

MARITIME LIENS AND RIGHTS *IN REM* IN UNITED STATES LAW

*David J. Sharpe**

1. INTRODUCTION

The United States law of maritime liens comprises an integrated system of law and practice that is quite different from the maritime lien law of other legal systems, even those in the Commonwealth of Nations. The United States is not a signatory to the 1926 International Convention for the Unification of Certain Rules Relating to Maritime Liens and Mortgages,[1] or to the 1952 International Convention Relating to the Arrest of Sea-Going Ships.[2]

In order to appreciate the conflict of laws problems that go with

---

*Professor Sharpe is co-editor of *Cases and Materials on Admiralty* (with Nicholas J. Healy). Vice-chairman, Committee on Continuing Legal Education, Maritime Law Association of the United States. Recent co-author of an essay on collision damages in *Damages Recoverable in Maritime Matters* (American Bar Association 1984).

1   6A Benedict on Admiralty, Doc. No. 8-2.
2   *Ibid.* Doc. No. 8-1. For an historical account of these Conventions, see Price, *Maritime Liens,* pp. 218-237 (1940); Comment, "The Difficult Quest for a Uniform Maritime Law . . .," 64 Yale L.J. 878 at 893-903 (1955); Kriz, "Ship Mortgages, Maritime Liens, and Their Enforcement: The Brussels Conventions of 1926 and 1952," 1963 Duke L.J. 671, 1964 Duke L.J. 70; and Note, "International Uniformity of Maritime Liens and Mortgages: The 1965 New York Conference of the Comité Maritime International," 41 N.Y.U.L. Rev. 939 (1966) (draft convention text at 960-963). The Comité Maritime International, conceding that the 1967 convention on maritime liens and mortgages, 6A Benedict on Admiralty, Doc. No. 8-3, was not a success, is currently working on a successor. Berlingerie, "Maritime Liens and Mortgages – A Progress Report," CMI Newsletter (Sept. 1983).

maritime lien litigation in United States courts, the Commonwealth maritime lawyer needs, first, to learn something about the indigenous United States law of maritime liens and actions *in rem;* second, to learn how courts of the United States have treated issues of enforcement and recognition of foreign maritime liens; and third, to accept the unfamiliar aspects of United States maritime law and practice as parts of an organic legal system, trying not to reject them as archaic and perverse legal curiosities – though that is the prevailing tone of the current single-volume treatise on United States admiralty law, *Gilmore and Black.*[3]

2. THE MARITIME LIEN LAW OF THE UNITED STATES

The United States posseses, by comparison with other nations, a very long list of maritime liens.[4] It enforces whole families of liens that may not exist elsewhere (for example, repairs, supplies, cargo damage, stevedoring, and breach of charter party); liens that arise from express contracts; and liens creating obligations that are enforced only *in personam* by other legal systems.

The maritime lien under United States law – including contract-based liens – arises by operation of law, not by the agreement of the contracting parties. By contrast with other legal systems, the United States district court in admiralty thereby acquires added power to give or to withhold relief *quasi ex contractu* as to the vessel, limited only by the clearest waiver of rights *in rem* by the creditor.[5]

The *in rem* concept also bears upon the choice of law question. If a charter party (a personal contract) is fixed in the United Kingdom, and even if it casts upon the charterer the obligation to provide and pay for bunkers, the furnishing of bunkers to the vessel by a United States supplier is treated by United States courts as a separate contract, executed between the supplier and the vessel, and calling for the application of United States law. Only if the supplier deliberately waives its option to rely upon the credit of the vessel does it lose the United States maritime liens.[6]

---

3   G. Gilmore & C. Black, *Law of Admiralty,* ch. 9 (2d ed. 1975).

4   For a compact survey, see Comment, "Developments in the Law of Maritime Liens," 45 Tul. L. Rev. 574 (1971). See also 2 Benedict on Admiralty § 51 (7th ed. 1982); and see *The Scotia,* 35 Fed. 907, 908 (S.D.N.Y. 1888).

5   *E.g., Gulf Trading & Tpt. Co. v. The Hoegh Shield,* 658 F. 2d 363, 1982 AMC 1138 (5th Cir. 1981) (Cir. J. John R. Brown), cert. denied, 457 U.S. 1119, 1982 AMC 2108 (1982).

6   See *Point Landing Inc. v. Alabama Dry Dock & Shipbldg. Co.,* 261 F.2d 861 at 866, 1959 AMC 148 (5th Cir. 1968).

Furthermore, the maritime lien created or enforced by United States law is "indelible" – not literally and forever, to be sure, but surviving the passage of a reasonable amount of time in which to arrest the vessel, and even surviving the transfer of a vessel to a bona fide purchaser for value without notice. The indelibility of the collision tort lien in *The Bold Buccleugh*[7] also applies in United States law to contract liens.[8]

Finally, a vessel may be liable *in rem* under United States law although her owners are personally immune to suit for one reason or another. The prime statement of the United States rule arose in a collision tort case involving compulsory pilotage,[9] but the rule also applies to actions for breach of maritime contract brought against vessels by creditors to whom the owners are immune.

The United States also has a well-developed and currently operating system of actions *in rem,* chiefly against ships,[10] in which neither the presence nor the absence of a parallel action *in personam* impedes the action *in rem.* For example, *The Barnstable*[11] is often cited as the basic United States case declaring that a chartered vessel may be liable *in rem* even though the owner is immune *in personam,* and the opinion so holds: the absence of the owner *in personam* is irrelevant.[12]

The classic *in rem* situation keeps recurring in United States litigation: the owner time-charters his vessel; the charterer orders fuel and supplies in a United States port without having the supplier rely exclusively on the charterer's credit; the charterer fails to pay; and the supplier arrests the vessel in a United States port.[13] The owner would win under a foreign law that gave no supply lien at all, or one that gave no right to arrest when the owner was not personally liable; but under United States law, the supplier wins consistently, and United States law applies where the furnishing took place in a United States port, regardless of foreign contracts otherwise.

The effect upon actions in United States courts of the pendency of actions in foreign courts has been explored to some extent. A United

---

7   (1852), 7 Moo. P.C. 267, 13 E.R. 884 (P.C.).
8   *The Key City,* 81 U.S. (14 Wall.) 653 (1871).
9   *The China,* 74 U.S. (7 Wall.) 53 (1868).
10 For the mechanics, see Rogers, "Enforcement of Maritime Liens and Mortgages," 47 Tul. L. Rev. 767 (1973).
11 181 U.S. 464 (1901).
12 The owner was very much present in fact, however, because the reason for the appeal was the impleading action by the owner *in personam* against the demise charterer *in personam;* the owner won.
13 *E.g., Gulf Trading & Tpt. Co. v. The Hoegh Shield,* 658 F.2d 363, 1982 AMC 1138 (5th Cir. 1981), rehearing en banc denied, 670 F.2d 182 (1982) (table), cert. denied, 457 U.S. 1119, 1982 AMC 2108 (1982).

States cargo claimant got a German judgment essentially *in rem* in 1971, but the vessel had been under charter, and the judgment exonerated the owner. While a further appeal in Germany was pending, the cargo claimant sued the owner in Norfolk *in personam* and attached a sister ship. The district court dismissed and the Fourth Circuit affirmed, holding that the German judgment *in rem* could not be the foundation for a United States action *in personam*.[14]

In 1984, the Fifth Circuit held that the three-year pendency of a United States bunkering company's action *in personam* in The Netherlands was no impediment to bringing the same claim *in rem* when the vessel visited the United States.[15] Once again, the action *in rem* was separate from the action *in personam* in United States admiralty practice, and whether the owner was absent or present was irrelevant. It has even been held that the district court having possession *in rem* may ignore orders of another district court seeking to delay the sale on behalf of *in personame* creditors.[16]

Of course, if both actions can be brought in or transferred into the same forum, they may be pleaded and tried together.[17] There is a small body of case law holding explicitly that a plaintiff's claim *in rem* against a vessel is not merged into the plaintiff's prior judgment *in personam* against the vessel's owner.[18]

The rationalization of doctrine in United States maritime lien and action *in rem* practice dates only from the mid-nineteenth century, but the doctrine receives the deference usually due to much more ancient origins. The United States maritime law in this respect has never been codified, although maritime lien[19] and ship mortgage statutes[20] have diverted and complicated the application of United States law. Both

---

14   *M.W. Zack Metal Co. v. Int. Navigation Co.,* 510 F.2d 451, 1975 AMC 720 (4th Cir. 1975), cert. denied, 423 U.S. 835, 1975 AMC 2159 (1975).

15   *Belcher Co. v. The Maratha Mariner,* 724 F.2d 1161 (5th Cir. 1984) (dismissal rev'd; action *in rem* remanded with directions to stay the United States proceedings pending decision of the Netherlands action, in which the owner had posted a letter of undertaking).

16   *Wong Shing v. The Mardina Trader,* 564 F.2d 1183 (5th Cir. 1977).

17   Fed. R. Civ. P. 20(a).

18   *E.g., The Eastern Shore,* 24 F.2d 443, 1928 AMC 327 (D. Md. 1928); followed in *The Henry S.,* 4 F. Supp. 953, 1933 AMC 1401 (E.D. Va. 1933). See G. Gilmore & C. Black, *Law of Admiralty,* p. 614, notes 72-73 (2d ed. 1975). The authorities in *Continental Grain Co. v. The FBL-585,* 364 U.S. 19 at 25, note 4, 1961 AMC 1 (1960), do not bear out Justice Black's statement to the contrary, though his statement is probably consistent with the current Supreme Court view that questions of claim and issue preclusion lie within the judge's discretion. See *Parklane Hosiery Co. v. Shore,* 439 U.S. 322 at 331 (1979) (not a maritime case).

19   46 U.S.C. §§ 971-975.

20   46 U.S.C. §§ 911-961, 981-984.

maritime lien law and specialized admiralty practice are alive and well today in the United States federal courts. Though constitutional due process challenge threatens the *in rem* practice, and codification threatens the substantive law, little thought has yet been given to replacing the United States system with any other system.

3. ENFORCEMENT AND RECOGNITION OF FOREIGN MARITIME LIEN LAW

(a) Maritime Lien Actions

When a United States court is confronted with the opportunity to apply foreign law that confers a maritime lien, the United States court already must have possession of the vessel in question; this factor seems to incline the court toward enforcing those liens under foreign law that resemble United States maritime liens. The practical effect is to apply the *lex fori,* although the announced United States policy is to apply the *lex loci contractus* as to contract-based liens.[21] United States courts in admiralty may and often do accept maritime lien actions between foreigners, having no United States contact except arrest of the vessel,[22] and this creates the pressure to find out what the foreign law is; but as one Court of Appeals frankly described its process some years ago, "There is no presumption that the law of foreign countries is unlike ours. One who would rely upon the difference between them prove its existence. If he does not, we apply our law to the case."[23] The court showed its relief at not having to choose between the *lex loci contractus* and the law of the flag, each of which was pressed strenuously. In the absence of proof of foreign law, the United States court is free to apply the United States law – especially when the law of the flag is also the law of the United States.[24]

Once upon a time the reason given for thus applying the *lex fori* was adherence to general maritime law. Chief Justice Marshall wrote in 1828:

> A case in admiralty does not, in fact, arise under the Constitution or laws of the United States [an allusion to one basis of federal court subject-matter jurisdiction appearing in the Constitution]. These cases are as old as navigation itself; and the law, admiralty and maritime [another allusion to constitutional subject-matter jurisdiction], as it has existed for ages, is applied by our Courts to the cases as they arise.[25]

---

21   *E.g., The City of Atlanta,* 17 F.2d 308 (S.D. Ga. 1924).
22   *E.g., The Maggie Hammond,* 76 U.S. (9 Wall.) 435 (1870).
23   *The Hoxie,* 297 Fed. 189 at 190, 1924 AMC 630 (4th Cir. 1924), cert. denied, 266 U.S. 608 (1924).
24   See *The Snetind,* 276 Fed. 139 (D. Me. 1921).
25   *Amer. Ins. Co. v. Canter,* 26 U.S. (1 Pet.) 511 at 545.

Justice Oliver Wendell Holmes, Jr., did not believe in the general maritime law; he called it scornfully a "brooding omnipresence in the sky."[26] Writing for the Court in 1922, Justice Holmes said of both foreign law and the general maritime law, "There is no mystic over-law to which even the United States must bow."[27] But many United States judges have referred to the general maritime law in terms that make its existence both real and dispositive by itself – neither as the domestic law of the United States nor the law of another nation.

In the long run, Justice Holmes's inlfuence has been strong, but a respected United states "admiralty" (really a federal district court) judge, Addison Brown of the Southern District of New York, was in good company when he used the general maritime law concept to explain why he enforced a Haitian maritime lien for supplies against a United Kingdom vessel arrested in New York. Yet in his holding, Judge Brown used the law of the place at which the obligation to pay became fixed, the *lex loci contractus*, not the law of the British flag (which deprived the master of power to incur this lien in his manner), nor yet the *lex fori* (which happened to enforce the Haitian type of lien.).[28] Judge Brown's opinion showed that he was well aware of the British legal history that produced doctrine, remedies, and statutes decidedly in flux and considerably at odds even with Commonwealth nations, to say nothing of France and the United States. What *The Scotia* shows is that the restricted British maritime law could not prevent the United States judge from enforcing a third-country maritime lien.

What *The Scotia* did not show was that a British supplier, who had no maritime lien for necessaries furnished in the United Kingdom, might yet have one if he could arrest the vessel in the United States. Exactly this situation arose in *The Snetind*,[29] where, in the absence of proof of United Kingdom law to the contrary (a dispositive absence), the judge gave English creditors a maritime lien on a United States flag vessel for supplies, repairs, and advances. In the same year, a New York federal court took the more patient view of ordering the complaint amended so as to plead the law of The Netherlands, where the work was done, in order to determine whether any lien arose in the *lex loci contractus*, thus avoiding prefering the no-lien Dutch creditor.[30] To complete the *lex loci contractus* variations, where English law was proven to give liens for insurance premiums and new-ship materials furnished to a Newfoundland vessel in ports governed by English law,

---

26   *Southern Pac. Co. v. Jensen*, 244 U.S. 205 at 222 (1917) (dissenting opinion).
27   *The Western Maid*, 257 U.S. 419 at 432.
28   *The Scotia*, 35 Fed. 907 (S.D. N.Y. 1888).
29   276 Fed. 139 (D. Me. 1921).
30   *The Woudrichem*, 278 Fed. 568 (E.D.N.Y. 1921).

the United States court enforced the liens, even though they did not exist in United States law.[31]

United States courts are still wrestling with these problems. Quite recently a Port of Québec ship chandler acquired a maritime lien for supplies furnished to the Panamanian *Caribbean Klif,* but he lost the lien under Canadian law when the owners sold the vessel to bona fide purchasers, who renamed her the Honduran *Leah.* The chandler arrested the *Leah* in Charleston, South Carolina, but the district court found that Canadian law barred the necessary lien,[32] and the court of appeals affirmed this part of the decision.[33] In as simple a case as this, the Canadian chandler got no better treatment in the United States than he would have had at home. Actually, counsel wisely but unsuccessfully tried to show that the supply contract had been made with the Canadian plaintiff's affiliate in the United States, but the courts held that the goods were furnished in Canada – the *in rem* connection again.[34]

Substantial United States contacts will call for the application of United States law, even though the bulk of the contacts seem to be foreign. Quite recently the United States Court of appeals for the Ninth Circuit (the West Coast) ruled that even though the law of Italy (which indicated the law of the flag, Norway, for bunker liens) and the law of Egypt (for Suez Canal tolls) did not give maritime liens, by means of balancing contacts with the United States (the charter party, the necessaries viewed as orders rather than deliveries, and visits of the vessel to the United States), United States law governed – thereby treating the furnishers of bunkers and canal passage better in the United States than they would have been treated in their home courts.[35] An East Coast circuit earlier took a similar balancing position where the vessel was arrested in the United States, she had been chartered under a United States time charter form, and a preponderance of other contacts were with the United States; the law of the flag (United Kingdom) was held not to be the single dominant contact, nor did the intent of the parties dictate United States law, as the lower court had held.[36]

The law of the flag seems to be applied most easily to wage liens, but the seaman's wage lien must be the closest approximation to a universal maritime lien, and conflicts of law do not arise. Conflicts have arisen for centuries, though, over the shipmaster's right to a maritime lien for his

---

31   *The Maud Carter,* 29 Fed. 156 (D. Mass. 1886).
32   *Ocean Ship Supply Ltd. v. The Leah,* 1982 AMC 2740 (D.S.C. 1982).
33   729 F.2d 971 (4th Cir. 1984).
34   *Ibid.* at 973-974.
35   *Gulf Trading & Tpt. Co. v. The Tento,* 694 F.2d 1191, 1983 AMC 872 (9th Cir. 1982), cert. denied, 103 S. Ct. 2091, 1983 AMC 2109 (1983).
36   *Rainbow Lines Inc. v. The Tequila,* 480 F.2d 1024, 1973 AMC 1431 (2d Cir. 1973).

services, and the United States gave the shipmaster a lien for his wages only in 1968.[37] In prior cases, if the United States court refused to enforce the foreign master's lien, the foreign master lost outright.[38] Somewhat more subtly, the United States court could recognize the foreign lien but apply the United States priority scheme, in which case the lienworthy master finished out of the money.[39]

"Interest analysis," the attempt to determine whether some other sovereign has a more significant relationship to the action, is now being used by United States courts in reaching their decisions on whose law to apply, in contract as well as in the more numerous tort cases. The analysis of contacts is still well-entrenched, though, partly because it offers a framework upon which to marshal facts,[40] and partly because United States contacts analysis developed in maritime cases under the "Jones Act," the United States' apparently world-wide seamen's injury and death statute.[41]

Considering the assortment of choice-of-law tests presently available for use, it may seem surprising that a United States court still occasionally applies the *lex fori* to a case that does not seem to yield to contacts testing or interest analysis. For example, where the plaintiff chartered a vessel in the United States, and where numerous other United States contacts existed, the court found that the place of loading cargo for export (Sweden), where the affreightment contract was also breached, did not prevent the application of United States law.[42] On the other hand, where the only United States contact was arrest of an Italian vessel, the repairman was Japanese, and the owner was Italian, the judge applied Japanese maritime lien law, the *lex loci contractus,* without hesitation.[43] The enforcement of foreign maritime liens in United States courts thus has a pragmatic foundation of *in rem* practice that does not fit predictably the changing fashions in conflict of laws analysis that are applied to transitory actions *in personam.*

(b) Ship Mortgage Foreclosures by United States Courts

By statute, the United States courts in admiralty have jurisdiction to foreclose foreign as well as domestic ship mortgages on vessels

---

37   Pub. L. No. 90-293, 82 Stat. 107, 46 U.S.C. § 606.

38   *E.g., The Graf Klot Trautvetter,* 8 Fed. 833 (D.S.C. 1881).

39   *The Olga,* 32 Fed. 329 (S.D.N.Y. 1887).

40   See Restatement (Second) of Conflicts of Law, §§ 6, 188 (1969), as applied in *Gulf Trading & Tpt. Co. v. The Hoegh Shield,* 658 F.2d 363, 1982 AMC 1138 (5th Cir. 1981), cert. denied, 457 U.S. 1119, 1982 AMC 2108 (1982).

41   46 U.S.C. § 688; application to a largely Danish-contacts case rejected in *Lauritzen v. Larsen,* 345 U.S. 571, 1953 AMC 1210 (1953).

42   *Cardinal Shipping Corp. v. The Seisho Maru,* 1983 AMC 2573 (S.D. Tex. 1983).

43   *Kawasaki Heavy Indust. Ltd. v. The Sorrento,* 1984 AMC 263 (E.D. Va. 1983).

arrested in United States ports.[44] Whether a vessel is foreign or domestic, the United States court will certainly apply the United States law as to the maritime liens of United States creditors. Under the statute, the United States suppliers' and repairmen's post-mortgage liens are senior to foreign mortgagees' security interests, but they are junior to United States mortgages that are properly registered.[45]

Foreign claims tend to be given maritime lien status according to the law of the place of furnishing necessaries, but to be given priority according to United States law.[46] For example, where a United States preferred ship mortgage was senior to an Italian supply lien under United States law, the priority of the Italian lien under Italian law became an empty promise when the United States court applied the United States' own priority system and let the mortgagee come first, wiping out the fund available to lien creditors.[47] The United States practice was explained by saying that the place of furnishing bunkers (Italy) established the existence of the lien, but the law of the forum (United States) assigned it priority. The court further held that the treaty of friendship and navigation did not require the United States to rearrange its maritime lien priority system so as to prefer the foreign creditor.

(c) Foreign Judicial Sales of Vessels

The recognition of foreign maritime judgments takes place in the context of foreign judicial sales of vessels, whether by foreclosing mortgages, by executing maritime liens, or by sales in bankruptcy. Here the consequences of United States *in rem* practice are projected upon the foreign sale, whether that would be the foreign practice or not, including the United States view that arrest of the vessel is constructive notice to all creditors.[48] Foreign judgments that sell vessels are not lightly subjected to collateral attack by United States creditors for reasons of contrary United States admiralty practice.[49] If the foreign court had possession of the vessel as nearly as might be in the same manner that a United States admiralty court must have, its possession was exclusive

---

44   Ship Mortgage Act, 1920, 46 U.S.C. § 951 (unnumbered second paragraph added in 1954, Act of June 29, 1954, ch. 419, 68 Stat. 323).

45   See *Payne v. The Tropic Breeze*, 423 F.2d 236 at 239, 1970 AMC 1850 (1st Cir. 1970), cert. denied, 400 U.S. 964, 1971 AMC 818 (1970).

46   *E.g., Potash Co. v. The Raleigh*, 361 F. Supp. 120, 1973 AMC 2658 (D.C.Z. 1973).

47   *Brandon v. The Denton*, 302 F.2d 404, 1962 AMC 1730 (5th Cir. 1962).

48   *E.g., Zimmern Coal Co. v. Coal Trading Ass'n*, 30 F.2d 933, 1929 AMC 334 (5th Cir. 1929).

49   See *Atlantic Ship Supply Inc. v. The Lucy*, 392 F. Supp. 179, 1975 AMC 1153 (M.D. Fla. 1975), aff'd per curiam, 553 F.2d 1009 (5th Cir. 1977).

and its judgment was valid everywhere;[50] and the foreign court's adjudication extinguished all maritime liens, even liens that were not recognized in the foreign court.[51]

In one recent case, the Netherlands sale of a vessel extinguished a United States supply lien that would not be enforced under Netherlands law;[52] in another case, the sale of a vessel by a Mexican bankruptcy court was recognized, since the Mexican court took possession of the vessel; it did not merely adjudicate her owners' rights *in personam*.[53] And in 1977, a United States court held that a Costa Rican court's foreclosure sale of a Costa Rican vessel mortgaged in Costa Rica cut off the maritime liens of the United States creditors: a supplier, a stevedore, and a bunkerer.[54]

If the foreign court did not have possession of the vessel when it foreclosed a ship mortgage, the United States court will not recognize the foreclosure as extinguishing the United States maritime lien of a creditor who was not a party to the foreclosure.[55]

If the foreign sale took place where the creditor happened to find the ship, the United States lienholder is completely without a remedy.[56] But where a United States ship mortgagee, like a cat playing with a mouse, deliberately let the ship incur a bunker debt in the United States so the ship could sail to the Bahamas, where the bunkerer had no lien, and then foreclosed and wiped out the debt, a United States court held that the mortgagee was unjustly enriched by the amount of these bunkers – though not as to prior supplies.[57] The question of letting the supplier arrest the ship in the United States did not and probably could not arise after the Bahamian foreclosure sale.

In a subsequent case, the mortgagor first arrested the defaulting borrower's vessel in the Canary Islands, which would have enforced a

---

50   *Hilton v. Guyot,* 159 U.S. 113 at 167 (1895).
51   *The Trenton,* 4 Fed. 657 (E.D. Mich. 1880) (Henry B. Brown, later Justice Brown – an American "admiralty judge").
52   *Alpine Gulf Inc. v. First Nat. Bank,* 1981 AMC 540 (N.D. Ill. 1979).
53   *Gulf & Southern Terminal Corp. v. The President Roxas,* 1983 AMC 435 (E.D.N.C. 1982), aff'd, 701 F.2d 1110, 1983 AMC 1521 (4th Cir. 1983), cert. denied, 103 S. Ct. 3115, 1983 AMC 2109 (1983). It has been and continues to be doubtful whether a foreign court would recognize the sale of a vessel free of maritime liens by a United States bankruptcy court, which is different from a United States admiralty court. See *Morgan Guaranty Trust Co. v. Hellenic Lines Ltd.,* 1984 AMC 1074 (S.D.N.Y. 1983).
54   *Atlantic Ship Supply Inc. v. The Lucy,* 392 F. Supp. 179, 1975 AMC 1153 (M.D. Fla. 1975), aff'd per curiam, 553 F.2d 1009 (5th Cir. 1977).
55   *Todd Shipyards Corp. v. The Maigus Luck,* 243 F. Supp. 8, 1966 AMC 1608 (D.C.Z. 1965) (excellent details of examining foreign law through expert witnesses).
56   *E.g., Gulf & Southern Terminal Corp. v. The President Roxas,* 701 F.2d 1110, 1983 AMC 1521 (4th Cir. 1983).
57   *Gulf Oil Trading Co. v. Creole Supply Inc.,* 596 F.2d 515, 1979 AMC 585 (2d Cir. 1979).

United States supplier's maritime lien; but in order to let perishable cargo be sold, the mortgagee let the vessel move to The Netherlands, which did not enforce the supply lien, and where the vessel was thereafter sold. When the United States supplier sued the mortgagee for unjust enrichment, seeking to establish a constructive trust on the proceeds to the extent of its supply claim, the district judge found that in the circumstances, the mortgagee was not unjustly enriched, commenting that maritime forum shopping is not a maritime tort, and distinguishing the *Gulf Oil Trading Co.* case on the basis that the supplier did not enable the vessel to flee the lien-enforcing forum.[58]

To state the same concept in reverse, the foreign judicial sale system that does not cut off maritime liens cannot protect the vessel in the United States. In a very recent case, the United States bunkering company had not been paid when the time charterer's agent went bankrupt after having itself been paid. The bunkering company attached the vessel in The Netherlands, which has no action *in rem;* the Netherlands attachment, then, dealt neither with the vessel's liability nor with a ship mortgage foreclosure, but with the personal liability of the owner as affected by the charter party. The bunkering company therefore arrested the vessel later in a Texas port, where her liability *in rem* was not really open to question under the United States doctrine of personification of vessels. The Texas district court dismissed the action *in rem* under the doctrine of *lis alibis pendens* because of the action in The Netherlands, but the Fifth Circuit reversed, stressing that the Netherlands action *in personam* against the owner was quite different from the United States action *in rem* against the vessel.[59] Apparently the United States separation of actions *in rem* from actions *in personam* means that the unpaid foreign maritime creditor can sue the ex-shipowner *in personam* in the United States, unless some other aspect of the foreign litigation, such as discharge of the owner in bankruptcy, also cuts off the creditor's personal remedy under recognized foreign law.

4. CONCLUSION

United States maritime lien laws and *in rem* practice have reached a high state of evolution as a legal ecosystem. The system works fairly well with other systems most of the time, although good interrelations are achieved only through the frequent and heavy expenditure of intellec-

---

58   *Alpine Gulf Inc. v. First Nat. Bank,* 1981 AMC 540 (N.D. Ill. 1979).
59   *Belcher Co. v. The Maratha Mariner,* 1983 AMC 2089 (S.D. Tex. 1983), rev'd, 724 F.2d 1161 (5th Cir. 1984). Counsel for the vessel have advised the author that the Netherlands court decided that the supplier had no lien, and that the vessel probably will take no further appeal.

tual effort and good will among attorneys. Improvement of the fit between the United States system and other nations' systems would call for structural alterations in the United States system, not minor cosmetic changes, and no major changes are to be expected in the foreseeable future.

THE LAW OF CONFLICTS AND MARITIME LIENS: THE UNITED STATES, CANADA, THE UNITED KINGDOM AND FRANCE

*W. Tetley**

*Professor of Law, McGill University. Visiting Professor Tulane University, New Orleans, Louisiana, and past President of the Canadian Maritime Law Association. Author of *Marine Cargo Claims.*

1. INTRODUCTION

(a) The Law Merchant

Until three or four centuries ago, the *lex mercatoria,* of which maritime law was a major part, extended beyond the boundaries of individual nations, being based as it was on such universally accepted edicts as the *Rôles of Oléron* and the *Consolato del Mare.*

A truly international law would avoid conflict of laws and a truly international maritime law would avoid conflict of maritime laws. This was true up to the sixteenth century, so that Graveson in writing of that period could declare:[1]

> But even in Admiralty there was no conflict of laws because, in cases to which the law merchant applied, there was only one law. And when, in the sixteenth century, the law merchant was taken over and administered in the courts of common law, it was applied on the theory that it was part of the common law, and not a law foreign to the court.

The civil law was also the source of much of the universality of the law merchant. In consequence, even in 1835, it could be reported that Sir D. Dodson K.C. (assisted by his "junior" Dr. Lushington) had pleaded for respondents in *The Neptune* as follows:[2]

> By civil law, and the laws of Oleron, which have been generally adopted by the nations of Europe as the basis of their maritime law, whoever repaired or fitted out a ship had a lien on that ship for the amount of his demand. It is useless to cite authorities on this head, for they are undoubted, and are collected in a note in Lord Tenterden's "Treatise on Shipping" Part 2, cap. 3, s. 9.

> The United States of America have in great measure followed the civil law (see the authorities cited in a note to this case, 3 Hag. Adm. p. 14). In England the same law prevailed.

---

1   R.H. Graveson, *Conflict of Laws* (7th ed., 1974), pp. 33-34.
2   (1835), 3 Knapp 94 at 103, 12 E.R. 584 at 587-8 (P.C.). For the appellant were Holt K.C. and his "junior" Dr. Phillimore. Note that the judge was none other than Thomas Erskine.

Unfortunately for us today, we have retreated into nationalistic shells; the great international codes are almost forgotten, the *lex mercatoria* and the civil law as an international maritime code have lost much authority. Unfortunately, as well, modern international conventions do not cover all the subjects of maritime law nor have the conventions been ratified by all the world's maritime nations. The result is conflict of maritime laws, a subject which has been dealt with only sporadically and occasionally and which would fill many volumes. The present observations are only intended to touch on a few major principles and problems in respect to liens and mortgages.

(b) Categories of Conflicts

Conflict of laws can be divided into three main categories: (i) choice of law, (ii) choice of forum and (iii) recognition of foreign judgments. Maritime law conflicts can be found in all three categories and a single case may involve problems in two or even three categories. For the purposes of this study, with respect to maritime contract liens and mortgages, choice-of-law problems will be looked at with some lesser reference to questions of choice of forum and recognition of foreign judgments. Tort liens (collision and damage) have few if any conflict problems because all jurisdictions give them a high ranking as traditional maritime liens.

(c) Theories of Conflict of Laws

Every philosophy or set of rules intended to resolve conflict of laws must be based on a basic first premise or doctrine. Various doctrines have evolved over the years. Graveson describes the modern theories as follows:[3]

1. *The Statutory Theory* settles disputes as to whether they are *real* or *personal*. *Real* issues are decided by the place where the property is situated and *personal* issues which are decided by the law of the person.
2. *The International Theory* holds there is ". . . a universal and customary body of principles of the conflict of laws to which municipal systems of law give effect".[4] Savigny, Westlake, Wharton, Zitelmann and Jitta are exponents of this school.
3. *The Territorial Theory* is that foreign laws will not be recognized, but rights vested under foreign laws will be admitted by the local government if proven as a fact, being an application of the doctrine

---

3   Graveson, *supra* note 1, at pp. 36 *et seq.*
4   *Ibid.* at 37.

of comity of nations and the doctrine of public policy. Dicey, Schmitthoff and Beale are exponents of this theory.[5] Beale was the author of the *First Restatement* on choice of law.

4. *The Local Law Theory* is American in concept and is an extension of the general doctrine of territoriality. It holds that courts never apply any law but their own. Professor W.W. Cook is the chief exponent.[6]

5. *The Theory of Justice* is that courts faced with a conflict problem will apply the law which provides the most justice, based on the ethical, sociological and legal premises of English law. This is the theory of Graveson[7] and of Jackson[8] when the latter commented on *The Halcyon Isle*.[9]

Apart from the above theories, there is in the United States the *Second Restatement, Conflicts of Laws 2d*,[10] a pragmatic theory of the conflict of laws which American courts have often accepted and followed.[11] Willis L.M. Reese was the reporter of this *Restatement*. Section 6 of the *Second Restatement* reads in part:[12]

> (2) When there is no such directive, the factors relevant to the choice of the applicable rule of law include (a) the needs of the interstate and international

---

5   *Ibid.* at 38.

6   *Ibid.* at 39-40.

7   *Ibid.* at 41. See also P.H. Graveson, *Comparative Conflict of Laws, Selected Essays* (1977), Vol. 1, p. 7.

8   D.C. Jackson, "Foreign Maritime Liens in English Courts – Principle and Policy", [1981] L.M.C.L.Q. 335.

9   *Bankers Trust Internat. v. Todd Shipyards Corp.; The Halcyon Isle*, [1981] A.C. 221, [1980] 3 All E.R. 197, [1980] 2 Lloyd's Rep. 325, 1980 AMC 1221 (P.C.).

10   The American Law Institute, *Second Restatement, Conflict of Laws 2d*. The *Restatement* can be looked upon as an attempt to create a "doctrine" for the common law similar to "la doctrine" of the civil law. Doctrine, or the writings of law professors, plays a major part in the civil law, a practice quite unheard of in common law. Codal interpretation or construction requires that a civilian look first at the civil code to determine the meaning of the law. If this fails, one next looks at the codifiers' reports written when the code was first presented to Parliament. Thirdly, one reads "la doctrine" or the opinion of the law professors. Only fourthly does one look at decisions of the highest courts. In law reports in France, such as *Droit Maritime Français*, the order of appearance is therefore as follows: First "la doctrine", then Supreme Court decisions, then Court of Appeal decisions and finally the judgments of the court of first instance.

11   *Gulf Trading v. Hoegh Shield*, 658 F 2d 363 at 367, 1982 AMC 1138 at 1142 (5 Cir 1981).

12   *Second Restatement, supra* note 10, at p. 10. Elliott E. Cheatham and Willis L.M. Reese in their article entitled "Choice of the Applicable Law" (1952), 52 Colum. L. Rev. 959, had earlier given nine expanded basic social concerns relevant to the choice of the applicable law. See art. 7 of the *Convention on the Law Applicable to Contractual Obligations*, Rome, June 19, 1980 (80/934/E.E.C.).

system (b) the relevant policies of the forum (c) the relevant policies of other interested states . . . (d) the protection of justified expectations (e) the basic policies underlying the particular field of law (f) certainty, predictability and uniformity of result and (g) ease in the determination and application of the law to be applied.

The above theory is often known as the "state of the most significant relationship" theory[13] and is found, for example, in *Romero v. Internat. Terminal Operating Co.,*[14] where the United States Supreme Court declared:

The controlling considerations are the interacting interests of the United States and of foreign countries.

The court had already noted that, in respect to maritime cases, ". . . due regard must be had for the differing interests advanced by varied aspects of maritime law".[15]

(d) Universality and Certainty and Justice

The practitioner, like the judge, is faced with a multitude of theories of which a number are mentioned above. Every theory of conflict of laws is based on certain premises as to the nature and the purpose of law. This writer's theory is based on three premises in respect of maritime law.

The first premise is that maritime law should, if at all possible, be universal. No nation's maritime law should be an island unto itself. As Marshall C.J. declared, [16] "The whole world, it is said, are parties in an admiralty cause; and therefore, the whole world is bound by the decision." The second premise is that maritime law should be certain and predictable to all persons – to judges, lawyers, merchants, even the professors and their students. Lastly, maritime law should also present the most just system of settling maritime disputes, but what is just, in respect to seamen and carriers or in respect to carriers and shippers or in respect to lien holders and mortgage holders, may differ from nation to nation.

Universality is important, if not essential, to facilitate trade and to avoid disputes. If maritime law cannot be universal because international maritime law conventions have not been accepted by the maritime nations of the world, local national versions of the maritime law should at the very least be certain and predictable to us all.

---

13 The theory was developed by others into the "governmental interest analysis theory". In particular, see Brainerd Currie, "Conflict, Crisis and Confusion in New York", 1963 Duke L.J. 1.

14 358 U.S. 354 at 382, 1959 AMC 832 at 854 (1959).

15 *Ibid.* at 383 [U.S.], 854 [AMC].

16 *The Mary,* 13 U.S. 125 at 143 (1815).

In order to have certainty (where there is no universal international convention), it is necessary to have common rules of conflict of laws. The rules suggested by the author are those set out below.

2. PROCESSING A CONFLICT PROBLEM

A conflict of laws problem only arises when one party attempts to apply a foreign law and that foreign law conflicts with local law. In such a case the problem is resolved by the process which follows.

(a) What Law of Conflicts Applies?

The first basic step to be taken in any conflict of laws problem is to decide which rules of conflict of laws will be applied in solving the conflicts problem. The answer is not difficult to find: the courts of all nations will almost always apply their own rules of conflict of laws.[17]

Thus, in *Meridian Trading Corp. v. S.S. Denton,*[18] section 7 of the *First Restatement* was applied and the court held:

> When the rule of conflicts of the forum refers to the law of a foreign state, it refers to the law of the foreign state applicable to the subject matter and not to the foreign states rules governing conflicts of law.

The *Second Restatement,* at section 7(2), states:

> (2) The classification and interpretation of Conflict of Laws and terms are determined in accordance with the law of the forum, except as stated in sect. 8 [s. 8 deals with *renvoi*].

(b) Characterization

After the choice of a nation's own conflict of laws rules, the next step is to categorize or characterize the problem – that is, to determine what type of problem is involved. Is it a case of contract or of tort, maritime or civil law, collision, salvage, necessaries, liens or one of many other subjects? Characterization is often understood to include the next steps outlined below, *i.e.,* the study of special directives, and the search for and study of connecting factors and decisions concerning public order, public policy, procedure, substance and attempts to evade the law. It is noteworthy that characterization is done under the laws and rules of the forum.[19]

---

17   Occasionally courts look to foreign conflict of laws rules; when those rules send the problem back to the law of the original jurisdiction, this is *renvoi.*

18   1960 AMC 2264 at 2270 (SD Tex 1960). See also *Mason v. Rose,* 176 F (2d) 486 at 490 (2 Cir 1949).

19   Castel, *Private International Law* (1960), pp. 34 and 76; Cheshire and North, *Private*

(c) Special Directives (in the contract or in the law)

One should next look to see if the law or the statute gives any direction as to the applicable law or if the contract itself specifies a particular law.[20]

The French *Civil Code*[21] was a revolutionary statement of human rights (civil rights as they were called then) which emphasized the rights of persons. Article 8 c.c. (France) contains a special directive when it states: "[Translation] Every Frenchman will benefit by the civil rights (of this Code)." Article 11 extended those rights to foreigners in France. There is a reference in art. 3 to the law with respect to where immovable property is situated but not in regard to where contracts are entered into.

Article 6 of the Quebec *Civil Code*[22] applies to immovable property (real property) within Quebec, while art. 8 contains a special directive as to contracts. Contracts are subject

> to the law of the country where they were passed, unless there is some law to the contrary, or the parties have agreed otherwise, or by the nature of the deed or from other circumstances, it appears that the intention of the parties was to be governed by the law of another place; in any of which cases, effect is given to such law, or such intention expressed or presumed.

The contract, too, may contain an agreement or special directive as to choice of law.

The *Canada Shipping Act*[23] at s. 274, contains a legislative directive. Part III of the Act entitled "Seamen", will apply if there is an express provision. Otherwise, the law of the ship's flag will apply.

(d) Connecting Factors

Assuming there are no *effective* directives in the law or in the contract as to the law to be used, one must then study the facts and circumstances of the problem which relate it to one law or another. These facts and circumstances are "connecting factors" or "contacts" and are the basic "raw materials" of conflict of laws, whereas the rules are the "tools". It is these factors that the court uses to link the particular set of circumstances of the case to a particular law. Usually there are many connecting factors to consider. They may be the place of the

---

International Law (10th ed.), p. 44; Graveson, *Conflict of Laws* (7th ed., 1974), pp. 46-47; Groffier, *Précis de Droit International Privé Quebecois* (2nd ed., 1982), p. 140.

20   *Cogsa*, 46 U.S. Code 1301-1315, *e.g.*, stipulates at s. 1300 that the Act shall apply to every bill of lading or similar document of title which is evidence of a contract or carriage *to* or *from* U.S. ports.

21   Adopted in 1804.

22   Adopted in 1866.

23   R.S.C. 1970, c. S-9, Part III at s. 274.

contract, the place of the delict or tort, the place of carrying out the contract, the flag of the ship, the nationality of the crew, the domicile of the vessel owners or the domicile of the charterers. All the connecting factors must be ascertained and valued in order to determine the applicable law amongst the laws of the competing states.

For example, in *Lauritzen v. Larsen*[24] (a tort case regarding an injury to a seaman), the United States Supreme Court held that the connecting factors to be considered were:

1. Place of the wrongful act;
2. Law of the flag;
3. Allegiance or domicile of the injured person;
4. Allegiance of defendant shipowner;
5. Place of the contract;
6. Inaccessibility of the foreign forum; and
7. The law of the forum.

Equal authority is not necessarily given to each connecting factor. The Supreme Court, because of the particular circumstances of the *Lauritzen* case, emphasized three factors: the law of the flag, the allegiance or domicile of the injured seaman and the allegiance of the shipowner.[25]

(e) Conclusion

The *Lauritzen* decision is especially important because, as the Supreme Court itself subsequently declared, its broad principles are to govern all choice of maritime law problems in the United States.[26] The connecting factors of *Lauritzen,* however, are neither exhaustive nor of equal value, as was pointed out again by the Supreme Court in *Hellenic*

---

24   345 U.S. 571 at 583-592, 1953 AMC 1210 at 1219-1226 (1953). See also *The Second Restatement, supra* note 10, at s. 188(2):

    In the absence of an effective choice of law by the parties, (see sect. 187) the contacts to be taken into account in applying the principles of sect. 6 to determine the law applicable to an issue include: (a) the place of contracting, (b) the place of negotiation of the contract, (c) the place of performance, (d) the location of the subject matter of the contract, and (e) the domicile residence, nationality place of incorporation and place of business of the parties.

    These contracts are to be evaluated according to their relative importance with respect to the particular issue.

25   See *Rainbow Line Inc. v. M/V Tequila,* 480 F 2d 1024, 1973 AMC 1431 at 1433 (2 Cir 1973). See also *Tjonaman v. A/S Glittre,* 340 F 2d 290 at 291, 1965 AMC 57 at 58 (2 Cir 1964).

26   *Romero v. Internat. Terminal Operating Co., supra* note 14, at p. 382 [U.S.], p. 854 [AMC]. See also *Tjonaman v. A/S Glittre, supra* note 25; *Mobil v. Pacific Bear,* 1980 AMC 1409 at 1410 (ND Cal 1979) and *Gulf Trading v. Hoegh Shield, supra* note 11, at p. 366 [F], p. 1142 [AMC].

Lines Ltd. v. Rhoditis,[27] who added an eighth connecting factor in respect of *Jones Act* cases – "the shipowner's base of operations". Connecting factors are, of course, what the beholder chooses them to be, but the case provides sufficient guidelines to prevent the choice from being too arbitrary.

3. RECOGNITION OF FOREIGN LAW

(a) The General Rule

It is a general principle of the choice of laws to recognize foreign law if it is the law of the place where the contract was entered into. There are a great many exceptions to the rule so that, at times, the exceptions seem to attain preponderance over the rule.[28]

Despite the exceptions, one must recognize that it is a principle of international law, particularly maritime law, that a local law should not be applied to foreigners, foreign events or foreign transactions, otherwise than by exception. In this respect, Lord Russell of Killowen stated in *R. v. Jameson:*[29]

> One other general canon of construction is this – that if any construction otherwise be possible, an Act will not be construed as applying to foreigners in respect to acts done by them outside the dominions of the sovereign power enacting. That is a rule based on international law by which one sovereign power is bound to respect the subjects and the rights of all other sovereign powers outside its own territory.

Marshall C.J. put it this way:[30]

> [A]n act of Congress ought never to be construed to violate the law of nations if any other possible construction remains, and consequently can never be construed to violate neutral rights, or to affect neutral commerce, further than is warranted by the law of nations as understood in this country.

(b) The Exceptions

Many reasons have been given for failure to recognize foreign law, but they can be grouped into three main exceptions to the general rule.

---

27   398 U.S. 306 at 309, 1970 AMC 994 at 996 and n. 4 (1970), followed in *Mobil v. Pacific Bear, supra* note 26.
28   Some theories even propose to never recognize foreign law unless it is identical to the local law. The majority decision in *Bankers Trust Internat. v. Todd Shipyards Corp.; The Halcyon Isle,* [1981] A.C. 221, [1980] 3 All E.R. 197, [1980] 2 Lloyd's Rep. 325, 1980 AMC 1221 (P.C.) in respect of foreign maritime liens can be read this way.
29   [1896] 2 Q.B. 425 at 430, cited in *Lauritzen v. Larsen, supra* note 24, at p. 578 [U.S.], pp. 1215-6 [AMC].
30   *The Charming Betsey,* 6 U.S. 137 at 143 (2 Cranch 64 at 118) (1804).

(i) Public policy/public order. Public policy or public order, as its civil law equivalent is called, is often employed by courts so that they may refuse to apply the foreign law of the contract because that foreign law violates a basic concept of the local law. For example, because of the doctrine of public order, many nations do not recognize assignment of seamen's wages.

Public order or *ordre public* of the civil law is quite different from "public policy" of the common law. In the first place, *ordre public* is a basic tenet in all civil codes which stipute that it cannot be contravened. Article 6 of the *Civil Code* of France reads:[31]

> On ne peut déroger, par des conventions particulières, aux lois qui intéressent l'ordre public et les bonnes moeurs.
> [Translation] No one may by private agreement validly contravene the laws of public order and good morals.[32]

Ordre public has a connotation of morality as well, specifically referring as it does to good morals.

If public policy is not as strong as public order, it is, nevertheless, used to invoke local law when foreign law would normally be applicable.

(ii) Procedural matters. Only substantive foreign law will be recognized, while foreign procedural law will not. This rule is obvious because the courts, their judges and officials are not equipped, even if they were so authorized, to conduct trials by any other means than according to the procedures, practices and rules of evidence that they know and have on hand.

Thus Dicey and Morris state:[33]

> The principle that procedure is governed by the *lex fori* is of general application and universally admitted.

Cheshire and North's *Private International Law* declares:[34]

> One of the eternal verities of every system of private international law is that a distinction must be made between substance and procedure, between right and remedy. The substantive rights of the parties to an action may be governed by a foreign law, but all matters appertaining to procedure are governed exclusively by the *lex fori.*

---

31   The *Civil Code* of France was adopted in 1804 and art. 6 has remained unchanged. It is identical to art. 13 of the Quebec *Civil Code* adopted in 1866. See also the Austrian Federal Statute of June 15, 1978, *Private International Law,* art. 6; the *Civil Code* of Spain, art. 11(3); the *Civil Code* of Italy, prov. 31; the *Civil Code* of Portugal, art. 22; the Decree 13 of the Presidential Council of the Hungarian People's Republic, *The International Private Law,* art. 7; the *Convention of the Law Applicable to Contractual Obligations,* Rome, June 19, 1980 (80/934/E.E.C.), art. 16.
32   This translation is the English version of art. 13 of the Quebec *Civil Code,* a bilingual code with each version having equal authority.
33   *The Conflict of Laws* (10th ed., London, 1980), p. 1175.
34   (10th ed., 1979), p. 691.

Castel,[35] Graveson,[36] Sykes and Pryles[37] all accept the same principle. Others, however, do not.[38]

It is important to note as well that the law of the forum determines what is substantive and what is procedural.[39] This is part of the characterization process. What is substantive and what is procedural is often difficult to determine.[40] With respect to maritime liens, the lien or the right would seem to be substantive and the ranking or priority, procedural.[41]

From the beginning, American courts have divided liens into substance and procedure. In 1809, Marshall C.J. stated:[42]

> The law of the place where a contract is made is, generally speaking, the law of the contract; i.e. it is the law by which the contract is expounded. But the right of priority forms no part of the contract itself. It is extrinsic, and is rather a personal privilege dependent on the law of the place where the property lies, and where the court sits which is to decide the cause.

In *Bethlehem Steel Lim Procs; The Steelton,* [43] Krupansky J. held that the limitation of liability paragraphs in s. 647(2)(*e*) and (*f*) of the *Canada Shipping Act* [44] were procedural and paras. (a), (b), (c) and (d)

---

35   *Canadian Conflicts of Laws* (1975), Vol. 1, p. 599.

36   *Conflict of Laws* (7th ed., 1974), p. 592.

37   *Australian Private International Law* (1979), p. 129.

38   D.C. Jackson, "Foreign Maritime Liens in English Courts – Principle and Policy", [1981] L.M.C.L.Q. 335.

39   The American Law Institute, *Second Restatement, Conflict of Laws 2d,* Vol. I, para. 122; Joseph H. Beale, *A Treatise on the Conflict of Laws,* (New York, 1935), Vol. 3, p. 1601. More recent writings question the full application of this rule and include some reference to the foreign law: Castel, *supra* note 35, at p. 602; Falconbridge, *Essays on the Conflict of Laws* (Toronto, 1954), at 304; Dicey and Morris, *supra* note 33, at p. 1175.

40   Lord Wilberforce, in *Chaplin v. Boys,* [1971] A.C. 356 at 392-393, [1969] 2 All E.R. 1085 (H.L.).

41   The Supreme Court of Canada, in *Todd Shipyards Corp. v. Altema Compania Maritima S.A.; The Ioannis Daskalelis,* [1974] S.C.R. 1248 at 1254, 32 D.L.R. (3d) 571 at 574, [1974] 1 Lloyd's Rep. 174 at 177, 1973 AMC 176 at 180, divided a foreign ship-repairer's lien – the right being declared substantive subject to foreign law and the ranking being declared procedural or subject to the law of the forum. The Privy Council, in *The Halcyon Isle, supra* note 28, at p. 331 [Lloyd's Rep.], p. 1233 [AMC], held that liens were remedies and although apparently unwilling to declare openly that liens were procedural, concluded that liens were subject to the law of the forum.

42   *Harrison v. Sterry,* 9 U.S. 289 at 298-9 (1809), relied on in *Potash Co. v. M/V Raleigh, infra* note 64, at p. 124 [F Supp.], p. 2662 [AMC].

43   435 F. Supp. 944 at 949, 1977 AMC 2203 at 2209 (ND Ohio 1976), upheld in appeal 631 F. 2d 441, 1980 AMC 2122 (6 Cir 1980). See also *Re Arctic Explorer Limitation Proceedings and Geophysical Service Inc.,* judgment dated May 8, 1984 (SD Tex. C.A. No. 81-3381).

44   R.S.C. 1970, c. S-9.

were substantive. In respect of the procedural sections of the Act, he applied the law of the forum, *i.e.*, American law. In *Ishizaki Kisen Co. v. U.S.A.*,[45] the Ninth Circuit also distinguished between substance and procedure. The court held that the collision rules, including the Pennsylvania Rule, were substantive rather than procedural, and therefore applied Japanese collision law to a collision in Japanese waters.

What court costs and attorneys' fees will be ordered, if at all, is clearly a question of procedure to be decided under the law of the forum.[46]

(iii) Evasion of the law. Courts may refuse to apply the law designated by the conflict of laws rule. This will happen when one of the parties acts or manoeuvres with the intention that the applicable conflict rules designate a law which would normally have governed.[47]

Evasion of the law is a particularly civil law doctrine[48] but is also American. Thus in *Rainbow Line Inc. v. M/V Tequila,*[49] a case involving evasion of law, the Second Circuit, in relying on *Lauritzen v. Larsen,* [50] held that:

> [I]f there were any doubt on the choice of law point, it would certainly be resolved against the United States citizen who wished to avoid its country's own laws.

(d) Proof of Foreign Law

Local law will normally be applied by the courts unless foreign law is pleaded and proven. Proof of foreign law is usually made by the testimony of a member of the foreign Bar association who is also a recognized expert of the foreign law.[51]

---

45   510 F 2d 875, 1975 AMC 287 (9 Cir 1975).

46   *Conte v. Flota Mercante del Estado,* 277 F 2d 664 at 672, 1960 AMC 1075 at 1086 (2 Cir 1960).

47   An example would be the mortgagee who has foreclosed on the mortgage, who then orders the ship from one jurisdiction into another, which latter jurisdiction favours ship mortgages over necessaries. See also Graveson R.H., supra note 36, at p. 170.

48   See the *Civil Code* of Portugal, art. 21; see also *Cour de Cassation; La Princesse de Bauffremont,* March 18, 1878, S. 78.1.193.

49   *Supra* note 25, at p. 1027 [F], pp. 1434-5 [AMC]; but see *Alpine Gulf v. First National Bank,* 1981 AMC 540 at 544 (ND Il1 1979).

50   *Supra* note 24, at p. 587 [U.S.], p. 1223 [AMC].

51   *Robinson v. SS J Lanasa,* 1958 AMC 1980 at 1984 and 1985 (D CZ 1957). This is a rule common to all jurisdictions.

4. CHOICE OF LAW – CONTRACT LIENS – UNITED STATES

(a) Introduction

American courts have not been consistent in their approach to choice of law with respect to contract liens. A reasonable body of law, nevertheless, has evolved over the years so that, for the most part, United States courts now apply the law of the place of the contract to define the type of lien and then apply the law of the forum to fix the priorities. A review of important American contract lien cases is revealing.

(b) Review of Decisions

In *The Scotia; Mills v. The Scotia,*[52] a British-flag ship received necessaries in Haiti and New York. The United States court noted that British maritime law did not give a maritime lien for necessaries[53] but that, on the other hand, American and Haitian law gave a lien to necessaries men. The court held that the necessaries' lien is subject to the law of the place where the supplies were provided and not to the law of the flag of the ship. Thus the contract liens were recognized and were then ranked according to the law of the forum. This is an early case and contains a confusing dictum which is often cited. It is an observation on what courts did at that time, rather than on what they should do:[54]

> In contracts to be performed elsewhere, such as contracts of affreightment, and of bottomry, other considerations arise as to the law applicable to the transaction; depending upon the reasonable or presumed intention of the parties, the conveniences of commerce, and the justice of the case. See *The Brantford City,* 29 Fed. Rep. 373, 383-396, and cases there cited. Whether a lien created by the local law shall be recognized and enforced in another country upon the *res* when found and seized there, depends upon the law of comity. If the law of the latter country does not recognize any similar liens, as between its own citizens, it will not ordinarily enforce the foreign lien in favor of a foreigner to the prejudice of its own citizens. Liens and privileges, when enforced in other countries than in those by whose laws they are created, are largely treated as remedies; and, unless affecting foreigners alone, take rank according to the law of the forum. Story, Confl. Law, ss 323, 423, b, d; 1 Desjardins, Droit Mar. ss 104; Whart. Confl. Law, ss. 324, 335-348.

Unfortunately, because of the above citation, when local citizens are involved in foreign lien contracts, even today, those liens are often treated as procedural "unless affecting foreigners alone".

---

52   35 F 907 (SD NY 1888).
53   *Ibid.* at 908.
54   *Ibid.* at 910, 911.

In *The City of Atlanta,*[55] the court applied the foreign law with respect to a claim for necessaries in Cuba, citing 1 Corpus Juris, p. 1262, s. 50:

> In the matter of foreign contracts the law of the place where the contract was made furnishes the rule of decision, unless the contracting parties clearly appear to have had some other law in view.

In *Meridian Trading Corp. v. SS Denton,*[56] an American preferred ship mortgage (a United States mortgage, on a United States ship, recorded at United States Customs where the ship has its port of registry, and recorded as well on the ship's documents) was given preference over an Italian supplier's lien for bunkers supplied in Italy. The lien was actually a maritime lien for master's disbursement away from the home port in virtue of art. 2(5) of the 1926 *Liens and Mortgages Convention,* to which Italy is a party. Italian law, however, recognizes the law of the flag in matters concerning ships of a foreign nation, when that nation is not a party to the 1926 *Convention.* The United States court accepted this *renvoi* to American law and applied American law, giving the preferred ship mortgage precedence over the lien, as though the lien were a supplier's lien. The court rather weakly noted that no proof had been made that an Italian supplier's lien had precedence over an American preferred ship mortgage (at p. 2269). The court added that, in any event, it was a matter of public policy that the preferred mortgage shall have preference over *all* claims against the vessel" (at p. 2273). If the Italian law of the flag rule had not existed, the court should have recognized the lien created by a master's disbursement away from the home port, noted that it had the same maritime lien status as wages, collision and salvage under the 1926 *Convention,* and given it that substantive status. Then when ranked under the United States law of the forum, it would have been ranked ahead of the preferred ship mortgage.

In *M/V Marifax v. McCrory,*[57] a ship was repaired in Miami and then sailed to the Bahamas where she was arrested. The initial suit in the Bahamas was apparently "dismissed on the grounds that the British law [unlike American law] does not provide a maritime lien for repairs".[58]

---

55   1924 AMC 1305 at 1307 (SD Ga 1924). See also *Liverpool & Great Western v. Phoenix Ins. Co.,* 129 U.S. 397 at 458 (1889); *Barge Waubaushene; Re Insurance Co.,* 22 F 109 (ND NY 1884); *The Maud Carter,* 29 F 156 at 157 (D Mass 1886); *The Scotia, supra* note 52, at p. 909; *The Woudrichem,* 278 F 568 (ED NY 1921); *The Coastwise,* 291 F 166 at 167, 1923 AMC 942 at 944 (D Mass 1923).

56   1960 AMC 2264 (SD Tex 1960), upheld in 302 F 2d 404, 1962 AMC 1730 (5 Cir 1962).

57   391 F 2d 909, 1968 AMC 965 (5 Cir 1968).

58   *Ibid.* at 909 [F]; 966 [AMC]. The initial Bahamas finding is not dissimilar to the decision of a British court in *The Christine Isle,* 1974 AMC 331 (Supreme Ct. of Bermuda 1974).

Suit was then taken in the Southern District of Florida. The maritime lien was properly recognized at trial and in appeal.[59]

In *Rainbow Line Inc. v. M/V Tequila*[60] a British-flag vessel was chartered to Rainbow Line and improperly withdrawn by the owner before cargo was loaded on board, thereby giving rise to a maritime lien under United States law but not under British Law. The ship was sold and registered under the Liberian flag and then mortgaged. The United States Second Circuit had first to determine what law applied. It found that the law of the flag and the allegiance of the parties were important connecting factors as per *Lauritzen v. Larsen*,[61] but it also relied on *Hellenic Lines Ltd. v. Rhoditis*[62] to look through the corporate facade. The court found that the buyer, the seller and the mortgagee were one and the same, being related and being subsidiaries of the same American company. They were therefore effectively American. The other parties also had substantial American connections. The only British contacts were the registration of the vessel and the nominal ownership of the vessel at the time the charterparty was breached. American law was therefore applied and the breach of contract lien, which arose before the mortgage, was given precedence. (This lien could also have been pleaded as a United States tort lien and the registration date of the mortgage would then have been immaterial.)

In *Basis v. Universal Line*,[63] the court seemed to indicate that, had Panamanian law not settled the matter, it would have recognized a foreign seaman's lien for wrongful dismissal.

In *Potash Co. v. M.V. Raleigh*,[64] the United States District Court in the Canal Zone applied its own law (*i.e.,* American law as it then was) to both the characterization of the lien and the ranking. A Canadian charterer contracted to have goods carried from Canada to Brazil. The vessel breached its contract by failing to leave Balboa C.Z. once it arrived there. This would be a tort under American law (the place of the tort), and the Canal Zone District Court held that American law applied and thus a United States tort lien was created. Seemingly ignored was the fact that the law of the flag, the law of the contract, the law of the place of shipment, the law of the destination, the law of the allegiance of the plaintiff and the law of defendant were not American. The court also assumed that tort liens for breach of contract exist in Canada and Brazil

---

59   *Supra.*
60   480 F 2d 1024, 1973 AMC 1431 (2 Cir 1973).
61   345 U.S. 571, 1953 AMC 1210 (1953).
62   398 U.S. 306, 1970 AMC 994 (1970). Reference was also made to *Bartholomew v. Universe Tankship Inc.,* 1959 AMC 273, 263 F 2d 437 (2 Cir 1959).
63   1970 AMC 1073 (ED NY 1970).
64   361 F Supp 120, 1973 AMC 2658 (D CZ 1973).

(the decision is not clear as to what proof if any was made in this regard), and then applied American priorities. At least the court correctly applied American priorities *i.e.,* the law of the forum.

In *Ramsay Scarlett v. Koh Eun,*[65] a United States District Court recognized that a Canadian stevedore had a right *in rem* but did not seem to realize that it was not a maritime lien. The court at this point incorrectly assimilated the right *in rem* to the maritime lien but properly applied American ranking, *i.e.,* the law of the forum.

In *Mobil v. Pacific Bear,*[66] an American bunker supplier entered into an agreement to supply bunkers to an American charterer of a United States flag vessel owned by an American owner. Although bunkers were supplied in Japan, all the other connecting factors pointed to United States law in virtue of *Lauritzen v. Larsen*[67] and the *Second Restatement,*[68] the court, in consequence applied American law to both the recognition of the lien and the ranking.

In *Gulf Trading v. Hoegh Shield,*[69] a Norwegian-flag vessel owned in Normay was under time charter to what appears to be a British company. By a contract reached in England with the time charterer, bunkers were supplied by an American company to the vessel in the Canal Zone which at that time was subject to United States law. If English law had applied, there would have been no maritime lien against the vessel, nor even a right *in rem* because there was no evidence that the bunkers were supplied on the vessel owner's instructions and credit. Under American law there was a presumption that the bunkers were supplied on the credit of the vessel resulting in a maritime lien against the vessel. The Fifth Circuit relied on the principle of connecting factors set out in *Lauritzen v. Larsen* and s. 188 of the *Second Restatement.* The court also relied on s. 6 of the *Second Restatement* which specifically set forth principles to be applied in choice-of-law matters including "(d) the protection of justified expectations" and "(e) the basic policies underlying the particular field". The court then held that Congressional intent was to protect stevedores and others by making maritime liens available and cited the House Report in respect of the 1971 Amendment of the 1920 *Ship Mortgage Act.*[70] It next cited the Congressional Record:[71]

---

65   462 F Supp 277, 1979 AMC 970 (ED Va 1978). A correct decision was taken by the District Court of South Carolina in *Ocean Ship Supply v. Leah, infra* note 73.

66   1980 AMC 1409 (ND Cal 1979.).

67   *Supra* note 61.

68   *Mobil v. Pacific Bear, supra* note 66, at p. 1412, referred confusingly to the *Second Restatement, Conflicts of Laws 2d,* 1971, at s. 251 comment (g), and ignored s. 188.

69   658 F 2d 363, 1982 AMC 1138 (5 Cir 1981).

70   H. Rep. No. 92-340, 92 Cong. 1st Sess., reprinted in (1971) U.S. Code Cong. & Admin. News, pp. 1363 and 1365; also cited in *Atlantic & Gulf v. Grand Loyalty,* 608 F 2d 197 at 201, 1980 AMC 1716 at 1721 (5 Cir 1979).

71   *Gulf Trading v. Hoegh Shield, supra* note 69, at p. 367 [F], p. 1144 [AMC].

Granting the materialman a lien encourages the prompt furnishing of necessaries to vessels so that they can be speedily turned around and put to sea. This is especially significant today when the emphasis on vessel performance is reduced port time and increased speed.

The court concluded that:[72]

Despite the fact the contract . . . was formed in Great Britain, it cannot be argued that Great Britain would have as great an interest as the United States in protecting an American supplier of fuel to a non-English vessel in an American port.

In *Ocean Ship Supply v. Leah,*[73] the District Court of South Carolina properly categorized the claim of a Canadian stevedore for services performed in Canada as only a right *in rem* under Canadian law and not a maritime lien. Such a right *in rem* in Canada, unlike a maritime lien, expires with the sale of the ship if no arrest has been made. The District Court in consequence properly concluded that the arrest in Florida, made after the sale of the ship, was invalid.

(c). Conclusion

American courts, it can be seen, are in general internationally minded in recognizing foreign maritime liens. They are nevertheless quick to apply American law when they find a preponderance of American connecting factors.[74] This practice of American courts can be regarded as an application of the exception of public policy based on the "centre of gravity" theory or state-interest theory. The practice is very probably the result of the policy enunciated in s. 6 of the *Second Restatement, Conflict of Laws 2d.*

5. CANADIAN DECISIONS ON CHOICE OF LAW OF CONTRACT LIENS

(a) Case Law

Canadian decisions, especially of the Supreme Court of Canada, have been relatively consistent with respect to conflicts and contract liens.

In *Coorty v. The George L. Colwell,*[75] necessaries were supplied in 1898 to an American ship by American suppliers in the United States.

---

72   *Ibid.* at 368 [F], 1144, 1145 [AMC]. See also *Gulf Trading & Transp. Co. v. M/V Tento,* 694 F 2d 191 (9 Cir 1982).

73   1982 AMC 2740 (D SC 1982), upheld in appeal on the conflict of laws question, March 13, 1984 (4 Cir No. 82-1433).

74   *Rainbow Line Inc. v. M/V Tequila, supra* note 60; *Mobil v. Pacific Bear, supra* note 66; *Gulf Trading v. Hoegh Shield, supra* note 69; to a lesser extent, *Potash Co. v. M.V. Raleigh, supra* note 64.

75   (1898), 6 Ex. C.R. 196.

The ship was arrested in Canada and the Quebec Admiralty District noted that it had jurisdiction *in rem* over "any" ship whether British or foreign under the *Admiralty Act, 1861*[76] as long as the necessaries were furnished at the port of registry other than the one "to which she belongs". The court then recognized the lien of the American supplier. Routhier L.J. added [translation]:[77]

> If it were necessary to add anything, I would say that it is the opinion of the most accredited international law lawyers, that the courts of every nation have jurisdiction over, and must not refuse to judge cases involving foreigners which come before them: to refuse to hear them is to commit a denial of justice.

In *Pittsburg Coal Co. v. S.S. Belchers,*[78] a Canadian-flag ship owned by Canadians was arrested in Canada for supplies provided in the United States by an American company. Canadian law, at that time, did not permit arrest for necessaries where the vessel owners were domiciled in Canada. The Exchequer Court of Canada erroneously held that it did not have jurisdiction and thus failed to recognize the American supplier's lien.

Shortly after the *Pittsburg Coal Co.* decision, the Supreme Court of Canada, in The *Strandhill v. Walter W. Hodder Co.,*[79] ruled with respect to an American supplier who had arrested an American ship in Canada for necessaries. The court noted that, although there was no equivalent lien in Canada, our courts would accept jurisdiction and recognize and enforce the foreign right. After an enlightened analysis of English precedent, Newcombe J. said:[80]

> Then it is clear, upon abundant authority, that a right acquired under the law of a foreign state will be recognized, and may be enforced, under the law of England, unless opposed to some rule of domestic policy or procedure which prevents the recognition of the right.

In *Baker v. The Astoria,*[81] necessaries were supplied in Connecticut to an American ship registered in New York by New York suppliers. Upon consideration of *The Strandhill,*[82] the Exchequer Court of Canada in Admiralty held that the court had jurisdiction to hear and enforce a foreign lien. The court noted:[83]

---

76   (24 & 25 Vict. c. 10), s. 5.
77   *Supra* note 75, at p. 201. See also *Marquis v. The Astoria,* [1931] Ex. C.R. 195, where the foreign maritime lien was *recognized* but erroneously *ranked* after the mortgage.
78   [1926] Ex. C.R. 24.
79   [1926] S.C.R. 680, [1926] 4 D.L.R. 801.
80   *Ibid.* at 685.
81   [1927] 4 D.L.R. 1022.
82   *Supra* note 79.
83   *Baker v. The Astoria, supra* note 81, at p. 1026.

In the first place that case [*The Strandhill*] clearly establishes the principle that a maritime lien acquired under the law of a foreign state, will be recognized and may be enforced here, if the tribunal to which the party asserting the right to the lien has resorted, has the requisite jurisdiction.

The court added, again relying on *The Strandhill*,[84] that whether or not the necessaries were supplied in the American ship's home port was immaterial to jurisdiction to hear a foreign lien in Canada.

The Exchequer Court referred yet another time to *The Strandhill*, in *Harney v. M.V. Terry*,[85] to prevent the Master of an American ship from claiming a lien on his ship, while Canadain law would have granted him one:[86]

There [in *The Strandhill*] the Court, distinguishing between the *lex loci contractus* and the *lex fori*, held that the former governed and thus recognized and applied the maritime lien for necessaries given by American law though it was unknown to Canadian law. I have no doubt that the converse must be equally true, viz., that the Court will refuse to enforce a maritime lien not given by American law though valid under Canadian law.

The decision confirms that the *Strandhill* rule is to be applied positively (when it recognizes a right) as well as negatively (when it does not recognize a right).

In *Todd Shipyards Corp. v. Altema Compania Maritime S.A.; The Ioannis Daskalelis*,[87] a Greek-flag ship, registered in Greece, was owned by a Panamanian company. In 1961 a Greek ship mortgage was registered, and in 1964 the ship was repaired in a United States shipyard. The ship was arrested in Canada after the mortgagee foreclosed and ordered the vessel to Canada rather than to the United States. Under American law, an American repairman is granted a maritime lien, which ranks ahead of all foreign ship mortgages, no matter when registered.[88] Under Canadian law the repairman does not have a maritime lien but only a statutory right *in rem* and is therefore outranked by the mortgage. On the other hand, a maritime lien in Canada ranks ahead of a mortgage.

Ritchie J., speaking for the Canadian Supreme Court, carefully analyzed British and Canadian decisions and recognized the foreign contract lien, because it was substantive. He then held that ranking was procedural and thus subject to the law of the forum, *i.e.*, Canadian law. In consequence the repairman's lien, having already been recognized as

---

84   *Ibid.* at 1027.
85   [1948] Ex. C.R. 27, [1948] 1 D.L.R. 728.
86   *Ibid.* at 30 [Ex. C.R.], 730 [D.L.R.].
87   [1974] S.C.R. 1248, 32 D.L.R. (3d) 571, [1974] 1 Lloyd's Rep. 174, 1973 AMC 176.
88   46 U.S. Code 971.

a maritime lien under foreign law (the *lex contractu*), was ranked ahead of the mortgage under Canadian law (the *lex fori*).[89]

With respect to *The Colorado*,[90] the court said:[91]

> Although the decision in *The Colorado* is somewhat clouded by the fact that the judges purport to follow the decisions in the cases of *The Millford*, and *The Tagus*, . . . in both of which the English courts disregarded the proper law of the contract and gave the master of a foreign ship the benefit of an English maritime lien for wages and disbursements, it nevertheless appears to me that *The Colorado* is authority for the contention that where a right in the nature of a maritime lien exists under a foreign law which is the proper law of the contract, the English courts will recognize it and will accord it the priority which a right *of that nature* would be given under English procedure.

The decision of Ritchie J. in *The Ioannis Daskalelis* seems to be a clear, logical and proper approach to conflict of laws in respect of contract maritime liens. Fortunately, it is binding in Canada.

In *Orient Leasing Co. v. The Kosei Maru*,[92] the Federal Court employed the *Ioannis Daskalelis* process. First, it recognized a particular Japanese law, the *Corporate Reorganization Law*, with respect to a Japanese mortgage and a Japanese ship. Then it applied the Canadian remedy, a writ *in rem*, to bring the right into fruition. *The Ioannis Daskalelis* was followed by Mahoney J. in *Ultramar Can. Inc. v. Pierson Steamships Ltd.*,[93] where American liens for towage and grain trimming were recognized as maritime liens under American law and therefore were granted preferred status by the Canadian court.

The consistency of the Canadian decisions is marred by *Marlex Petroleum Inc. v. The Har Rai*[94] in first instance. Here it was held, relying on the *Federal Court Act*,[95] that the shipowner must be liable *in personam* in order for the court to enforce a right *in rem*. To confuse the matter even more, this erroneous judgment is couched in a language

---

89   That the ranking under Canadian law was the same as under American law is purely the result of having applied the *lex fori* to the ranking and does not make the decision ". . . authority for the proposition that a foreign maritime lien, which is given precedence over a registered mortgage by its *lex loci*, will be given the same precedence under Canadian maritime law", as was stated in *Marlex Petroleum v. The Har Rai, infra* note 94, at p. 620 [F.C.], p. 1397 [AMC].

90   *Infra* note 121.

91   *The Ioannis Daskalelis, supra* note 87, at p. 1256 [S.C.R.], p. 576 [D.L.R.], pp. 177-178 [Lloyd's Rep], pp. 181-182 [AMC]. The Supreme Court later on, in its reasons, disposed of the decision in *Marquis v. The Astoria, supra* note 77, with dispatch.

92   [1979] 1 F.C. 670, 94 D.L.R. (3d) 658.

93   [1983] E.T.L. 404, 43 C.B.R. (N.S.) 9 (Fed. Ct.).

94   [1982] 2 F.C. 617, 1982 AMC 1395 (Fed. T.D.), reversed (1984), 4 D.L.R. (4th) 739, 53 N.R. 1 (Fed. C.A.).

95   R.S.C. 1970, c. 10 (2nd Supp.), s. 22(1), (2)(*n*) and (3)(*a*), (*c*).

reminiscent of *The Halcyon Isle*[96] of the House of Lords. The defects in *Marlex Petroleum Inc. v. The Har Rai* have been dealt with elsewhere by the author.[97]

(b) Directives in the Law

The *Canada Shipping Act*[98] contains a directive as to applicable law at s. 274. With respect to Part III of the Act ("Seamen"), the express provisions of Part III will apply. Otherwise, the law of the flag will apply.

6. CONTRACT LIENS – CONFLICT OF LAWS – UNITED KINGDOM

(a) Introduction

Conflict of laws as a science, particularly with respect to *maritime* law, has not developed in British courts[99] in the same way that it has in the United States and other parts of the world. This is perhaps because British maritime and commercial law led the world for centuries, until after World War II. The British courts were secure in the knowledge that, in applying British law, they were rendering justice, because they were rendering the law that the rest of the world relied on, accepted and imitated.[100] Foreigners often appeared before British courts, and today the High Court on its commercial side, because of its efficiency and the competence and integrity of its judges, hears a large proportion of cases between foreigners who choose British jurisdiction. Lloyd's Open Form of Salvage Agreement (L.O.F.), for example, first created in the 1890's, called and still calls for arbitration in London. The courts have held that, when the parties use these forms, they have chosen English law by which to settle their dispute over a salvage claim.[101]

---

96 *Infra* note 103.
97 Tetley, "Canadian Maritime Law Judgments in 1982", [1983] L.M.C.L.Q. 603 at 610-611. *The Har Rai* was fortunately reversed on appeal: *supra* note 94. *The Har Rai* has apparently been appealed to the Supreme Court of Canada, where it may be decided on a question of jurisdiction.
98 R.S.C. 1970, c. S-9.
99 British authors, on the other hand, have developed an extensive and excellent body of conflicts principles, but there is little in respect of maritime law, except perhaps recently as a result of *The Ioannis Daskalelis, supra* note 87, and *The Halcyon Isle, infra* note 103.
100 Up to 1949, appeals from Canada's Supreme Court could be made to the Judicial Committee of the Privy Council in London. The practice continues with respect to certain British dominions and colonies.
101 Lord Diplock in the *Tojo Maru*, [1971] 1 Lloyd's Rep. 341 at 361. The 1980 version

Lord Denning, M.R. summed up the attitude of British courts to foreigners, and vice versa, as follows:[102]

> The right to come here [before English courts] is not confined to Englishmen. It extends to any friendly foreigner. He can seek the aid of our courts if he desires to do so. You may call this "forum shopping" if you please, but if the forum is England, it is a good place to shop in, both for the quality of the goods and the speed of service.

This great tradition of English courts rendering justice to the world under English law has perhaps caused the English courts to choose the *lex fori, i.e.,* English law, even when the connecting factors would indicate that the foreign law of the contract should be applied.

English courts do provide quick, efficient, very competent and utterly untainted justice, but in agreeing to hear foreigners it is essential that the courts apply the proper law of the contract or the tort and not necessarily English law. English justice can include the recognition of foreign law. The ancient merchant courts of England prided themselves on deciding cases between two foreigners under the foreign law.

Unfortunately, British courts today have not built up any accepted theory or set of rules on conflict of maritime laws which will give a predictable result. The majority opinion expressed in *The Halcyon Isle,*[103] the most recent and authoritative British decision on maritime conflicts, virtually deals only with precedents; there is no basic premise on conflict, no elevating or inspiring theory that can guide future decisions. *The Halcyon Isle* majority simply review previous decisions and conclude that a maritime lien is a remedy and therefore, presumably, procedural.[104]

A study of English conflict of laws decisions involving maritime liens illustrates what appears to be a strong chauvinistic attitude of British courts by their characterization of what others would call rights as remedies and their thus resulting conclusion that they are procedural. The basis for the argument seems to be precedent but, unfortunately,

---

of Lloyd's Open Form, being LOF 1980, takes no chance and invokes English law at art. 1(d). See [1980] L.M.C.L.Q. 304.

102   *The Atlantic Star; Atlantic Star v. Bona Spes,* [1972] 3 All E.R. 705 at 709, [1973] 1 Q.B. 364 (C.A.), reversed [1973] 2 All E.R. 175, [1973] 2 W.L.R. 795 (H.L.). Denning's comment was specifically questioned "with all respect", in appeal to the House of Lords, by Lord Reid at p. 181 [[1973] 2 All E.R.]. But see *Alpine Gulf v. First Nat. Bank of Chicago,* 1981 AMC 540 at 544, where Decker D.J. states: "There is no indication in the statute [*Ship Mortgage Act,* 46 USCS 911 *et seq.*], direct or indirect, that Congress intended to make maritime forum shopping a federal tort."

103   *Bankers Trust Internat. v. Todd Shipyards Corp.; The Halcyon Isle,* [1980] 2 Lloyd's Rep. 325, 1980 AMC 1221, [1981] A.C. 221, [1980] 3 All E.R. 197 (P.C.).

104   The minority decision in *The Halcyon Isle* takes a much more international view of maritime law: *ibid.* at 334 *et seq.* [Lloyd's Rep], 1239 *et seq.* [AMC].

English precedent has not developed any consistent maritime conflict of laws rules.

The emphasis on remedies illustrates a major difference between the common law and the civil law. The civil law deals with rights which appear chapter after chapter in the civil code and these rights are granted virtually the same recourses: either rescission of the contract or damages or both. The common law emphasizes remedies rather than rights. "Remedies" is taught in common-law law schools, but is not a subject known to the civil law or taught in civil law faculties and law schools. It is also important to realize that a maritime lien is a civil law concept, and that it is a right or privilege found in the civil code, not in the code of procedure. To a civilian, it is clearly substantive. Admiralty law, too, is civil law rather than common law in origin and nature.[105] Common law courts should recognize that maritime liens are rights, not remedies.

(b) British Decisions on Choice of Law Involving Contract Liens

The following is a sampling of English maritime conflicts decisions. At times foreign liens are recognized, and at other times they are not. When the cases directly involve seamen's or masters' wages as in *The Golubchick*,[106] *The Milford*,[107] *The Tagus*,[108] *The Arosa Star*,[109] *The Fairport*[110] or *The Westport*,[111] the courts seem either to ignore conflicts rules or to apply those rules in a random manner. In this way, masters and seamen are permitted to recover as much as possible. This coincides with the Justice Theory of some authors.

In *Don v. Lippmann*,[112] a note was drawn up in France in 1809 and a judgment obtained upon it one year later in France. There were insufficient assets to satisfy the judgment and, in 1829, suit was taken in Scotland, the domicile of the defendant. A clear and valid distinction was made betwen the law of the contract and the law of the remedy. It was held:[113]

> The law on this point is well settled in this country, where this distinction is properly taken, that whatever relates to the remedy to be enforced, must be determined by the

---

105 See *History and Definition of Maritime Liens*, chap. 1.
106 *Infra* note 114.
107 *Infra* note 115.
108 *Infra* note 119.
109 *Infra* note 127.
110 *Infra* note 128.
111 *Infra* note 129.
112 (1837), 5 Cl. & Fin. 1, 7 E.R. 303 (H.L.). This is not a maritime law case, but is cited in *The Halcyon Isle, supra* note 103.
113 *Ibid.* at 13 [Cl. & Fin.], 307-8 [E.R.].

> *lex fori* ... Then assuming that to be the settled rule, the only question in this case would be, whether the law now to be enforced is the law which relates to the *contract* itself, or to the *remedy*. [Emphasis added].

In *The Golubchick,*[114] Spanish seamen sued for wages against a Russian-flag ship. Dr. Lushington held that he had jurisdiction because

> ... this Court, administering as it does, a part of the maritime law of the world, would have a right to interpose in cases of the present description.

He does not seem, however, to have applied British law to the contract. In *The Milford,*[115] an American master of an American ship sued for his wages in England and seized the freight. Under American law, the master would have had no right against the freight, but he would so have under English law. Dr. Lushington applied the English statute and noted the inconvenience to him of *lex loci contractus:*[116]

> It is impossible not to be struck with the inconveniences which might ensue if the Court is to be governed by the *lex loci contractus;* in every case in which a foreign seaman or master sued, the Court would have to enquire into the contract and into the law of the country under which it was made;

He nevertheless admitted that the *lex loci contractus* would have applied had the matter been a question of contract:[117]

> ... the next question is, whether the law of the United States is applicable? It may be, for if I am to construe a contract, its meaning and extent must doubtless be governed by the *lex loci contractus;*

Yet he concluded that ". . . the proceeding originated in this country; it is a question of remedy, not of contract at all."[118]

In *The Tagus,*[119] a foreign master of an Argentine ship sued for wages and disbursements in an English court and was granted a lien for wages and disbursements under English law, the *lex fori.* If the law of the contract had applied, *i.e.,* Argentina, the master would have had only a lien for wages and disbursements *on the last voyage.* Phillimore J., in applying English law, relied on *The Milford.*[120]

The Court of Appeal, in *The Colorado,*[121] applied the law of the contract and recognized the foreign hypothec over the English necessaries man. Scrutton L.J. was quite clear:[122]

---

114   (1840), 1 W. Rob. 143 at 147, 166 E.R. 526 at 528.
115   (1858), Swab. 362, 166 E.R. 1167.
116   *Ibid.* at 362 [Swab.], 1169 [E.R.].
117   *Ibid.* at 366 [Swab.], at 1169 [E.R.].
118   *Ibid.* at 366 [Swab.], at 1170 [E.R.].
119   [1903] P. 44.
120   *Supra* note 115.
121   14 Ll. L. Rep. 251, [1923] All E.R. Rep. 531, [1923] P. 102 (C.A.).
122   *Ibid.* at 252 [Ll. L. Rep.], at 534 [All E.R.], at 108 [P.].

The nature of the right may have to de determined by some other law, but the nature of the remedy which enforces the right is a matter for the law of the tribunal which is asked to enforce the right.

Scrutton concludes:[123]

The fallacy of [the appellants'] argument appears when they argue that because the French Courts would give a French necessaries man, or a necessaries man suing in the courts of France, priority over the French claimants under a "hypothec", therefore, an English court should give an English necessaries man a similar priority. The answer is that their client is not asking for French remedies, but English remedies; and the English law postpones him to a person who has what is equivalent to a maritime lien.

In *The Zigurds (No. 1)*[124] it was held that, whatever the position of German necessaries men under German law, the question of priorities was to be decided by the law of the forum. The court refused to turn to German law to characterize the necessaries claim because such claims were already known – albeit differently – in English law. It is upon this basis that he distinguished the present case from *The Colorado.*[125]

In *The Christine Isle,*[126] a Liberian ship, charged with a Liberian mortgage, subsequently received stevedoring services in the United States. Such services give rise to a maritime lien under American law, but the Bermuda trial judge, on the basis of English precedent, applied English law both for the recognition of the lien and for its ranking. He thus held that the mortgage outranked the lien.

In *The Arosa Star,* [127] the Chief Justice of the Bermuda Supreme Court applied English law to the master's and seamen's claims for wages. The *lex fori* applied as it was held to be a question of remedy. The seamen were given priority for their salaries not merely for the last voyage, as would have been done under Greek law. Thus, the *lex fori* was applied because justice for seamen was to be done.

In *The Fairport,*[128] an uncontested case, Greek law seems to have been recognized. Here again, justice was done for the benefit of seamen.

In *The Westport,*[129] Karminski J., recognized the responsibility of the master of a Greek ship under Greek law to pay taxes on crew's salaries and pensions, and ranked this sum ahead of the mortgage, although there was no equivalent claim by the master under English law. Thus, in this case, where equity pointed in the other direction, the court did not apply the *lex fori.*

---

123   *Ibid.* at 252 [Ll. L. Rep.], at 535 [All E.R.], at 109 [P.].
124   43 Ll. L. Rep. 156, [1932] P. 113.
125   *Supra* note 121.
126   1974 AMC 331 (Supr. Ct. of Bermuda, 1974).
127   [1959] 2 Lloyd's Rep. 396.
128   [1965] 2 Lloyd's Rep. 183.
129   [1968] 2 Lloyd's Rep. 559.

(c) The Halcyon Isle

Banker's Trust Internat. v. Todd Shipyards Corp.; The Halcyon Isle[130] is the leading English judgment on the conflict of laws with respect to maritime liens. The facts are almost identical to *The Ioannis Daskalelis.*[131] A British ship with a British mortgage was repaired in the same Todd Shipyards in Brooklyn, U.S.A., and then arrested by the mortgagee (in this case in Singapore where English law applied, rather than in Canada).

The Judicial Committee of the Privy Council effectively decided, three to two, that maritime liens for repairs in the United States (and presumably all liens) are remedies under English law and, because all remedies are subject to the law of the forum, the repairman's lien could not be recognized in the United States, not being recognized under English law.

The court seemed reluctant to openly reject the normal conflicts rule that the law of the foreign contract is usually applied. Yet the majority did not rely on the normal conflicts exceptions to the rule of applying foreign law – (i) evasion of the law, or (ii) public policy. Evasion of the law could not be applied, except against the mortgagee who had kept the ship out of American waters and then had it arrested in Singapore. Nor was the court willing to invoke the principle of public policy, *i.e.,* that it was against English policy or national interest to recognize the very peculiar and chauvinistic American lien law which favours all American liens, even suppliers and repairmen, over foreign mortgages.[132] Instead the court, without the benefit of or real reference to conflicts rules, relied on earlier English decisions and concluded that "maritime claims" which give rise to maritime liens would be enforceable by actions *in rem* in English courts "where and only where" there is a maritime lien under English law.[133] This is a strict and absolute application of the law of the forum and nothing else. It can also be described as the Justice Theory,[134] which is that the court, in deciding which law will apply, looks to see that justice be done.

The court summed up and concluded:[135]

---

130   [1980] 2 Lloyd's Rep. 325, 1980 AMC 1221, [1981] A.C. 221, [1980] 3 All E.R. 197 (P.C.).

131   *Todd Shipyards Corp. v. Altema Compania Maritima S.A.; The Ioannis Daskalelis,* [1974] S.C.R. 1248, 32 D.L.R. (3d) 571, [1974] 1 Lloyd's Rep. 174, 1973 AMC 176.

132   The court nevertheless came close to condemning the United States policy on maritime liens: see pp. 333 and 334 [Lloyd's Rep.], pp. 1236-1237 and 1238 [AMC].

133   P. 332 [Lloyd's Rep.], p. 1234 [AMC].

134   R.H. Graveson, *Conflicts of Law* (7th ed., 1974), p. 41. When viewed so narrowly, this doctrine washes its hands of the notion of the protection of legitimate expectations, which arguably could be part of a broader justice theory.

135   P. 332 [Lloyd's Rep.], p. 1234 [AMC].

In their Lordship's view the English authorities upon close examination support the principle that, in the application of English rules of conflict of laws, maritime claims are classified as giving rise to maritime liens which are enforceable in actions in rem in English Courts where *and only where* the events on which the claim is founded would have given rise to a maritime lien in English law, if those events had occurred within the territorial jurisdiction of the English Court.

Diplock L.J. was explicit in stating that both the right *and* the ranking were to be decided by the *lex fori*:[136]

> But any question as to who is entitled to bring a particular kind of proceeding in an English Court, like questions of priorities in distribution of a fund, is a question of jurisdiction. It too under English rules of conflict of laws falls to be decided by English law as the lex fori.

> Their Lordships therefore conclude that, in principle, the question as to the right to proceed in rem against a ship as well as priorities in the distribution between competing claimants of the proceeds of its sale in an action in rem in the High Court of Singapore falls to be determined by the lex fori, as if the events that gave rise to the claim had occurred in Singapore.

The court did note another option (the process suggested here):[137]

> The choice would appear to lie between (1) on the one hand classifying by reference to the events on which each claim was founded and giving to it the priority to which it would be entitled under the lex fori if those events had occurred within the territorial jurisdiction of the distributing Court; or (2) on the other hand applying a complicated kind of special renvoi by (i) first ascertaining in respect of each foreign claim the legal consequences, *other than those relating to priorities in the distribution of a limited fund,* that would be attributed under its own lex causae to the events on which the claim is founded; and (ii) then giving to the foreign claim the priority accorded under the lex fori to claims arising from events; however dissimilar, which would have given rise to the same or analogous legal consequences if they had occurred within the territorial jurisdiction of the distributing Court. To omit the dissection of the lex causae of the claim that the second choice prescribes and to say instead that if under the lex causae the relevant events would give rise to a maritime lien, the English Court must give to those Courts all the legal consequences of a maritime lien under English law would, in their Lordship's view, be too simplistic an approach to the questions of conflicts of law that are involved.

Having rejected the procedural/substantive analysis as "too simplistic", Diplock L.J. then went on to adopt the first alternative for "the merit of simplicity".[138]

Diplock L.J., speaking for the majority, seems to have misunderstood what the Court of Appeal had concluded in *The Colorado,*[139] nor did he seem to understand that the French hypotheque is much like a lien, that it requires suit, unlike the British ship mortgage which

---

136   P. 330 [Lloyd's Rep.], p. 1229 [AMC].
137   P. 327 [Lloyd's Rep.], p. 1223 [AMC].
138   *Ibid.*
139   14 Ll.L. Rep. 147 and 251, [1923] All E.R. 531, [1923] P. 102.

transfers ownership to the mortgagee by the simple notice of foreclosure, without benefit of suit.

The majority decision in *The Halcyon Isle* is questionable on the following grounds:

1. It ignored conflicts rules, whether its own, or those of English authors or of others.

2. It relied solely on English precedent and ignored or confused the leading case, *The Colorado*.[140] That decision, in applying the conflict of laws, noted the difference between right and remedy and clarified the term "remedy" as relating to the order of payment:[141]

    [W]hen the Court is ordering that payment should be made to claimants in a particular order, it is merely awarding a remedy, and therefore will apply the *lex fori*. But as I have said, it must first ascertain whether there is any claim at all.

    The favourable decisions relied on in *The Halcyon Isle* are for the most part early English judgments when both conflict of laws and the laws of liens were in their earliest development.

3. It created a rule of law that is very dangerous – that because a suit has been taken, a remedy is involved; and that, as remedies are the subject-matter of the forum, the law of the forum applies for all aspects of the case. But how else does one come before a court, except by suit? And, if a remedy is the guide, it is interesting that it was the mortgagee who took the action *in rem* to arrest the ship in Singapore.[142] Does this not mean, because the suit of the mortgagee is remedial, that the mortgage must comply with the prerequisites of English law to be valid, *i.e.,* registration in England, under English forms, *etc.?*

4. There is little moral purpose or justice to be found in the majority judgment, in fact quite the opposite, and the dissenting judges, Lord Salmon and Lord Scarman, pointed this out clearly:[143]

    If it were otherwise, injustice would prevail. The respondents would be deprived of their maritime lien, valid as it appeared to be throughout the world, and without which they would obviously never have allowed the ship to sail away without paying a dollar for the important repairs upon which the respondents had spent a great deal of time and money and from which the appellants obtained substantial advantages.

    It is suggested in the majority judgment that the respondents were well aware that the lex loci contractus, conferring upon them their maritime lien, was likely to be disregarded by overseas lex fori in its determination of priorities. We entirely disagree. The importance which the respondents attached to their maritime lien is clearly shown by the shiprepair contract which included the term:–

    Nothing herein shall be deemed to constitute a waiver of our maritime lien.

---

140 *Ibid.*
141 *Ibid.* at 253 [Ll. L. Rep.], 111 [P.].
142 *The Halcyon Isle,* at p. 326 [Lloyd's Rep.], p. 1222 [AMC].
143 P. 337 [Lloyd's Rep.], p. 1244 [AMC].

5. The majority in the Privy Council particularly failed to realize that a maritime lien is a substantive right, a "privilege" which finds its source in substantive civil law rather than in the common law of remedies.

6. The majority in the Privy Council failed to note that, by its decision, maritime law would not be international, but uncertain and dependent not on the desires of the parties in a contract lien or the law of the place of the contract or the law of the place of delict, but on the law of the forum.

7. The majority decision in *The Halcyon Isle* added a new criterion to the traditional definition of a maritime lien – that it travels with the ship. Now a maritime lien would travel with the ship *only if the ship arrives at a jurisdiction which recognizes that lien in its law.*

(d) The Minority Decision in the Halcyon Isle

The minority decision in the *Halcyon Isle,* rendered by Lord Salmon and Lord Scarman, also looked to English precedents, but came to a different conclusion, particularly with respect to *The Colorado.*[144]

The minority decision noted that a maritime lien is a right of property, noted the international nature of maritime law, predicted the chaos of refusing to aid international law and concluded:[145]

> In our opinion the English Court of Appeal in *The Colorado* adopted the approach which is correct in principle. A maritime lien is a right of property given by way of security for a maritime claim. If the Admiralty Court has, as in the present case, jurisdiction to entertain the claim, it will not disregard the lien. A maritime lien validly conferred by the lex loci is as much part of the claim as is a mortgage similarly valid by the lex loci. Each is a limited right of property securing the claim. The lien travels with the claim, as does the mortgage: and the claim travels with the ship. It would be a denial of history and principle, in the present chaos of the law of the sea governing the recognition and priority of maritime liens and mortgages, to refuse the aid of private international.
>
> For these reasons, we think that the Court of Appeal reached the correct conclusion and would dismiss the appeal.

(e) Other Solutions to The Halcyon Isle

Most modern maritime lien conflicts cases are concerned with chauvinistic American law which favours American suppliers' liens[146] and American ship mortgages over foreign mortgages.[147] American

---

144 *Supra* note 139.

145 *The Halcyon Isle,* at p. 339 [Lloyd's Rep.], p. 1249 [AMC].

146 The result of elevating *American* suppliers liens to the rank of full maritime liens by 46 U.S. Code 971.

147 The result of reducing all foreign mortgages to lesser status by 46 U.S. Code 951 and 953.

maritime lien and ship mortgage law is the cause of considerable justified opposition, as well as the source of considerable blind animosity, so that the discussion of conflict lien cases deprecates American law, but rarely does so outright in writing. The majority of the Judicial Committee could have grasped the nettle and denounced American maritime lien law, if it were odious to them, and to do so the majority could have invoked public policy or public interest. Instead the subject was left to allusions and almost silent critiscm.

The ranking of liens is subject to "discretion" in the United States and "equity in other jurisdictions".[148] The majority of the Judicial Committee, in finding the application of normal conflict rules and the recognition of foreign contract liens to be odious, might have taken another course by recognizing the lien, but invoking equity and ranking the mortgage ahead of the United States repairman's lien.

The majority decision in the *Halcyon Isle* is dangerous and will be regretted as a precedent.

7. FRANCE – CONFLICT OF LAWS

(a) Introduction

France has not solved the problem of conflicts of maritime liens any better than any other of the world's shipping nations. The adoption of the *Civil Code*,[149] probably the most important achievement of the Napoleonic era, gave the civil law as a right to every Frenchman, no matter where he was resident, "even in foreign lands."[150] The principle of nationality has ever since been a cornerstone of French conflict of laws rules,[151] yet the law of the flag of the ship has not been adopted by France as the basic determinate in respect to maritime lien conflicts. Rather there have been various theories, most of them leading to the chauvinistic conclusion that the *lex fori* should apply.

France, to its credit, has adopted the *Liens and Mortgages Convention* 1926,[152] so that it has more justification than non-signatory nations

---

148   *The William Leishear,* 21 F 2d 862, 1927 AMC 1770 at 1774 (D Md 1927); *U.S. v. Cornell Steamboat Co.,* 202 U.S. 184 at 194 (1906); *The Leoborg (No. 2),* [1964] 1 Lloyd's Rep. 380 at 383; *Montreal Dry Dock & Ship Repairing Co. v. Halifax Shipyards Ltd.* (1920), 60 S.C.R. 359 at 371, [1920] 3 W.W.R. 25, 54 D.L.R. 185.

149   1804.

150   Art. 3.

151   That French citizens should be bound by the *Civil Code* was not surprising in 1804 because the *Civil Code* was such an advance on the civil laws of most nations at that time.

152   Signed at Brussels on April 10, 1926. France brought the *Convention* into force by the law of February 19, 1949, replaced by the Law No. 67-5 of January 3, 1967, at arts. 49-50.

in imposing its own law, because that law is the international convention.

(b) Hypothèques

France is a signatory of the *Liens and Mortgages Convention* of 1926, [153] and therefore is bound by art. 1 of the *Convention,* which directs that contracting states will recognize and treat as valid, mortgages and hypothecs duly effected in accordance with law of the contracting state to which the vessel belongs. This law is usually both the law of the flag of the ship and the law of the contract (the hypothèque).

The foregoing is an important first rule or directive in conflict of maritime lien cases in France and in most other countries as well, because of the good sense of the rule.

(c) Doctrine

In France, where "la doctrine", or the exposition of the law by experts is so important, it is fitting to study how the leading authorities have solved French conflict of laws problems in respect of maritime liens. Ripert, Rodière, du Pontavice and Batiffol and Lagarde give varying views. [154]

(i) Georges Ripert. Ripert has concisely reviewed the various possible conflict rules with respect to liens and mortgages, dividing the subject into five main areas. [155] He favours, with some reservation, the law of the flag of the ship as the law which should be applied in any conflicts case.

1. A French ship arrested in France:
(a) When a French ship is seized in France, a French court will apply a foreign privilege if the privilege is one which is recognized or exists under French law. [156]
(b) A French court will not recognize a foreign privilege on a French ship if the privilege is not one recognized under French law.

Ripert has no comment here.

2. Where a foreign ship subject to a foreign lien is arrested in France, a French court should recognize the foreign lien, but in practice usually applies the *lex fori, i.e.,* only recognizes a lien which is known to French law. Ripert regrets this practice of the French

---

153 *Supra* note 152.
154 See *infra* notes 156-163.
155 Georges Ripert, *Droit Maritime* (4th ed.), Vol. II, paras. 1161 *et seq.*
156 *Ibid.,* at para. 1162. This is an application of the nationality principle.

courts. He notes that it is inconsistent with the 1926 *Convention* whereby foreign hypothecs are recognized.[157]

3. When a foreign ship is arrested in France for a lien contracted in France, the French courts apply the law of France when, according to Ripert, they should apply the law of the flag to establish the existence of the lien in order to create a situation parallel to the practice in foreign countries.[158]

4. Proof of the Lien: Ripert believes that proving a lien should be according to the law of the flag of the ship.[159]

5. The Ranking: Ripert notes the difficulties of ranking by the law of the flag and notes that the French courts apply the *lex fori*.

Ripert's general conclusion is that a uniform international convention is necessary.[160]

(ii) René Rodière. Rodière spends little time on conflict of laws of maritime liens.[161] He cursorily discards the law of flag, which he says is unlikely to be known because liens are not subject to publicity, lacking as they do, public registration. He rejects the law of the place of the contract, because one presumably cannot learn that law and because he declares some liens are in tort. (Actually, very few liens are in tort and those few are full maritime liens with virtually a uniform international ranking.)

Again without reasons, he quickly disposes of the theory of recognizing the contract according to the *lex causae,* while at the same time applying the *lex fori* to the ranking.

He recognizes the "conflict mobile" problem without offering a solution and finally resigns himself to the *lex fori,* which he concludes is the least wrong solution.

(iii) Du Pontavice. Du Pontavice, without any in-depth discussion, suggests that the law of the forum (the *lex fori*), which necessarily coincides with the law of the place of the ship (*lex sitae*), is the solution.[162]

(iv) Battifol and Lagarde. Battifol and Lagarde briefly suggest that, because the law of the ship's flag is the law governing hypothecs, one should apply the law of the flag (which coincides with the *lex sitae* to maritime liens).[163]

---

157   *Ibid.,* at para. 1163. See also para. 1148.
158   *Ibid.,* at para. 1164.
159   *Ibid.,* at para. 1165.
160   *Ibid.,* at para. 1166.
161   René Rodière, *Le Navire* (1980), para. 138.
162   Emmanuel du Pontavice, *Le Statut des Navires* (1967), p. 142.
163   *Droit International Privé* (7th ed., 1983), para. 508.

(d) Conclusion

The courts of France as well as the writers on conflict of laws seem to apply the law of the flag of the ship if it does not *contradict* the law of the forum. In effect, it is therefore the law of the forum which is applied.

8. SUMMARY AND CONCLUSION

The foregoing description of conflict of maritime lien laws in the United States, the United Kingdom, Canada and France, if nothing else, underlines the need for a uniform and international maritime liens and mortgages convention. Failing the adoption, in the near future, of such a convention by the world's shipping nations, it is essential that consistent rules of conflict of maritime lien laws be agreed upon or at least informally accepted.

Such acceptance may, at first glance, seem unlikely, yet maritime lien law is fortunately so strongly grounded in common sources and traditions that national maritime lien conflict rules necessarily have a principal common purpose – international uniformity. This is an encouraging sign.

National maritime lien and mortgage laws also have much in common. First, a single historical source – the ancient codes, the *Rôles of Oléron,* the *Consolato del Mare, etc.,* culminating in the *lex maritima,* the *lex mercatoria,* the *Ordonnance de la Marine* of 1681 and the maritime law of Doctor's Commons. There is therefore a fairly uniform general maritime law with a common tradition and a common origin – the codified *lex maritima* and *lex mercatoria* which is civilian in nature. From this common source and tradition it is clear that the maritime lien is a "privilege" – it is a right, not a common law remedy.

Secondly, maritime lien conflict cases are usually a confrontation between liens and mortgages and, if the applicable law of maritime lien is still in doubt in some jurisdictions, the law of the ship mortgage (hypothec) is almost universally judged to be the law of the ship's registry, which is the law of the flag. Thus is solved a very major problem of liens and mortgages conflict of laws. That there is a solution for hypothecs should give heart to those attempting to find a solution for conflict of lien laws.

Thirdly, maritime law has a great tradition of universality and uniformity, as seen in its basic source, the *lex maritima* and *lex mercatoria.* The desire for uniformity along ith a desire for predictability of law and the belief in just solutions are the three essential basic purposes of any conflict of laws theory. And these three criteria provide the stimulus and the authority for courts to recognize foreign law under which foreign contracts have been made. The courts, nevertheless, are left with valid occasions when they may justifiably refuse to recognize foreign laws:

(a) when the foreign law violates local public policy or public order requirements;
(b) when there is an evident case of evasion of local law or some other law; and
(c) where matters are purely procedural.

Despite the direction in which the foregoing purposes point, three leading methods of deciding conflict of maritime liens have unfortunately emerged.

The first method is to consider all maritime liens, no matter where they arose, as subject to and to be interpreted by the law of the place of arrest, the *lex fori*. Put another way, liens are considered to be remedies or to be procedural and therefore to be decided by the *lex fori*. Such a solution is the antithesis of the three principles of international uniformity, of predictability of law, and of justice. Unfortunately, it was the solution adopted by the majority in *The Halcyon Isle*. Fortunately, it was challenged with eloquence by the minority court in the same case.

The second method is to accept maritime liens as rights, to recognize the law of the place of the contract or of the event and then to rank the liens (once accepted) according to the law of the forum (ranking being procedural). This is the unanimous solution of the Supreme Court of Canada in *The Ioannis Daskalelis* and of the minority of the Privy Council in *The Halcyon Isle*. In the author's view, it complies with the three criteria of international uniformity of law, of predictability of law, and of justice.

Another method is to classify liens according to the law of the flag and then to rank them presumably by the *lex fori*. This is similar to the contract/procedure method above in many respects. Unfortunately, "the law of the flag" concept raises considerable problems. The law of the place of the contract is the natural, normal law of a contract, being the law of the party providing the services, supplies, repairs, stevedoring, pilotage, *etc.* Each supplier would be obliged to know the law of each nationality of ship with whom he does business and to have appropriate contracts written according to that law. Such a solution results in uncertainty and unpredictability of the terms of a contract and is impractical.

It is hoped that, if a universal liens and mortgages convention is not adopted, the courts of the world will base their conflict of law rules on the three principles of uniformity, predictability and justice. That being the case, they should accept maritime liens as rights subject to the law of the place of the contract and then rank them according to the law of the place of the forum.

THE IMPACT OF TECHNOLOGY
ON SHIPPING DOCUMENTATION

THE CHANGING FACE OF DOCUMENTATION IN THE CARRIAGE OF GOODS

*A.R. Elliott**

1. INTRODUCTION

With the ability of computers to accurately manipulate masses of numerical data, many firms first enter the "electronic world" by applying computers to their internal financial and administrative systems. If the firms are heavily involved with the manufacture of goods and their shipment, automation is usually also applied to keeping track of the inventory to produce the goods. Often a "cargo-tracking program" is developed to give up-to-date information on the location of many of the goods shipped. This information, until recently, was gathered by telephone, or by entering it into a computer from the various documents received at a headquarters location.

In the past few years, many international trading firms have established electronic networks for tracking the shipment of goods between countries. Remote terminals, some with local intelligence, are used to capture required data. Companies such as Atlantic Container Lines, Canadian Pacific and Air Canada are typical of those that have established extensive networks to simplify their documentation handling. Information is entered from remote terminals, while bills of lading, for example, are printed at different locations world-wide. Other required forms for the formal transfer of goods between countries and companies

---

*Ph.D, President, COSTPRO.

are printed as needed. In some firms, this computerized international document-processing ability has become a marketing advantage, allowing a firm to state that it can expedite shipments faster because it knows almost instantly where the goods are located.

The significant point to notice is that the automation advances being promoted by companies today describe the systems available *within* a company. Each company can establish management control parameters that satisfy legal requirements. They can specify their own security controls on the system and can produce the necessary documentation when required to meet any special demands. Occasionally, other firms might be linked into a network operated, for example, by a carrier. But the interconnection will be on the carrier's terms, and usually only with terminals owned or certified by the carrier. In this way, control is maintained.

The true trading problem is much more complex, involving the buyer, the seller, the shipper, customs authorities, insurance agents, banks, freight forwarders, brokers and a multitude of intermediaries in the transaction of an order. Once computers are brought into this complex situation, at least an extra order of difficulty is evident. The problems involved in electronically transmitting information between various companies and agencies in different countries, generally using different computer systems, different terminals, with different ways of printing the information, as well as ensuring that the proposed system can be integrated into manual processing operations, appear insurmountable.

Companies and governments, however, are quickly establishing systems for the electronic interchange of data. For example, the United States Census Authorities permit the transfer of statistical export and import information by magnetic tape, with some 70 per cent of the information collected now arriving in this way. The growing use of micro-computers by smaller firms will likely force the technical, regulatory and legal aspects of trade document processing to be addressed at a more rapid pace, as these companies apply quick solutions to perceived operational problems. The fast installation of different systems leads to incompatibilities and more inefficiencies, and to concerns about reliability and security, once they become interconnected.

The optimum solution for intercompany and interagency interconnection being developed world-wide calls for standards for the electronic interchange of documents. The standards, however, need to allow for local variations. For example, some companies may wish to print the date of shipment in one location on a form; other companies may wish to put it in another location. Different languages with different symbols must be incorporated in any solution. The banking community, which is directly involved in many international shipments through letters of credit, demands a high level of security in order to satisfy the requirements of that community. Key questions now being asked by most companies which examine the electronic linking of the parties to a trade transaction are, what is the legal status of documents transmitted electronically, and can a signature be authenticated in such a system?

The systems and standards being promoted by the UN/ECE (Economic Council for Europe) Working Party on Trade Facilitation, and national facilitation groups such as COSTPRO, have addressed most of these issues. The systems that have been developed from years of research represent cost-effective solutions to many of the problems raised. The basis of this paper is to present: (i) an overview of the multi-company interconnection problem; (ii) an assessment of current activities; and (iii) evidence that the rapid growth of pilot systems testing intercompany interaction will require the skills of lawyers in the next few years.

2. A BRIEF HISTORY OF THE TRADE FACILITATION EFFORT

As early as 1959, the International Chamber of Commerce (ICC) produced a brochure entitled *Merchant Shipping on a Sea of Red Tape.* It was decided at the Washington Conference of the ICC in the same year that the Intergovernmental Maritime Consultative Organization (IMCO), as the International Maritime Organization (IMO) was then known, should adopt facilitation procedures along the lines of those already used by the International Civil Aviation Organization (ICAO).[1] IMCO established a group of experts to prepare a draft convention for the Conference on Facilitation of International Maritime Traffic, which was held in London from March 24 to April 9, 1965. In total, 57 states were represented by delegations,[2] with eleven states sending observers.[3] Moreover, more than 16 international organizations sent observers.[4]

The Convention consisted of 16 articles which, generally, outlined the willingness of the contracting parties to co-operate in facilitating matters related to ship arrival, stay and departure[5] and in promoting documentary uniformity.[6] Sample forms and guidelines were annexed

---

1   Erler, Jochen, "The New Convention on Facilitation of International Maritime Traffic" (1967), 13 McGill Law J. 323.

2   IMCO, *International Conference on Facilitation of Maritime Travel and Transport, 1965* (1968), p. 1.

3   *Ibid.*

4   *Ibid.* at 1, 3.

5   Art. II(1).

6   Art. III.

to the Convention.[7] The Convention entered into force on March 5, 1967.[8]

Unfortunately, the cumbersome amendment process in article VII of the Convention "frustrated" efforts to bring the Convention in line with developing shipping practices.[9] As a result, two more conferences were convened by IMO in London. The second conference produced appropriate amendments which resulted in easier amendment procedures for the Annex. These amendments to article 7 have been effective since July 31, 1978.[10]

The Convention has been ratified or acceded to by more than 49 states including Canada, the United Kingdom, the U.S.S.R. and the United States. Moreover, while there are on-going efforts to produce uniform documentation at IMO, other efforts were also underway to simplify trade documentation outside of the maritime arena.

In the 1960's many industries were very concerned about the amount of paper required for an international trade transaction. The phenomenon was noted world-wide. The Economic Council for Europe was recommending closer linkages for their member countries. Sweden had made a presentation to the ECE in 1960 that one of the key problems to be resolved in making a more united Europe was the elimination of the many different customs documents used between the countries and the establishment of a uniform standard. The Swedes recommended that an ECE committee be formed to deal with this matter and other approaches that would facilitate trade. The current extensive studies into trade documentation processing began with the establishment of this committee.

In time, the ECE trade facilitation committee recognized that the most effective solution to the documentary simplification problem would need a world-wide effort. United Nations experts were assisting the ECE committee from its earliest days. By 1968, formal UN involvement was common, and in 1972, with the formation of the UN/ECE Working Party on Trade Facilitation, the United Nations offices in Geneva became the key location for analysis of the problems involved with processing trade documents. It continues in this role today, though many of the technical details have moved to formal standardization committees. Representatives of other interested groups (not just countries) attend and participate in the meetings. For example, the United Nations Legal Advisory Group (UNCITRAL) sends representatives to

---

7   See Annex B, reproduced in IMCO, *supra* note 2, at pp. 28-57.
8   Singh, Nagedra, *International Maritime Law Conventions: (Vol. 4) Maritime Law* (1983), p. 3116.
9   *Ibid.*
10   *Ibid.*

the meetings to comment on various legal issues. Representatives from international standards organizations such as the I.S.O. and the C.C.I.T.T. also attend.

Many of the countries studying trade facilitation at the United Nations created "national" facilitation organizations to act as the focal point for studying the document-simplification problem within a country. Most countries modelled their approach on the SITPRO (Simplification in Trade Procedures) organization established in Britain in 1968. The mandate of the national facilitation groups was to examine ways and means to reduce and simplify the number of paper documents required for a trade transaction, and to harmonize recommended solutions with other international organizations with the objective of producing world-wide improvements in trade documentation processing. In Canada, the national facilitation group was called COSTPRO (The Canadian Organization for the Simplification of Trade Procedures). It was formed in Canada in 1972 as the result of meetings of the Shippers Council of Canada, the Canadian Export Association and the Government of Canada.

The international community, through the national organizations, tackled the problems by first questioning the need for various forms and the need for the many data elements (*i.e.,* items of information) required on a form. There was a recognition that only certain information items were essential to the trade transaction and to governments. As a result of much conversation and negotiation, many of the trade forms have been withdrawn or combined with other forms. As an example, when Canada first became involved in studying the trade simplification problem, some 30-35 forms were required for an international trade transaction with Europe. Today, only eight to ten forms are necessary. Over 135 data elements had been specified. Today, only 80 (and more typically 50-60) are necessary.

This reduction in the requirements for information on forms has meant significant savings to the trading community. It is estimated that, in Canada, over one billion dollars in administrative costs have been eliminated through this concerted international effort to minimize the paper requirements.

Along with this effort to eliminate paper, it was evident that some paper would still remain. Much effort was spent on examining ways and means of processing the remaining paper to minimize the work effort in filling in the required forms. The result has been a set of common approaches and standards for international trade transactions that fall into three categories.

First, there is the definition of each of the data elements themselves. A common understanding of the meaning of various trade terms such as "consignee", "shipping date", etc. has been developed for over 350 trade terms. They are published in a United Nations Trade Data Elements Directory. These "dictionary definitions" have been approved by the 40 national facilitation organizations now active and are promoted by these groups within their countries. The recommendations of the national facilitation groups have often been formally adopted by officials in the countries. In Canada, the Trade Data Elements Directory has been published by both the Canadian General Standards Board and COSTPRO. It is expected that, through a voting process, Canadian industry will adopt the definitions as a Canadian standard.

The second standard relates to the way in which the necessary information is organized on a trade form. The layout of the information follows a standard approach developed by the UN/ECE Working Party. It is called the UN/ECE Layout Key. In this approach, the information is divided into four main groups – four areas on the form. The upper left of the form contains consignee information; the upper right contains shipping information; the central area is reserved for the description of the goods being shipped; and the lower portion of the form is set aside as a "free" area which allows many of the different forms to be made nearly identical, yet allow for local variations within a country or a company. With this standard, "aligned" forms can be easily created.

Aligned forms have the same information located in the same location on each form. Carbon "snap-sets" of the forms used for shipping an order can then be typed once, eliminating the need for multiple typing. Snap-sets, and the COSTPRO developed "overlay" system, are one-run methods that will save about 50 per cent of the time to type the documents using manual typewriters.

By using computers (and noting that most companies tend to ship to the same company, using the same carriers and generally the same items), it is possible to prestore the common information required in each shipment and to have the computer type this information quickly and accurately on a form. The only new information is usually the date, a new quantity and perhaps a price change. Adding a computer (or word processor) for typing the snap-sets, or overlays, will achieve a further 35 per cent time saving in the day-by-day operation.

In Canada, COSTPRO produced the Canadian Trade Document Alignment System (the CTDAS), based on this UN/ECE Layout Key. This was adopted by the Canadian General Standards Board in December 1982 as a Canadian standard. The CTDAS is promoted by COSTPRO and schools in Canada as an effective way of producing trade documents. The same system is incorporated into research prototype software developed by COSTPRO, which has been verified by our member companies.

Inherent in the location co-ordinates is the "size" (*i.e.,* how many characters are required to contain the information related to the data element) of the data element. For example, the consignee information is specified to be 35 characters by 5 lines long. This means that normally no more than 175 characters are required to specify a consignee. This information is very useful for calculating the amount of computer storage needed for information on a form and also the time needed to electronically transmit a form. The time is useful to know, since most communications carriers charge for data transmission by some measure of the number of characters transmitted.

The third area of standardization is just now reaching finalization. It deals with the electronic transmission of the trade data elements through computer/communications networks. Once again, the UN/ECE Working Party has been the focal point for the research in this area. In Canada, COSTPRO has been deeply involved with researching this area as well as the use of computers for processing the forms. Three proposed standards for describing trade information for electronic messages are now being closely analyzed by world organizations concerned with trade simplification. The three message formats are:

1. the Trade Data Interchange (TDI) Standard, developed initially in Britain, and adopted by the UN/ECE as their first general standard;
2. the Electronic Data Interchange (EDI) Standard, developed in the United States, (with some minor modifications) adopted by the American National Standards Institute (ANSI) as the Business Data Interchange (BDI) and given the designation "X.12"; and
3. a recent proposal by the French government called the Commercial File Exchange (the CFE).

For the exchange of commercial information electronically, the key decision is the "size" of the data element, which has been defined in the deliberations of the UN/ECE Working Party. The remaining effort has been devoted to determining how to describe (electronically) what data element is being transmitted, when a computer would know that the data element had been transmitted, and how to define the beginning and end of the form itself. A conceptual explanation of the process is given below.

The face of documentation has changed. The emphasis is on standards, a common set of definitions, a common way of displaying the information on a form and a common technique for allowing computers to move the information electronically between companies and countries. The balance of this paper will present the current status of the use of computers in the carriage of goods, and describe some of the difficulties for legal authorities in dealing with the world of paperless information flow.

3. THE GROWING USE OF ELECTRONIC MESSAGES

Internationally, many large shipping companies, and airlines in particular, have tested and installed very effective computer-based systems for the electronic transmission of trade documents. TELEX is still the dominant intercompany electronic mail system, with facsimile machines also being used extensively. However, as more computer-to-computer interchanges are tested, the need for systems that can interconnect directly is growing.

The key problem administratively with TELEX and facsimile is the need for human intervention in either reading the information sent or in re-entering the information into another system. When shipments may average 100 a day, each requiring a set of documents, computer generation of the information is being used to save time and improve the accuracy of the documents produced. Re-entering this information into a TELEX, or using a separate machine (facsimile) to move the information, offsets the time saving and can lead to transcription errors. However, the production of facsimile documents from an original and the use of TELEX present fewer legal problems. Indeed, the use of TELEX has resulted in legal cases that have strengthened its application, because of the creation of paper documents at each end that can be verified and authenticated. The ability of third parties to produce the TELEX is sometimes cited in legal cases as an authentication of the message.

Direct computer-to-computer message interchange is seen by the technical operators of systems as promising even more savings. By not creating even the document, savings on paper costs, inventory storage and labour are often cited by information analysts in cost-justifying this solution. If the customer enters the data and electronically mails it as well, then even further labour costs are saved. As mentioned earlier, if all this activity takes place *within* the same company, very effective systems can be installed, with significant cost savings. By controlling the network within a company, the legal aspects can be taken into account.

Though many firms are using automation to handle much of their administrative work within the confines of the company and for generating internal forms (packing slips, acknowledgements, etc.), it is only in the past year that tests of the technology for intercompany and international exchange or trade information have become significant. Because some of the forms transmitted (such as purchase orders, bills of lading, etc.) have a legal or quasi-legal status, an understanding of the growing use of electronic message systems and how they work is necessary for legal authorities.

4. A TECHNICAL VIEW

To understand what happens when a message is sent electronically, an analogy of two fundamental components is useful. The message and the envelope carrying the message are common enough in the business world to be used as the main analogy. With electronic mail, the message consists of the composed words. The communications network constitutes the envelope.

Consider how one sets up a letter. A standard heading, is commonly used:

Mr. Smith,
1456 Somewhere,
Someplace, Canada,

Dear Mr. Smith,

This format is a protocol we all follow. It is placed in a standard position on the paper and is followed by the message. We normally terminate with one or two standard endings, "Yours truly" or "Yours sincerely", etc., and a signature. The ending and the signature can be called the "trailer". A key point to understand from a legal aspect is that the letter as composed usually has the signature added as an authentication mark unique to the sender. The receiver of the letter uses the signature to verify that the letter was indeed sent by the sender. It is also assumed that the signature is added after the letter is composed, and constitutes an integral part of the letter.

Once the letter is composed, we place it in an envelope. The envelope also contains a certain protocol. The name and address of the person to whom we are sending the letter go on the envelope. The name and address of the sender are usually placed in the upper left-hand corner. The reason for this return address is to allow the letter to be returned if it is undelivered for any reason. A stamp is placed on the envelope showing that it has been prepaid for delivery. The mail carrier normally adds its own "stamp" showing that the letter is in its system. This "stamp" generally includes a time of sending.

Electronic mail is composed on a word processor or a computer terminal. A "header" (usually the name of the person to whom we are sending the message) and a "trailer" (our name) surround the message. We then mail it electronically. The electronic network we use is the "envelope" for the message we wish to send.

In the electronic world, the main difference in the envelope is that the address of the receiver of the message is a phone number, as is the return address. These "addresses" are maintained by the communications carrier inside its network and are used to return the mail if it cannot be delivered, as well as to bill for the mail transmission after it is sent.

(This "after-sending-billing" does distinguish the two message-carrying groups. Another distinguishing character is that the mail carrier bills on weight, while the electronic carrier bills on time of usage of the network, or a function of the number of characters for data.) The communications carrier also includes the time of sending the message, much the same as the mail carrier.

Standards are needed for the electronic "envelope" in order for messages to be transmitted. ASCII codes; the type of plugs; transmission protocols such as the HDLC, SDLC, and X-25 designations: all fall into this category. These standards, for the purpose of this paper, can be grouped into a category called "the network protocol". For two systems to interconnect, their "network protocol" must be identical. There is still a lot of time spent connecting two data networks together, ensuring that the "baud" rate, parity and similar technical parameters are all compatible. This "network protocol" ensures that point A is connected correctly to point B so that a message can be sent.

If the message being sent is a set of words, designed to be read by a human at the other end, then usually no further protocols are necessary (other than ensuring that the message is in a language that can be understood by the receiver). In the case of trade documents however, a "trade message protocol" is essential. Often these messages are being sent from one computer to another, with no human intervention. The forms printed at both ends of the transaction must have the data printed in the correct location and with the correct information, since often the forms are read only after the shipment is under way. The *message* protocol is different from the *network* protocol.

Consider the form itself. Bills of lading, commercial invoices, export declarations, etc., all have standard clauses imprinted on them. The data required for all the forms consists of some 50 different elements. There is a duplication of about 35 of these elements on each form. Each element is in a "box" on a form, and each "box" has a heading. For example, one "box" will be labelled "Consignee", another "Date of Shipment", another "Port of Lading". Each one of these boxes can be considered to be a mini-letter. It has its own "heading" (*i.e.* – Consignee, Date of Shipment, etc.). The "trailer" will designate that all the information in that box has been sent. With this understanding, it should be evident why trade message protocols are being designed.

Since each form consists of about 35 "boxes", 35 mini-letters, each with its own "header" and a symbol stating that that was all the information in that mini-letter, must be transmitted if the form is to be correctly interpreted at the other end. As mentioned earlier, if one company prints the "Date of Shipment" in the upper left corner, while the other prints the "Date of Shipment" in the middle of the paper, the message must allow this to happen. The standard for transmission only requires that each party to the message agree on what the "header" means (the definition), how long the message is (its size) and what will determine that the message is complete. Once that is received, a program in the local computer can decide where to print the information. All the current proposed systems (TDI, EDI, and CFE) use this approach for setting up (formatting) the content of the trade documents.

A grouping of these mini-letters constitutes a form. Usually the protocols for trade messages contain another set of "headers" and "trailers" indicating what form is being transmitted. An electronic signature for the document is included in this portion of the protocol. If several documents are transmitted at the same time, "headers" are used to indicate which documents are being sent, and the redundant information between documents is only sent once.

5. ACTIVITIES ON THE CANADIAN SCENE

In the mid-seventies, Canada was extremely interested in digital communications. Major carriers such as Canadian Pacific and Air Canada were developing systems for tracking the goods carried and for electronically transmitting related information. Canada Customs installed and tested its CEPAC system for monitoring shipments at major ports. Many firms were experimenting with the production of forms for shipments using computers. The systems were internal to the companies.

One of COSTPRO's major research efforts from 1978 to 1982 was to examine the automation of the trade documentation process, in particular, the electronic mail aspects for intercompany mail. The legal issues were studied at the same time. It was evident that there would be a need for security about the data, and a special concern about the validity of an electronic signature was raised. Tests of message systems internal to a company were conducted with several members of COSTPRO in Ottawa, Toronto and Montreal. All are now using these approaches in their day-to-day operations. However, only one, Canadian Marconi, is testing its system for intercompany interaction. That has happened just in the past few months.

COSTPRO has tested both the Trade Data Interchange (TDI) Protocol, in trials with European organizations, and the Electronic Data Interchange (EDI) Protocol with companies interested in linking with trade systems in the United States. The experience allowed COSTPRO to transfer messages between the two different protocols, and to become a significant voice in the world community for developing a standard approach to the electronic transfer of trade documents. The President of COSTPRO is also Chairman of the Canadian Advisory Committee to the Internation Standards Organization (ISO) which deals with these protocols.

Though these tests were mainly research studies, COSTPRO, during the past 18 months, focussed its research on producing practical operational software for transfer to private industry. During April 1984, COSTPRO formally transferred, through a bidding process, the rights to several of these products to certain Canadian companies. One can expect to hear more about automation in trade documentation from these firms during the next few months. The members of COSTPRO have also decided that COSTPRO has completed the majority of its *raison d'être,* and voted on May 16, 1984 to dissolve the organization within a few months. Their reasoning was that the research results have been disseminated effectively, with many Canadian companies developing their own systems, based on the Canadian standards developed by COSTPRO. The Canadian Export Association has agreed to act as a focal point for any further industrial concerns in the area of trade facilitation, while the Department of External Affairs will maintain a liaison with the United Nations Working Group on Trade Facilitation.

Other firms in Canada, notably in the automotive, grocery and drug industries, are testing the EDI protocol for the transfer of information for the carriage of goods. Several of these groups are interfacing with similar companies in the United States to test the international linkages of the software. At the moment, some 10-15 Canadian companies are in pilot mode, while about 50 U.S. companies are experimenting with electronic mail for trade data. The numbers are expected to double within a year. Companies from the retail and warehousing sectors are expected to become interested in developing systems that can interconnect using a standard message format.

6.   ACTIVITIES ON THE INTERNATIONAL SCENE

In the United States, pilot trials of electronic interchange of trade documents are mainly with the grocery, automotive and warehousing industries. For example, a wholesaler such as Kraft Foods will be involved in trials with a retailer (*i.e.,* supermarket) such as Safeway. General Motors is testing the electronic mail with several of its suppliers. The EDI protocol is the common system being tested.

In Europe, an important trial is called the Mercador project. In this project, Vauxhall parts are being shipped from Europe to Britain. The documentation flow is carried out through electronic networks that link the motor plants in Belgium and Britain with customs authorities in both countries, as well as shippers. Tentative links to other plants in Holland and Germany are being planned. The trial is just now reaching operational status. The objective is to test the TDI protocol in a multi-company, multi-agency network system. SITPRO in England is a key group in this trial.

France is currently planning trials of the CFE protocol with companies located in Africa and France. In the Nordic countries, a network called the DEDIST system has been planned to test message protocols amongst different companies and computer systems.

In Europe, SITPRO has developed software for handling trade documents and electronic messaging. SITPRO offers its software for sale to companies throughout the world. Their SPEX and INTERBRIDGE systems support SITPRO's version of aligned documents and the TDI protocol, respectively. SIMPROFRANCE is strongly promoting the use of the CFE system, while in the United States, the Trade Data Coordinating Committee, (the developers of EDI) are a dominant influence in EDI software, offering packages for sale. Several small firms (two in the United States, two in Canada, and manufacturers in the United Kingdom) are now offering software systems for use by companies in handling trade documents in North America. Some Canadian service bureaux are also offering electronic trade protocols for handling trade messages. World-wide about 80 to 100 organizations are testing intercompany trade document interchange.

7. INTERCOMPANY AND INTERNATIONAL TRADE DOCUMENT INTERCHANGE TRENDS

Most large firms are testing intercompany interchange with their suppliers, and are working closely with government agencies to minimize the regulatory paperwork. Wholesalers will work with major carriers and brokers, interacting with each other in pilot trials for the electronic transmission of trade information. Several government agencies are also willing to be involved in pilot trials of transferring information. Most of these trials are operating without the controls usually associated with legal requirements. However, the legal issues are often understood. The reasons for the trials are mainly technical at this time. Testing the protocols and searching for easier ways to interconnect the systems automatically, while maintaining a high level of reliability and security, are dominant objectives of most of the tests.

By working closely with only one or two suppliers, companies usually assume that any legal problems can be addressed in the contracts setting out the trial. Often clauses are incorporated in such contracts covering the perceived issues. But as the trials become more operational and involve different participants, particularly those in another country, the need to address the legal complexities will be even stronger.

With the interest in such interchange being shown by companies and countries, several communications network companies are offering services that promise to handle the interchange of trade information on goods. General Electric's world-wide network is being tested by some of the automotive aftermarket industries, while TYMSHARE (in Canada and the United States) is the test vehicle for the warehouse industry. These service bureaux networks are usually offering a proprietary software protocol for document interchange.

Many large companies are also examining how micro-based systems can be used to process their documents in a decentralized mode, while using their data bases stored on larger systems as central files for access to information required on the documents. With the growing use of micro-computers by small businesses for the handling of business forms, the economic advantage evident to the small shipper from the electronic linking of trade transaction document-handling are becoming clearer. Many firms will adopt these systems in order to remain competitive with the bigger firms, but will only be able to demonstrate such competitiveness by being able to intercommunicate with similar firms internationally.

The technical solution for a global interconnection is a standard method of communicating trade messages between the companies. This requires a common understanding of the components of a trade message, and international agreement on how to generate, interpret and transmit these messages. Once this standard is agreed upon, trade messages can be communicated either through special hardware devices incorporating the standard, or with software capable of running on different hardware systems.

The efforts of the UN/ECE Working Party on Trade Facilitation, and the international standards organizations are now focussed on this problem. The various standards are being tested in several trials to study their effectiveness and ease of use. In the opinion of COSTPRO, it is expected that one or two standards will dominate within three to six years. In that same time-frame, the interconnecting parties will grow exponentially. From the 10-20 companies testing intercompany systems two years ago to the nearly 100 now testing the concept, it is anticipated that close to 500 firms will be testing the intercompany electronic interchange of trade documents by 1987. These companies will more clearly recognize the legal problems raised. The legal issues will need to be resolved soon.

WHEN BITS REPLACE BILLS, WHAT SHALL THE LAW BYTE ON? LEGAL CONSEQUENCES OF AUTOMATING CARRIAGE DOCUMENTATION

*Hugh M. Kindred**

1. Introduction: Automating Bills of Lading
2. Receipts for Goods
3. Contracts of Carriage
4. Documents of Title
5. Conclusion

1. INTRODUCTION: AUTOMATING BILLS OF LADING

Few of us are yet comfortable with the bits, bytes and binary theory underlying the computer revolution of this information age. Therefore it may be helpful to rephrase the topic in more familiar maritime language. This paper is an attempt to map the legal sunkers for the new generation of merchant adventurers on the sea of automation.

This is a time of upheaval in the procedures of international trade and transport. Though the technological capacity of computers for overseas trade has been achieved, universally compatible and acceptable systems for automating individual transactions have yet to be adopted operationally. A number of shipping companies, especially in the North Atlantic container service, have had fully automated systems for their own internal use for several years. None have yet instituted external electronic connections with their cargo-owning clients, though trial projects are in progress.[1] It is the legal problems resulting from this

---

*Professor of Law, Dalhousie University. Professor Kindred is co-chairman of the Carriage Documentation Committee of the Canadian Maritime Law Association, and lecturer in the carriage of goods by sea.

1   *E.g.,* the Mercator Project in Europe.

critical step into inter-corporate communication which will be discussed here.

Some of the solutions to the legal problems which will be raised may, in the end, depend upon the particular formats and protocols of the computer systems employed. However, a warning is in order. Judging by the extraordinary speed of development and deployment of computers of late,[2] the time available to perceive and prevent consequent legal problems is short indeed.

International trade and transport are typically conducted by means of documentary transactions. The documents are the means to cement the transaction. They constitute the medium by which commercial information and legal rights are transmitted. The paper medium is not important to the transacting parties, indeed it is almost worthless. It is the transmitted commercial messages that are significant and frequently very valuable. Even so, the paper medium does influence the message it carries. The documentary character of international trade and transport does affect their execution.

Electronic processing, as Dr. Ron Elliott's paper has described it for us,[3] is obviously a very different medium from paper. The substitution of electronic data processing (EDP) in the traditional documentary transaction will cause many changes in the conduct of international trade and transport. This discussion will address only those changes which appear to create issues of legal concern. Even so, little more than an exploration of the problems to be expected will be presented here.

Canadian law has been highly developed to regulate documentary transactions. The general rules of private law, the *Criminal Code,* evidence and procedure are the basic ingredients of this system of regulation. To them have been added special rules, both judicial and statutory in origin, to support the conduct of trade. Most of this body of laws directly affects the information exchanged between the trading parties, their agents and carriers, regardless of the medium of its transmittal. But not infrequently these laws achieve their purpose indirectly, by controlling the use of the documentary medium. As a result it is necessary to review Canadian law for its obstacles to the use of the new medium of EDP in trade and transport as well as for its adequacy to support the consummation of automated transactions.

This review will be conducted for the carriage of goods by sea in the context of the law governing bills of lading. It is trite knowledge that a bill of lading has a three-fold character. It acts as a receipt for the goods being transported, as evidence of the contract for their carriage and as a

---

2   See Dr. Elliott's remarks in the previous paper, "The Changing Face of Documentation in the Carriage of Goods".

3   *Ibid.*

document of title to them. In combining all these functions, the bill of lading appears to throw up for consideration the widest range of legal problems of automation compared to any of the other forms of ocean transportation, such as charterparties and sea waybills. It will therefore be assumed that a discussion on the computerization of each of these three characteristics of a bill of lading in turn will serve to illustrate the kinds of legal concerns that EDP will bring to any and all contracts for the carriage of goods by sea.

2. RECEIPTS FOR GOODS

Regarding the bill of lading merely as a receipt is to consider its simplest attribute. A carrier, on taking charge of the goods as bailee, issues a written acknowledgement of receipt to the shipper, their bailor. This strikingly simple transaction consists of an exchange of goods for a piece of paper. Of course, the contents of the receipt have commercial significance, which will be discussued later. Here it should be pointed out that this kind of documentary procedure is so much a part of international trade and transport that an account of the legal problems consequent on the introduction of EDP in its place would be incomprehensible without first considering the functions performed by the paper that carries the commercial purposes into reality.

As a medium of transmittal, the paper document does not determine what commercial information may be carried by it. The contents of the receipt may be any sort of carriage data. However, paper documents have distinct characteristics which do control how they themselves may be handled. Perhaps inevitably, the mode of transferring a document – that is physical delivery – does influence the effects of its contents. For instance, the delivery of goods by the carrier is dependent on the surrender of the bill of lading.

Although the traditional convenience of paper is being overtaken by electronic processing, the change is merely in the medium and so should not, in principle, affect the messages carried. Indeed, if computers could not transfer trade data at least as well as paper documents do, there would be no reason to make the change in the message carrier. However, EDP obviously involves a very different mode of message transmittal from documentary routines. Hence, differences may also be expected in the consequences EDP will have on the effects of its messages. To revert to the previous example of surrender of the bill of lading, the delivery of goods cannot be made to depend upon the physical presentation of a whole computer system.

The immediate task is to identify those characteristics of documents like bills of lading which are given commercial or legal significance. Other characteristics of the medium are of no consequence, since the paper itself is virtually valueless and its data content is all that matters. The resulting information will draw attention to the medium-dependent incidents of carriage for which EDP must account, in addition to its message-carrying capacity.

First, information in a document is personal to its keeper. Thus transfer of the document, in order to transmit the information, results in a loss to the transferor as well as an accretion to the transferee. It is common to keep a copy of the document so that knowledge of its contents is retained, but the original cannot be held if the information is to be transmitted by it. The physical difference between original and copied documents is perhaps much less than it used to be, but is still apparent, especially where a signature is also appended.

Secondly, information on paper acts as a record. The medium has to be destroyed in order to erase the information. A document provides a kind of permanency and specific identity to its contents which is not easily altered or forged without being apparent.

Shipping practice and law have both made significant use of these distinctions.[4] One example is the issuance of a received-for-shipment bill when goods are taken in charge of a freight terminal or a carrier. This receipt is a convenient and essential record of the goods in the hands of the owner who has parted with their custody. Another example is the statements about the quantity and condition of goods made by a carrier when he receives them on board by "clausing" the shipped bill of lading. These statements constitute amendments of the record in the hands of the cargo owner. A further example, already mentioned, is the practice of surrendering the bill of lading against receipt of the goods themselves.

The physical delivery of the document also conveniently establishes the moment of transmittal of the data it contains. The timing of this event may be important in determining what merchants may be expected or relied upon to know. Thus the giving of a notice of readiness by the carrier will fix when the time allowed to the cargo owner for loading or discharging his goods will begin. The transfer of the bill of lading may signify the moment when the ownership and title to the goods shift from the shipper to the consignee.

EDP has to take account of all these features of bills of lading as receipts, though it need not duplicate them in a literal fashion. Indeed, the unique possession or the physical transfer of an original record of goods in transit is quite contradictory to the world of computer commu-

---

4   Some of these are discussed in K. Gronfors, "The Legal Aspects and Practical Implications of Non-Documentary (Paperless) Cargo Movements", in NORDIPRO, *Legal Acceptance of International Trade Data Transmitted by Electronic Means* (Oslo, 1983), p. 156.

nication that reduces everything to electronic impulses. Yet, by all accounts, computers are marvelously adaptable to creating, keeping and transferring all kinds of records, so there is little doubt they can cope with the process of acknowledging bailment of the goods to a carrier, which the bill of lading currently performs.

Such problems as may be expected in automating the receipt functions of a bill of lading are more likely to arise from impediments in the law rather than any limitation of EDP.

Since shipping data are frequently extremely valuable, much Canadian law has developed about them. However, the law's attempts to govern the contents of carriage documents have often been effected through the medium of their transmittal. Since paper documents were universally and exclusively used by merchants and shipowners, it is not surprising that the law should refer to them explicitly. But the advent of EDP now makes this operation of law outmoded, even though its regulatory objectives are in no way diminished.

Use of EDP will run afoul of any legal requirements connected with paper. Hence, it is necessary to canvas our statute books for all the instances when paper documents are expressly or impliedly required in ocean transportation. The statutory references to paper are quite varied. The law may require written notice (*e.g.,* of a carrier's lien under the *Canada Shipping Act*[5]) or it may refer explicitly to a document (*e.g.,* a bill of lading in the *Bills of Lading Acts*[6]). This kind of explicit statutory restraint may be overcome by a deeming amendment. For instance, to the *Bill of Lading Acts* a section might be added stating:

> A bill of lading is deemed to include an electronic or computer generated message or series of messages which, by the custom of merchants, is treated in a manner analogous to the manner in which a bill of lading is treated.[7]

At best, this suggestion is a temporary reprieve rather than a remedy for a problem that is widespread. Use has been made of a library computer in a different mode, *i.e.,* as an information retrieval system, to reveal that references to bills of lading occur in 44 different federal statutes alone.

Sometimes law is more indirect. Thus, a statute may specify the contents of a shipping communication in such a way that it implies that a paper document is the means of its transmittal (*e.g.,* the information to be provided in a bill of lading under the *Carriage of Goods by Water Act*).[8] Legal requirements for an "original" or a "signed" copy of a

---

5   R.S.C. 1970, c. S-9, s. 667.
6   *E.g.,* R.S.C. 1970, c. B-6; R.S.N.S. 1967, c. 22.
7   Suggested by Adam Roberts, LL.B., in an unpublished paper.
8   R.S.C. 1970, c. C-15.

carriage transaction also imply the use of a paper document. These are some examples of the inadvertent statutory obstacles to EDP in Canada. Until they are all identified and removed they will block the development of a completely paperless, fully electronically-processed system of ocean transport.

3. CONTRACTS OF CARRIAGE

Bills of lading come in long forms and short forms. The long forms carry a great many fine-print conditions on their reverse sides which are supposed to represent the terms of the carriage contract. The short forms achieve the same purpose by incorporation clauses referring to the carrier's standard conditions in its long forms or on file in its offices. Storing and accessing these contractual terms by electronic means is little different from the record-keeping aspects of automated receipts. In fact, EDP may offer easier access than printed forms to the shipping companies' conditions of carriage, since they may be held on line and continually available. The legal problems that present themselves when the contract of carriage is recorded in this way are concerned with its authentication and its proof. While a bill of lading signed by the carrier is accepted as good evidence of a contract of carriage, will an electronic arrangement command similar respect at law?

Carriage documents are customarily authenticated by autograph. Signatures perform several important functions in shipping,[9] varying according to the purpose of the documents on which they are placed. A signature is an acknowledgement of authorship of a document.[10] It assigns an origin to the communication and a personal responsibility for its preparation and contents. A business letter is a typical example. A signature may also signify purposeful intent in making or approving a document.[11] It distinguishes, for example, cargo-data doodles from offers of shipping space and freight rates, and offers from carriage contracts. Furthermore, a signature may be relied upon as certifying the accuracy of the contents of the document. Thus the carrier's signature on a bill of lading will be treated as his acknowledgement that the goods

---

9   Re Henricksen, "Signature and Evidence in the International Trade and Transport Society Without Documents", and B.S. Wheble, "The Legal Problems In the Use of Automated Data Processing in International Trade", in NORDIPRO, *Legal Acceptance of International Trade Data Transmitted by Electronic Means* (Oslo, 1983), at pp. 44 and 262 respectively.

10   "The essence of signature whether made by writing or stamp or print must be to authenticate or identify the contract by the party to be charged": *per* Boyd C., in *Nasmith Co. v. Alexander Brown Milling Co.* (1905), 9 O.L.R. 21 at 23 (Ch. D.).

11   *Ogilvie v. Foljambe* (1817), 3 Mer. 53, 36 E.R. 21 (Ch.); *Caton v. Caton* (1867), L.R. 2 H.L. 127.

described have been received by him, until the contrary is proved to be a fact.[12] Signatures to sworn documents obviously carry even greater certifying force.

All of these uses of signatures are intimately tied to the documentary processing of bills of lading. In some sense a signature is physically transferred with the document to which it is attached for the benefit of the recipient. It cannot be taken back or erased unless the document itself is returned or altered. To transmit a personal autograph on an original bill of lading is to give up some power or control over goods that cannot be recreated or recovered without the recipient's consent. Signatures personify the documents in the shipping paper routine.

The introduction of EDP must provide similar personalized consequences for automated carriage contracts. One civil law commentator, Professor Roger Henricksen,[13] has suggested that there are three characteristics of signatures which must be fulfilled by EDP. Signatures are personal, are associated with recognizable data and are created by a deliberate and distinct act. The trade literature on EDP[14] seems to suggest that "electronic signatures" may be attainable with as much security as handwritten autographs, though as fast as one expert claims an invincible system, another proceeds to break it.

The question consequently arises whether there are legal impediments to electronic signatures. This inquiry divides into three parts. First is a definitional issue as to what is meant by "signature" in the general law. Second is a quest into the particular forms of signature required by individual statutes. Third is a question of criminal responsibility for forged signatures.

Does Canadian law ascribe any particular or limitative meaning to a signature? The variety of styles in use, and apparently acceptable in law, does not suggest that form controls a signature's significance. Thus handwritten signatures may be replaced by rubber-stamped names, personal or corporate seals, perforations or embossings.[15] The common feature of all these more or less mechanical signatures is not the name or the writing, but the deliberate act of attaching a personal sign.[16] In any

---

12   Hague Rules, art. III(4), enacted by R.S.C. 1970, c. C-15, Sched.

13   *Supra* note 9.

14   Gronfors, *supra* note 4 and Henricksen, *supra* note 9.

15   "Today's business could not be conducted if stamped signatures were not recognized as legally binding. The affixing of a stamp conveys the intention to be bound by the document so executed just as effectively as the manual writing of a signature by hand": *per* Hallett J. in *Re United Canso Oil & Gas Ltd.* (1980), 41 N.S.R. (2d) 282 at 289, 12 B.L.R. 130, 76 A.P.R. 282 (T.D.). *Cf. Goodman v. J. Eban Ltd.,* [1954] 1 Q.B. 550, [1954] 1 All E.R. 763 (C.A.).

16   "Speaking generally, a signature is the writing, or otherwise affixing, a person's name, or a mark to represent his name, by himself or by his authority . . . with the

case, handwritten initials and autographs are frequently so illegible and undecipherable that discernable identity cannot be their decisive feature. Indeed, the illiterate may sign documents; their marks are enough.

If the common law is not particular about the form of signatures, then Henricksen seems equally applicable in Canada with regard to the three characteristics that electronic signatures must satisfy. In a sense, electronic authentication is only the addition of another, if somewhat more sophisticated, form of mechanical signature.[17] There is no obvious reason why law should reject electronic signatures, provided they can be satisfactorily proved.

However, the universal practice of committing signatures to paper and doing so by handwritten autograph has influenced law in the way it regulates some shipping transactions. Here again Canadian law sometimes employs the medium of paper on which the signature is placed to control its effect in the transaction. By prescribing the form of authentication for the carriage data being transferred in terms of documentary procedures, the law prevents substitution of EDP and electronic signatures. Examples include the right of a shipper to demand a bill of lading under the *Carriage of Goods by Water Act*,[18] and the process of endorsement of such a bill of lading under the *Bills of Lading Acts*.[19] These examples are all particular situations created by statute, and occur where there are also other controls respecting the use of paper documents. It is therefore necessary to search the commercial statutes, not only for instances when bills of lading and other paper procedures are mandated, but also when authentication by handwritten signature is expressly or impliedly required.[20] The statutes will have to be pruned of both limitations on the form of carriage communiqués before EDP can be made fully operational.

Finally, the criminal responsibility for misappropriated signatures may be mentioned. Misuse of computer systems is clearly a much larger issue than fraudulent authentication of electronic carriage contracts. In

---

intention of authenticating a document as being that of, or as binding on, the person whose name or mark is so written or affixed": *Stroud's Judicial Dictionary* (3d ed.), Vol. 4, quoted with approval in both cases in note 15, *supra* [see now (4th ed.), Vol. 5, p. 2547].

17   "A valid replacement for signature can be offered by computer systems, giving verifiable guarantees as to the identity of the parties; these could permit themselves to recognise messages exchanged by the system and to sign a written agreement to this effect": from E.C.E. Working Party on the Facilitation of International Trade Procedures, *Recommendation No. 14* (Geneva, 1979), para. 23.

18   Hague Rules, art. III(3), *supra* note 12.

19   *E.g.*, R.S.C. 1970, c. B-6, s. 2; R.S.N.S. 1967, c. 22, s. 1.

20   For instance, *Sale of Goods Acts* require signed contracts in certain circumstances: *e.g.*, R.S.N.S. 1967, c. 274, s. 6.

times of swelling concern about the growing volume of maritime fraud, it is appropriate that the problems of computer crime have already attracted the attention of the Federal Department of Justice. Amendments to the *Criminal Code* to modernize the definitions of "theft" and "fraud" have been tabled in Parliament.[21] The *Criminal Law Reform Bill, 1984* will also create new computer-related offences. As a memorandum from the Department upon the introduction of the Bill explains:

> Proposed amendments would include as an offence in the *Code,* the wilful destruction, alteration or interference with the lawful use of computer systems data. In addition, a proposed new section would make it an offence to use a computer system without authorization, with intent to alter, destroy or interfere with the lawful use of data; to obtain a computer system; or dishonestly and knowingly, without authorization, to obtain the services of a computer system.[22]

Supposing that we are prepared to adapt law to respect electronic signatures, attention must still be given to the question of proof of an automated carriage transaction. In the event of a difference of opinion between a cargo owner and a carrier, each contracting party will find it necessary to establish objectively what has been done or agreed between them. Authentication may serve the purpose of verifying each item of carriage data that passed between the parties when it is produced. It does not help to assemble the record of their transaction. If the parties cannot settle their differences by further agreement, they will likely seek legal protection of their interests. Since the courts will normally enforce the contractual intention of the parties,[23] there has to be proof of their carriage agreement.

While a bill of lading issued by a carrier is readily accepted as sufficient evidence of the existence and contents of a contract of carriage, until the cargo owner demonstrates otherwise, there are plenty of reasons to be concerned about how an electronically made and recorded agreement may be proved. Part of the difficulty stems from the fact that computer records and communications are only machine readable. Though printouts in human readable form may be had, they may be viewed at best as copies, not originals. It is equally possible that the computer's output is the result of processing stored data into completely different material.[24] There are three dimensions to the problem of legal

---

21   Bill C-19, 1984. The Bill has since died on the order paper with the dissolution of Parliament.
22   February 7, 1984, at p. 10.
23   See *e.g., Fridman, The Law of Contract in Canada* (1976), pp. 33-45.
24   C. Tapper, "Evidence From Computers" (1974), 8 Ga. L.R. 562 at 565-566. As to when printouts may be treated as original records, see *R. v. Cordell* (1983), 39 A.R. 281 (Alta. C.A.).

proof of an electronically-processed carriage contract. They go to discovery, admissibility and credibility of carriage data. Each shall be outlined in turn.

Procedural rules of discovery are designed to establish the facts and issues between the disputing parties. Often the facts necessary to the proof of one party's case are in the possession of the other litigant or some third party. By the discovery procedures, the relevant information may be elicited for use in achieving a settlement or in the court at trial.

Canadian procedures for the discovery of facts are some of the most open. They vary on significant details from province to province, but, even so, none are obviously directed to the discovery of computer data. The principal methods are the disclosure of documents and the oral or written examination of persons involved in the matter in dispute.[25] In carriage transactions, documents play such a significant part that their full disclosure to each side is essential. When EDP is substituted for the documents, discovery of the shipping data will be no less important and necessary. It cannot be assumed that all parties will have authorized access to all relevant data just because they may be linked electronically.

Since the present discovery rules are partly couched in terms of documents, there is immediate uncertainty as to whether they are applicable to electronic carriage data at all. "Documents" are not usually defined exclusively,[26] and so may perhaps include information recorded or stored by any device. Further, discovery is commonly limited to those documents in a person's possession,[27] which is hardly an appropriate referent to EDP. The other mode of discovery by oral or written examination may provide an alternative way to obtain relevant shipping data through requests directed to computer operators. However the rules in many jurisdictions restrict this method when they state that only the parties to the litigation may be examined,[28] except perhaps where they also require a party under examination to obtain and produce related information from others.[29] There will evidently be a variety of such questions about the suitability of discovery procedures to elicit relevant carriage data from computer systems. The appropriate solutions may turn out to require amendment of our discovery rules.

While the discovery of all relevant shipping data is an essential procedure towards the resolution of a carriage dispute, the information obtained may only be used in accordance with the law of evidence. So much experience has been had with business records in the form of

---

25 A.J. Meagher and R.A. Meagher, *Civil Procedure Simplified* (1983), c. 5.
26 *Ibid.* at 147.
27 *Ibid.* at 151.
28 *Ibid.* at 163.
29 *Ibid.* at 165.

paper documents that a well-developed set of special rules about their admissibility in evidence has been achieved in Canada.[30] The introduction of EDP as a means of keeping carriage records, as well as a method of transmitting cargo information, raises anew the issue of admissibility as a matter of principle. The computer material, which will be sought to be put in evidence, includes the data files as well as the hard-copy printouts. The data bank in the computer system will be wanted as proof of its contents but obviously will have to be transcribed into a humanly perceptible form before it can be presented. Will the law accept such machine-readable material? Computer printouts may be offered as proof of their contents or as proof of the identity of a party to the carriage contract. How will the law regard such products of EDP?

In principle, Canadian law admits direct evidence.[31] That means there usually has to be a human witness who can give a first-hand account of it. With computer evidence, that is hardly possible. Fortunately, this judicial rule against hearsay is subject to a great many exceptions, including one elaborated by statute to admit business records. Thus at present, trade and transport documents are admissible according to these statutory rules.[32]

If computer data files and printouts can be regarded as documents by analogy, then they may be admissible evidence by statute. The prospect has to be investigated for each provincial jurisdiction, but there are already indications that the federal statute can be stretched to cover computer evidence.

Section 30 of the *Canada Evidence Act*[33] makes business records admissible where oral evidence of the same matter would be admissible. If the record is in a form that is unintelligible, a transcript of it, sworn to by the maker, is admissible in its place. The statute defines a "record" to include any "tape or other thing on or in which information is written, recorded, stored or reproduced."[34] Such a definition appears to be broad enough to include all the current forms of computer memories. Though they are incomprehensible as such, a transcription in the form of a printout should be acceptable in their place. At least two appeal courts have been prepared to admit computer records under this section when

---

30 J. Sopinka and S.N. Lederman, *The Law of Evidence in Civil Cases* (1974), c. 5.
31 *Ibid.* at 31 and 39.
32 The applicability of the business records exception to EDP was suggested by F. Constantine, LL.B., in an unpublished paper. There may also be an independent basis for the admission of computer data as real evidence. The approach is not discussed here, but see J.C. Smith, "The Admissibility of Statements by Computers", [1981] Crim. L.R. 387.
33 R.S.C. 1970, c. E-10.
34 *Ibid.*, s. 30(12).

handling criminal cases.[35] However, the statute is not well designed to facilitate computer evidence, as both these courts and various Law Reform Commissions have noted.

No doubt these attempts to present computer data under the existing rules of evidence will be overtaken in due course by statutory reforms to them.[36] Following reviews of the entire law of evidence by both the Ontario and the Canada Law Reform Commissions, the Uniform Law Conference of Canada adopted a set of new uniform rules.[37] They were introduced in the Senate in November 1982,[38] but have since been allowed to languish in the Commons. These rules make explicit reference to computer evidence for the first time in Canada. Some short extracts are quoted here:

> 153.(1) A business record is admissible whether or not any statement contained in it is hearsay or a statement of opinion, subject, in the case of opinion, to proof that the opinion was given in the usual and ordinary course of business.
>
> 131. Subject to this Act, the original is required in order to prove the contents of a record.
>
> 130. "original" means . . . (c) in relation to stored or processed data or information, any printout or intelligible output that reflects accurately the data or information or is the product of a system that does so;

Such a definition of "original" may strain the English language, but it clearly covers electronic processing of carriage contracts and admits shipping-data printouts as evidence.

A final obstacle to the admissibility of computerized shipping data may arise from the recurrent penchant of Canadian law to regulate carriage contracts through the medium of paper by which they have traditionally been conducted. There are occasions in other statutes when proof is required to be made by production of the original document. Thus under the *Bills of Lading Acts,* the bill of lading, when held by the consignee, may be presented as conclusive proof of the shipment of the goods described therein.[39] This statutory presumption is a distinct advantage to consignees of goods because it is irrebuttable, and so will not readily be given up. Consequently, the translation to EDP in carriage transactions will be hindered unless these legislated modes of documen-

---

35   *R. v. Vanlerberghe* (1976), 6 C.R. (3d) 222 (B.C. C.A.); *R. v. McMullen* (1979), 25 O.R. (2d) 301, 47 C.C.C. (2d) 499, 100 D.L.R. (3d) 671 (Ont. C.A.).

36   As has already taken place in the United Kingdom: see *The Civil Evidence Act,* (1968) (Eng.), c. 64, s. 5; and in South Australia, see *The Evidence Act Amendment Act,* 1972.

37   See the *Report of the Federal/Provincial Task Force on Uniform Rules of Evidence* (1982).

38   Bill S-33, now lapsed with the dissolution of Parliament.

39   *E.g.,* R.S.C. 1970, c. B-6, s. 4; R.S.N.S. 1967, c. 22, s. 3.

tary proof are also discovered and transcribed to computer-friendly standards.

Turning from the issues of admissibility of automated carriage data, attention must be given to the reliability of such evidence. When paper documents are produced in evidence, there are recognized ways to determine whether their contents are credible.[40] If computer records are introduced, what probative force should be ascribed to them? They should not be believed implicitly because the computer system which generated them is a highly technical set of equipment that may go wrong in a variety of different ways.[41] Many kinds of breakdowns in the hardware, faults in the software, mistakes in programming and human errors in the operation of a computer may occur. Some of these will lead to obvious failures in the system, such as shut-down, but others may create data files or may print out records that apparently are normal but in fact are incorrect. Further, inaccuracies may result from lack of security against deliberate human interference with the computer's operation.

Though these problems of accuracy, security and reliability of EDP are increasingly obvious and commonplace, it seems they have only been addressed seriously in Canadian law in the context of criminal responsibility, as mentioned earlier. Neither courts nor legislatures appear to have had nearly as much experience or forethought about the civil law aspects of computer reliability. Proving the security and the operational accuracy of the system of EDP has yet to be set on a regular basis in Canadian law.[42]

Section 30 of the *Canada Evidence Act,* mentioned above,[43] to admit computerized carriage data, does not ascribe any particular weight to such evidence. Section 29, dealing with the special case of bank records, declares them to be *prima facie* evidence. By contrast, section 30's silence requires the parties in litigation to contest the credibility of the computer data put in evidence. The *Uniform Evidence Bill*[44] implies the obligation more forcefully. Section 130(c) defines a computer printout as an acceptable original only when it is "shown to reflect accurately the data or information" stored or processed in the system.

---

40   Sopinka and Lederman, *supra* note 30.
41   See Tapper, *supra* note 24, at pp. 566-567; J.J. Roberts, "A Practitioner's Primer on Computer-Generated Evidence" (1974), 41 U. Chicago L.R. 254.
42   Compare the relatively sophisticated understanding in the United States to be found, *e.g.,* in *King v. State ex rel. Murdock Accept. Corp.,* 222 So. 2d 393 (Miss. S.C. 1969); *People v. Gauer,* 288 N.E. 2d 24 (Ill. C.A. 1972); *Grand Liquor Co. Inc. v. Dept. of Revenue,* 67 Ill. 2d 195 (S.C. 1977); and Roberts, *supra* note 41.
43   *Supra* note 33.
44   *Supra* note 38.

Given the extremely technical character of EDP, one might expect highly specialized and experienced experts to appear before the courts. Yet, in one of the two cases above referred to,[45] the computer evidence was accepted by the British Columbia court without comment on its reliability. In the other, the Ontario court made remarks that showed it was aware of the need to scrutinize the system of EDP which generated the evidence submitted. However, this decision has since been cast in doubt, at least in cases involving bank records.[46] It seems that a judicially acceptable pattern of inquiries into the reliability of the computer system is slow in developing as part of the proof of authentic carriage data.

4. DOCUMENTS OF TITLE

The commercial practice of treating a bill of lading as a transferable document of title adds quite a different legal dimension to its functions as a contract of carriage and as a receipt for bailed goods. Instead of looking to its contents as evidence of rights to the cargo being carried, the law grants rights in the bill of lading itself. It treats the shipping document on which carriage data is inscribed as representative of the goods so described.[47] In other words, the medium becomes the message; the paper takes on a symbolic role in place of the actual goods.

The negotiable function of certain shipping documents, such as bills of lading, is a great practical convenience because it allows a cargo owner to deal with goods merely by the possession of a piece of paper and without suffering the time, expense and difficulty of physically moving them about. Remember the three situations when cargo owners typically make use of this convenience.[48]

Reference has already been made to one concerning the delivery of goods. By means of a negotiable bill of lading the exporter of goods can control them even after he has put them in the hands of the carrier and so can prevent the foreign buyer receiving them until he authorizes their delivery. Typically the exporter wants this power of disposition of the goods in case he is not paid. He achieves this power by consigning the goods in the hands of the carrier to his own order and endorses the bill of lading in favour of the buyer only at the time the documents are accepted and the invoice is honoured by cash or credit, as previously agreed. The importer is satisfied because he does not have to pay unless and until the documents arrive and can be seen to be in good order. Upon endorse-

---

45 *Supra* note 35.
46 *R. v. Bell* (1982), 35 O.R. (2d) 164, 26 C.R. (3d) 336, 65 C.C.C. (2d) 377 (Ont. C.A.); but see also *R. v. Burns Foods* (1983), 42 A.R. 70, 74 C.P.R. (2d) 60 (Prov. Ct.).
47 Carver, *Carriage of Goods by Sea* (13th ed. R. Colinvaux, 1982), para. 1596.
48 Discussed *ibid.*, paras. 1596-1627.

ment and receipt of the bill of lading, the importer has an immediate right of access to the goods. The carrier must refrain from delivering them to anyone but the person who can produce and surrender the bill of lading properly endorsed in his favour.

Although the transfer of the trade documents is frequently conducted through the agency of banks, with or without the support of a letter of credit, their intervention does not displace the commercial function of synchronizing the transfer of the right to possession of the goods with payment of their price. Indeed, the services of the banks are intended to facilitate this essential exchange in each trade transaction.

Closely related to the documentary control on delivery of goods is the power to resell them. While the procedures just outlined afford access to the goods, they may also be used to transfer ownership too. Law imbues the holder of a negotiable bill of lading with rights to ownership, as well as to possession, of the described goods. Thus the endorsement and delivery of the bill of lading by the exporter will transfer ownership in the goods to the buyer. Hence, the buyer is clothed with the power to retransfer the goods himself. In short, instead of seeking delivery of the goods from the carrier, the buyer may resell them by further endorsing and delivering the bill of lading to another purchaser. Although this practice of forward selling of the goods has apparently decreased, it is still desired by cargo owners and remains very convenient in some trades.

The third situation in which an owner of goods may wish to employ his title by documents is as security for a loan. He may intend simply to raise cash against the goods afloat. Alternatively he may seek credit for the purchase price, less a discount, on cargo agreed to be sold but before payment is due. In either case, the financier, typically a bank, may take either or both of two kinds of documentary security in the goods. Their owner may simply pledge the document of title, such as the bill of lading, with the bank. This transaction involves the physical transfer of the bill of lading and no more. Since no endorsement is made on the document there is no transfer of ownership.

Canadian law treats the pledge of the title document as if it were a pledge of the goods[49] and thus the bank acquires possessory control of them. Possession of the bill of lading itself is enough to prevent anyone else dealing with it, for instance presenting it for delivery of the goods. In addition the pledge of the goods gives the bank a right to their possession too. Hence, the disposition of the goods may be restrained by the bank even though it does not own them.

If the bank desires greater security, it may demand full ownership.

---

49   *Factors Act, e.g.,* R.S.N.S. 1967, c. 97, s. 3.

In this situation the borrower will endorse the bill of lading to the order of the bank, which thereby becomes the consignee of the goods for the time being.

Banks apparently differ in their attitudes towards security for the financing they provide to support overseas trade. The typical form of bank financing is the documentary letter of credit. Some banks like to handle a letter of credit purely as a documentary transaction and will not take any interest in the goods for fear of being lumbered with them if the deal sours. Other banks take the opposite view. They demand full security in the goods so that they have some recourse to recoup their advance when the transaction breaks down.

In sum, these three functions of negotiability continue to play a very important, if less frequent, part in international trade and transport. The course of commerce will always demand that cargo owners be able to deal in goods while they are in transit. The ingenuity of the documentary transaction lies in the substitution of the document for the goods. Since the bill of lading is treated in law as if it is the goods, it can continue to be transferred in their stead until some owner wishes to take delivery of them. Moreover documents are transferred in exactly the same way as goods, though very much more conveniently. They are personally possessed until they are physically delivered. Thus there has not been a need to provide many special rules about possession, title, ownership or delivery in documentary sales.[50]

The use of EDP, however, introduces a new medium that not only differs in operation from the documentary procedures it replaces, but also departs from the mode of transfer of goods. Thus negotiability of title to goods seems likely to pose two kinds of problems in the translation to EDP. First, computer programmes must be developed to fulfil the functions of negotiability. Theoretical work has already been undertaken on this task, but apparently no programmes have been tested. Further, the couple of systems suggested in the literature[51] are not obviously commendable to cargo owners or carriers. In addition, any commercially acceptable form of negotiability by EDP will require reforms of law and changes in banking standards to facilitate its operation. Since EDP determines its own modes of transmittal, which are different from both paper and goods, existing Canadian law may well be inadequate. However, this matter is very dependent upon the mode of negotiability of title to goods in carriage that may be contrived elec-

---

50   There are some, of course, most notably the law of documentary credits.
51   Henricksen, *supra* note 9; and K.H. Reinskou, "Bills of Lading and Automated Data Processing", in NORDIPRO *Legal Acceptance of International Trade Data Transmitted by Electronic Means* (Oslo, 1983), p. 102.

tronically, so there is not much that can be said yet about the sort of legal reforms that would support its operation.

The significance of banking standards lies in the importance of banks in the financing of international trade and transport. Where a letter of credit is used to support a sale of goods, the participating bankers regularly demand that the performance of the transaction complies with the ICC's Uniform Customs and Practice for Documentary Credits.[52] These rules demand the issuance and transfer of a clean document of carriage.[53] In cases of ocean carriage that document at present is invariably a bill of lading. Banks will say that they deal in any documents agreed upon by the shipper and the foreign buyer. The choice belongs to the parties in making their agreement for sale, delivery and payment. However, the standard bank application form for a letter of credit only provides one choice-of-carriage document in the event of ocean transport, namely, the bill of lading.

This situation is about to change. In 1983 the ICC concluded a lengthy review of its rules on documentary credits. The revised rules,[54] which will come into effect in October 1984, will broaden the range of acceptable carriage documents in the sea mode. In addition to bills of lading, they include, for instance, sea waybills and combined transport documents.[55]

Regretably, even though the ICC rules have been amended to conform with the most modern paper routines, they will not honour a transaction by EDP.[56] Although the banks themselves may issue and pay credits by teletransmissions[57] and although the ICC rules permit the use of documents produced by automated or computerized systems,[58] still the cargo data required under a letter of credit must be made available on paper.[59]

It is apparently possible to execute an electronic equivalent to a letter of credit which fulfils all the documentary functions the ICC rules

---

52   H.C. Gutteridge and M. Megrah, *The Law of Bankers' Commercial Credits* (5th ed., 1976), p. 7; L. Sarna, *Letters of Credit* (1984), p. 45.

53   UCP, 1983 Revision, art. 34.

54   I.C.C. Publication No. 400.

55   *Ibid.,* arts. 25-27.

56   This is also the conclusion of Adam Roberts, LL.B., in an unpublished paper. See also P.J. Davidson, "The UCP and the Need For Amendment in the Light of Technological Advances", Conference Proceedings, Singapore (1982), p. 38.

57   UCP, 1983 Revision, *supra* note 54, art. 12.

58   *Ibid.,* art 22(c).

59   "In credit operations all parties concerned deal in documents, and not in goods, services and/or other performances to which the documents may relate": UCP, 1983 Revision, *supra* note 54, art. 4. This initial principle underlies all the subsequent detailed rules about credits.

demand.[60] However, bankers would have to handle these electronic credits outside the ICC rules. It seems more likely for the foreseeable future that EDP will not be acceptable for the execution of any transaction that is financed by banks through a letter of credit until the ICC rules are further altered. Given the recency and slowness of the review of the ICC rules, bankers are not expected to be quick to accommodate cargo owners wishing to trade by electronic means.

5. CONCLUSION

In concluding this discussion about the automation of the functions of a bill of lading, the above remarks are far from being an exclusive itemization of the legal problems that will arise with the automation of trade and transport. This commentary will now touch briefly upon two other areas in which legal difficulties may be anticipated.

The advent of computers has raised a new ground for well-founded concern about privacy. The capacity of computers to amass such great data banks, which are so easy to transfer, scares many people and governments at the prospect of unacceptable invasions of personal privacy and national security. The response has been a flurry of legislation.[61] Some of this activity strikes directly into the field of automating carriage transactions when enactments are passed to place controls on what are called trans-border data flows.

Canada has not yet taken any legislative action of this kind. Other states, including Great Britain and the Nordic countries, have begun to pass restrictive statutes[62] that may become an international trend. While there are very few controls on the movement of paper documents across national frontiers, considerable government interest has been aroused by the prospect of international transmissions of data electronically. Such legislation presents a new obstacle to foreign trade and transport. Broadly-worded enactments, intended to prevent the transfer of personally or governmentally sensitive information out of the country, may inadvertently limit the transmittal of perfectly ordinary cargo data such as is customarily required between exporters, importers and carriers. Any proposals for similar legislation in Canada must permit distinctions to be made between the claims to protection for sensitive and

---

60   Reinskou, *supra* note 51.

61   *E.g.,* the *Privacy Act,* R.S.B.C. 1979, c. 336; the *Freedom of Information Act,* S.N.S. 1977, c. 10; and the *Privacy Act,* S.C. 1980-81-82-83, c. 111 (Sched. II).

62   Discussed in R. Henricksen, "A Nordic Legal Analysis", in NORDIPRO, *Legal Acceptance of International Trade Data Transmitted by Electronic Means* (Oslo, 1983), p. 9. In May, the Minister for External Affairs announced that Canada would adhere to the voluntary Guidelines on the Protection of Privacy and Transborder Flow of Personal Data promulgated by the O.E.C.D.

confidential data without prejudicing the customary information transfers made in the ordinary course of overseas trade and transport.

The other area of renewed legal difficulty, which will be mentioned briefly, is very appropriate in light of the theme of conflicts of law involved in automating carriage transactions. Fresh twists to old problems are certain to arise, as well as entirely new ones. Here is one illustration.

A choice of law may depend in part upon the geographic association of significant connecting factors to a particular jurisdiction.[63] In carriage cases, the place of issuance of the bill of lading is relevant. When the paper document is replaced by EDP, who knows where the transaction takes place? The electronic impulses of the telecommunications systems used to transfer shipping data are not obviously locatable. The computer hardware in which the shipping data is stored and processed may be in several places, including a country foreign to both the shipper and his international trading partner. Forwarders, carriers, ships' agents, banks and other participants may execute their parts by adding, modifying or calling on this stored data from distant terminals in yet other locations. Even when the functions of a bill of lading may be replaced by EDP, we have still to consider how a resulting conflict of laws shall be resolved.

Hopefully, this paper has presented some idea of the magnitude of legal change which will be wrought in carriage matters through full-scale substitution of paper documents by EDP. In 1677, over 300 years ago, the *Statute of Frauds*[64] created legislative pressure to conduct commerce in writing. By 1787, the famous case of *Lickbarrow v. Mason*[65] had recognized the transfer of title to goods by endorsement and delivery of their bill of lading. Even though amongst merchants the practice was then already old, the case was a milestone decision in law. It adopted the commercial custom of dealing in goods by documentary transactions. It is the form in which we have continued to execute overseas trade to this day. Now automation challenges us with the undoing of the whole documentary superstructure. Another legal revolution will have to take place under the pressure of practice of EDP in trade and transport as surely as it did almost 200 years ago.

---

63   J.G. Castel, *Canadian Conflict of Laws* (1977), Vol. 2, pp. 515-519.
64   29 Car. 2, c. 3.
65   (1787), 2 T.R. 63, 100 E.R. 35 (K.B.), reversed (1790), 1 Hy. Bl. 357 (Ex. Ch.), reversed and venire de novo awarded (1793), 4 Bro. P.C. 57 (H.L.); Benjamin, *Sale of Goods* (2d ed., Guest, 1981), para. 1463.

THE ROLE OF GOVERNMENT
IN THE PROVISION OF
SALVAGE SERVICES

THE ROLE OF GOVERNMENT IN MARINE SALVAGE: AN INTERNATIONAL PERSPECTIVE

*David G. Hebden**

1. Introduction
2. Countries Providing Salvage Facilities
   (a) France
   (b) Turkey
   (c) Other Examples
3. The Role of the Navy in Salvage
4. Current Issues: Government and the Low-Valued Vessel and Cargo

1. INTRODUCTION

Governments are able to perform two basic functions in matters of salvage. One such function is to fund or operate their own salvage facility with the prime object of protecting their coastal waters from pollution. This has the added benefit of protecting the shipping community and, hopefully, of making money. The other basic function is to ensure that a satisfactory domestic legal regime exists in which proper relations between competing salvors, and between salvors and salved property, can be maintained. Governments can also participate in international deliberations to seek favourable international salvage law in the hope that an orderly salvage system will develop on a world-wide basis.

Within these two basic functions there exists, on a world-wide basis, a wide range of variations, combinations and mixtures of activities – under the control of government.

This paper deals with the practical aspects of salvage in a practical way. First to be considered is the function of government in those countries which provide their own salvage capacity; this involves the purchase of powerful tugs with trained crews and shore bases – a very

*Mr. Hebden is a solicitor with the London firm of Thomas Cooper & Stibbard and master mariner who specializes in salvage litigation and arbitration, and whose firm represents many professional salvors and the Canadian government in salvage claims.

costly business. An extensive legal apparatus is necessary to protect the heavy investment made in such equipment.

2.   COUNTRIES PROVIDING SALVAGE FACILITIES

(a) France

The government of France, following the *Amoco Cadiz* disaster, instituted wide control of shipping off the coast of France and set up their own salvage capability. If, for example, a laden tanker is in difficulty near France, as soon as the authorities learn of the presence of the vessel, they demand information as to the difficulty and usually deliver a timed ultimatum to the ship to leave the locality, whether or not it be within the territorial waters of France. If the ultimatum is not effective, the ship will be taken, usually by a tug, to a suitable port for repairs. Units of French Naval Forces are available to enforce this system and have done so on numerous occasions.

The "services" so rendered have to be paid for, and the shipowner has the option of paying a levy fixed by the government of France or of signing a Lloyd's Form (LOF).

The Lloyd's Form option is almost always favoured by shipowners since it ensures that cargo will be required to pay its share of the expense involved, at least in the first instance. The other option would, inevitably, be a charge only on the shipowner who would find it extremely difficult to obtain any contribution from cargo.

In the early days of this regime there were some misguided attempts by lawyers to oppose the system in the arbitration process in London. On these occasions the ship and cargo interests complained to Lloyd's arbitrators that salvage was not payable since the "salvors" were not "volunteers". Arbitrators were reluctant to accept this argument and it was not pursued with any vigour. It was realized that the only alternative to the LOF option and London arbitration was a system solely in the hands of the government of France.

In support of their policy, the French government invited the French tug companies to obtain two or three very large tugs and stationed them on the Atlantic and Mediterranean seaboards of France. The cost of these vessels must be astronomic; certainly the awards earned would not pay the full costs involved.

Recently there are signs that the French authorities are making it extremely difficult for foreign tugs to operate on salvage matters within the territorial waters of France.

(b) Turkey

France is not alone in her policy. There are other countries which adopt a fairly vigorous salvage posture; these include South Africa and

Cuba. The forerunner of the system was the Turkish salvage operation. Turkey, with a long and difficult coastline and the hazardous navigational passage of the Dardenelles, has for many years been a fruitful area for salvage endeavour. Turkey is a country which requires foreign exchange; the Turks have established a law which provides for exclusivity of Turkish salvors within Turkish territorial waters. Any competing salvors are given very curt treatment and chased away by the Turkish navy. The Turks insist on the use of Lloyd's Form.

The system is relatively simple. If salvage services are required by a ship, they can only be rendered by a Turkish salvor and the Turkish salvor will only operate on Lloyd's Form. A relatively simple decision is required from the ship master or shipowner. One either signs the contract or the ship is eventually lost.

There have been innumerable attempts to attack the Turkish monopoly in the Lloyd's arbitration process with little success. The attacks by "ship and cargo" upon the Turkish system have been met by the refusal of the arbitrators to alter their view that, since the law of Turkey is the governing law within their territory, there is little alternative to them but to make the awards in the usual way. The only real concession to the "ship and cargo" standpoint is that arbitrators have refused to accept submissions from the Turkish salvors that there is no alternative assistance available. If no other salvors are allowed by the Turkish government to operate, it is nonsense to give credit to the salvor based on a lack of alternative assistance.

Under the Turkish system there have been several examples where vessels lost on the coast of Turkey would almost certainly have been saved if international professional salvors had been involved. This point highlights the difficulty of how a shipowner proceeds when there is damage caused by the negligence of a salvor operating under a state monopoly.

In Turkey the problem is acute. If a shipowner feels that the Turkish salvors are being negligent, have been negligent or are likely to be negligent, he would normally wish to fly in an expert to assess the situation. The Turks are, in the author's experience, not above putting considerable difficulties in the way of such expert's attendance. On one occasion where it was considered desirable to send a team of divers in to assess the salvage prospects on a vessel, it took almost a week for them to arrive at the scene of the casualty, their diving gear never arrived and there was none available locally.

The advantage, for the salvors, of a monopolistic system is that there is never any difficulty obtaining adequate security for a salvage award. The vessel and cargo will not be released until adequate security is provided.

(c) Other Examples

Many third world countries have adopted laws similar to that used by the State of Turkey. In such cases the government takes a monopoly of salvage and similar related services in their territorial waters and seas so that any foreign national seeking to operate in their waters must seek official permission.

The system of government salvage monopoly varies from state to state. Somalia, for example, has contracted a Dutch salvage company to undertake the responsibility for salvage operations on its long and dangerous coast.

Other countries such as Morocco, Libya and Algeria have a limited salvage capability of their own and demand participation with foreign salvors. As part of the basic agreement, the government's share is usually a high percentage of the award. Some countries with absolutely no salvage capability whatsoever require a licence to be obtained before salvage operations start; this involves a "fee" for the licence, and one is never quite sure how the funding of such licences is achieved. It is an obscure aspect of the salvage business, with details of payments being very difficult to obtain.

Where the coastal state has salvage capabilities, there will be local participation and, on occasions, this can be extremely useful. While the local equipment may not be able to assist in the real operation of refloating a particular vessel, useful services of ferrying equipment, personnel and similar logistical duties can be provided. Over the years professional salvage organizations have acquired a considerable amount of knowledge about operations in various distant locations.

The fact that these operations might involve payment of local taxes, licence fees and payments of several kinds is an inconvenience. Such amounts are frequently brought before a Lloyd's arbitrator in London and claimed as an expense of the operation. The arbitrators and Lloyd's are realistic in such matters.

In addition to the third world countries which have restrictive salvage laws for operations on their coasts, one can add any country which includes the word "Democratic" in its form of national title. The countries behind the Iron Curtain are, inevitably, state-controlled and all operations, of any kind, are within their sway. The Russians and Poles have impressive salvage capabilities and do operate on a world-wide basis on occasion. The Russian role appears to be, almost exclusively, to service its own large national merchant and fishing fleet, but they have on occasion assisted other vessels – usually on Lloyd's Form.

Countries which rely on commercial salvage organizations to perform operations on their coast and allow freedom of access include the

United Kingdom, Canada and most European countries, with the exception of France.

Even those countries which allow complete freedom of salvage on their coasts are tending towards nationalism. The United Kingdom has introduced legislation (*The Prevention of Pollution Act, 1971*) which, while aimed at preventing pollution of the coasts, has the effect of permitting the government or governmental agencies the facility of exercising control over the operations of salvors. This must generally be regarded as unsatisfactory, since salvage is a high-risk business and the freedom of operations of the salvor does not always operate comfortably with government control.

3.   THE ROLE OF THE NAVY IN SALVAGE

Finally, on this aspect of the role of governments in salvage, one must consider the operation of naval units in matters of salvage. Canada, France and the United Kingdom all, upon occasion, have permitted their naval units to engage in salvage operations on a commercial basis. The Royal Navy has for many years been heavily involved in salvage operations.

There are always questions being asked about the fabulous rewards of salvage: the proverbial pot of gold at the end of the rainbow. Once in a while – as with the gold from HMS *Edinburgh* – there is a huge return for a huge investment. The figures generally tell another story.

During the period 1979 to 1983 there were 1,306 Lloyd's Forms handled by Lloyd's; 540 were settled and 642 went to at least original award. The differences, presumably, are still in the pipeline. Total awards, for five years, were £96,602,000 out of funds of £1.62 billion, a percentage of 6 per cent.

The full statistics are as follows:

Year	Cases B/F	Arbtrs Orig.	Apptd. App.	Settle- ments	Awards Orig.	Pub- lished App.	Total Awards £1,000	Total Values £1m.	Percent- age Awards to Values
1979	263	250	65	97	126	57	£11,752	£ 228.6	5.2%
1980	290	249	64	124	158	50	£15,674	£ 263.2	4.3%
1981	261	227	67	109	129	50	£20,651	£ 265.4	7.8%
1982	251	207	60	94	125	47	£27,962	£ 410.5	6.8%
1983	241	193	51	116	104	37	£20,563	£ 350.1	5.9%
	1,306			540	642		£96,602	£1,617.8	
			Total	1,182					

It will be noted that little has been said about the United Kingdom. There is no government-controlled salvage capability in the United Kingdom as such. The government has statutory rights to control any casualty which appears to be likely to cause a pollution threat. Since most vessels have fuel oil on board, this covers practically all cases of any consequence.

International salvors do operate from salvage stations on the coastlines of the United Kingdom and have done so for many years. The private companies which operate tugs in various ports and have salvage capability cover the vast majority of cases. The Royal Navy, of course, is heavily involved in salvage and has an impressive record. In the past ten years the Royal Navy has conducted some 250 salvage operations under Lloyd's Form, approximately one a fortnight.

There appears to be a modest amount of debate in Canada about salvage being performed by military units of the defence forces.

In the past few years, units of Canadian defence forces have performed salvage operations on ships in trouble in both the Atlantic and Pacific Oceans. The debate appears to centre on the issue whether government servants should receive additional benefit for simply doing their job. In the author's opinion, the answer lies in the expression "doing their job".

The job of the forces is to be ready to defend the state against its enemies. With naval forces, their function is to defend their country's shipping and that of any allies in time of war.

A necessary element of salvage is that there be voluntariness on the part of the salvor. If naval forces beat off an attack on civilian shipping in time of war, their service is not salvage. In times of peace, the duty to save lives rests heavily on all mariners – there is no duty to save property.

There are other objections to salvage being performed by military forces. There is, for example, the question of cost to the taxpayer, competition for local salvage companies, interference with training and the fact that obtaining salvage money by the Navy is thought to be unfair to other "non-marine" elements such as the Army or Air Force.

These objections will now be looked at briefly. The first matter concerns the basic cost of naval units being borne by the state. The capital costs of the operation, wages and maintenance of the crew is incurred in any event. Extra charges such as fuel, stores, equipment and helicopter time can be computed and charged to the salved property. Only if the operation is unsuccessful is there any burden on the government.

The question of whether salvage by military forces is competition to local salvors is an argument without merit. The Royal Navy sub-contracts to local salvors on many occasions. A basic naval unit is sometimes first on the scene, such as a minesweeper on fishery duty. This vessel may obtain a Lloyd's Form and then hire in the equipment or subcontract the work to other salvors. The Canadian experience is that the operations, to date, have not involved any direct competition with local salvors; they have competed with foreign salvors. If a situation of competition arises, a local salvage company can always compete by offering to perform the job on a lump-sum basis. Further, where there is sufficient salvage work to justify a major salvage presence, the competition is good for the shipping community and, in such areas, naval salvors rarely become involved in salvage operations. An example is the River Scheldt near the port of Flushing. The high state of readiness of the several professional salvors in the area effectively excludes competing salvors, including military vessels.

Sometimes the objection is to "unfair competition", a more realistic argument, since the requirement of commercial viability does not exist for a naval unit. But the worst thing a naval unit could do would be to offer to perform salvage for nothing – this would ensure that every ship in trouble would opt for naval rather than commercial salvage.

The "interference with training" argument and the view that salvage is unfair to other members of the defence forces can be dealt with together. Salvage is essential in peace and war. Naval forces must have a deep understanding and capability for salvage in wartime. Real operations provide first class training which test both men and equipment. It should also be remembered that the men who perform these operations are frequently putting themselves in situations of considerable danger. When up to the chin in surging oily water, lugging a Coventry Climax pump around a smoke-filled and flooding Engine Room, the salvor might be forgiven for envying the man on sentry duty outside Buckingham Palace. The reality is that salvage awards to the crews of naval vessels are modest, the Crown takes the largest share and the tax man has a go at what is left.

4. CURRENT ISSUES: GOVERNMENT AND THE LOW-VALUED VESSEL AND CARGO

This paper now addresses the role of government in providing a suitable legal regime under which salvors may operate. This involves modifying salvage law to deal with new developments – offshore rigs, for example – and a current concern in international salvage circles – the service rendered to a low-valued vessel with or without cargo on board.

The depressed shipping market has reduced vessel values by considerable amounts. Low profitability has resulted in many badly-maintained vessels being at sea. If they suffer a casualty and salvage services result, the shipowner may refuse to accept the re-delivery of the vessel at the end of the services.

At the start of this section it was pointed out that government may have two possible functions when matters of salvage are considered: first, to be actively involved in the business of salvage; and secondly, to ensure that a satisfactory legal system is available so that the parties to salvage matters organize themselves in an orderly manner.

Salvage, unlike other aspects of marine activity, cannot be planned, programmed or fitted into stereotypes in a style that is now fashionable. The events which give rise to the need for salvage services usually occur in a totally unpredictable way, in hostile weather and environmental conditions and, more often than not, success depends on a speedy and knowledgeable response.

It is also a feature of salvage operations that success depends upon the taking of risks by the salvors which would be totally unacceptable to normal commercial concerns, let alone some national department of state. In this respect governments, as salvors, may find themselves at a serious disadvantage. In many actual cases, where the operation is obviously a high-risk situation, the government concerned will employ an independent professional salvage contractor to undertake the work and thereby seek to gain some credit for success or provide itself with an excuse should the services fail and unpleasant consequences occur.

In general, this writer favours the view that government should not seek to be directly involved in salvage operations. It should, in the public interest, do everything possible to encourage any organization, with the appropriate capability, to salve ships and cargo within their territorial waters and sea approaches.

Finally, the need for governments to provide a system or regime to assist salvors to deal with the difficult and dirty salvage cases should be emphasized; this would involve powers to dispose of the ship and/or cargo to cover costs and remunerate the salvor and perhaps involve participation of the P. & I. Market in some realistic manner – where prevention of pollution has been achieved.

THE ROLE OF GOVERNMENT IN THE PROVISION OF SALVAGE SERVICES: A CANADIAN PERSPECTIVE

*Peter M. Troop**

1. INTRODUCTION

It is difficult now to see any decisive reason why the general body of taxpayers should bear the expense of salvage rather than the particular shipowners or underwriters who have benefited by it. The case is even less obvious when the ships salved are foreign or the underwriters are foreign in whole or in part.[1]

---

*Assistant Deputy Attorney General, Admiralty and Maritime Law, Department of Justice, Ottawa, Ontario.

I am not speaking on behalf of the government of Canada or the Department of Justice and the opinions I express are my own. I would like to acknowledge the assistance of Robin Carter, solicitor, in the preparation of this paper.

1 *Admiralty Commrs. v. The Valverda,* [1938] A.C. 173 at 189, [1938] 1 All E.R. 162 (H.L.), per Lord Wright.

These words, delivered in a salvage case where the Admiralty was denied salvage by the House of Lords, are an early recognition of the principle of "User Pay", *i.e.,* that the user should pay for government services and not the taxpayers.[2]

It is important to distinguish between military salvage and civil salvage. Military salvage, being part of the law of prize, consists in the rescue of property from the enemy in time of war.[3] The elementary principle of prize law is that all prize belongs to the state.[4] However, from early times the Crown has granted rights in, or a bounty for, captures by kings' ships and privateers. This practice amounted to distributing the proceeds known as prize money.[5] (Any similarity between military salvage and piracy is purely coincidental.)

The concept in maritime law of civil salvage is traceable to a period as early as the ninth century B.C., at which time Rhodian law provided that any person who rescued property at sea should receive one-fifth of that property which he saved.[6] Roman law also recognized that a volunteer who saved property at sea was entitled to compensation from the owner.[7] Later, Italian law of the 11th century A.D.,[8] the laws of Oleron[9] and of the Hanseatic towns of the Middle Ages[10] also recognized the principles of salvage.

Salvage is unique to maritime law. It is the only system of law which compensates the volunteer for saving property from imminent peril.[11] Maritime law also gives the salvor a lien on the property saved to protect his right of reward.[12]

2. SALVAGE CLAIMS AGAINST THE CROWN

Prior to the coming into force of the *Crown Liability Act* on May 14, 1953,[13] the Crown in Canada was not liable to pay civil salvage in respect of ships or aircraft owned by the Crown.[14] Subsection (3) of section 3 of

---

2   For a recent consideration of the subject of salvage generally, see Geoffrey Brice, *Maritime Law of Salvage* (London, Stevens & Son, 1983).

3   Viscount Tiverton, *The Principles and Practice of Prize Law* (London, Butterworth & Co., 1914), p. 33.

4   *The Elsebe* (1804), 5 C. Rob. 173, 165 E.R. 738.

5   See Tiverton, *supra* note 2, at pp. 45 *et seq.*

6   Martin J. Norris, *The Law of Salvage* (Baker, Voorhis & Co., Mount Kisco, N.Y., 1958), pp. 4-5.

7   *Ibid.* at 5-7.

8   *Ibid.* at 7.

9   *Ibid.* at 7-13.

10   *Ibid.* at 13-14.

11   *Falcke v. Scottish Imperial Ins. Co.* (1886), 34 Ch. D. 234 at 248 (C.A.).

12   *The Sabine,* 101 US 384, 25 L ed. 982 (1879).

13   S.C. 1952-53, c. 30 [now R.S.C. 1970, c. C-38].

14   *Young v. The Scotia,* [1903] A.C. 501 (P.C.); *The Broadmayne,* [1916] P. 64 (C.A.).

the *Crown Liability Act* extended the law relating to civil salvage to salvage services rendered in assisting any Crown ship or aircraft in the same manner as if the ship or aircraft belonged to a private person:

> except that all claims against the Crown . . . shall be made by petition of right[15] and shall be heard and determined by a judge of the Exchequer Court of Canada.[16]

Since that time, the Crown has paid salvage claims for salvage services rendered to Crown ships. Apparently, no salvage claims have been paid in respect of services to Crown aircraft.[17]

(a) HMCS Saguenay Salvage

The most important salvage case against the Crown was that of HMCS *Saguenay* when it went aground in the harbour of Port Hood on Cape Breton Island in July 1970.

1. On July 16, 1970, *Saguenay* entered Port Hood, Nova Scotia, to go to anchor. *Saguenay* went aground at approximately 08:48 when Smith Point Light was bearing 138 1/2°, distant 3,230 feet. The wind was southerly approximately 25-30 knots and visibility was estimated to be approximately eight to ten miles.
2. The Commanding Officer of *Saguenay* signed two Lloyd's Standard Forms of Salvage Agreement dated July 16, 1970, with the tugs *Arctic Shore* and *Pacific Shore* respectively, under which agreements the tugs were to salve *Saguenay* by refloating her and taking her into deep water.
3. The two tugs left Mulgrave, Nova Scotia, at about 18:35 on July 16 and proceeded on passage to Port Hood. They reached *Saguenay* at 22:50 and found her lying on a westerly heading about six cables from Smith Point Light. She went aground on a narrow spit, the seabed consisting of fine mud and sand.
4. Because some sand and shells had been sucked into the *Saguenay's* starboard engine intake, the engineer, in consultation with the Commanding Officer, had decided to shut down the main engines to prevent possible damage and overheating. However, her auxiliary engines continued to give her power, heat and light.
5. After the tugs had arrived at the position of the grounding, it was decided that the major effort to refloat the vessel would be made by

---

15 Now by statement of claim in the Trial Division of the Federal Court of Canada: see the *Federal Court Act,* R.S.C. 1970, c. 10 (2nd Supp.), s. 64(2).
16 *Crown Liability Act,* R.S.C. 1970, c. C-38, s. 3(3).
17 On June 6, 1983, the Royal Navy Sea Harrier from HMS *Illustrious* was forced to land on the Spanish cargo ship *Alraigo* after losing contact with her carrier and running out of fuel. The shipowners were awarded salvage of £478,500, about 10 per cent of that aircraft's value.

pulling her astern. The two tugs made fast to *Saguenay* shortly after midnight and, using various manoeuvers, were engaged in pulling her astern from time to time until approximately 03:00 when *Saguenay* came astern off the bank. The two tugs then towed *Saguenay* to an anchorage position about one and one-quarter miles east of Henry Island.

6. It was alleged by the salvors that due to the winds, which were increasing to Force 7, *Saguenay* was tending to be pushed more onto the bank. Because the depth of water was only ten to eleven feet around the bow of *Saguenay* and the mean draft of the two tugs was 12½ feet, it was alleged that there was a serious danger of the tugs themselves going aground and sustaining damage and loss throughout the refloating operation. Each tug was said to have a value of £1.25 million sterling.

7. There was some dispute on the evidence regarding the state of the weather and the effect of the tide.

8. The two tugs were released from *Saguenay* between 05:00 and 05:30, after which time they returned to Mulgrave where they berthed at 08:30 on July 17.

9. As of July 16, 1970, the Department of National Defence assessed the value of *Saguenay* at $11,677,316.

10. Notwithstanding that Lloyd's Form had been signed by the Commanding Officer of the *Saguenay,* the Department of National Defence took the position with the salvors that under the *Crown Liability Act,* claims against the Crown in right of Canada in respect of salvage had to be heard and determined by the Exchequer Court of Canada.[18]

(b) Distinctions in Claims Against Crown

It can be concluded, therefore, with respect to salvage claims against the Crown, that the Crown is in the same position and subject to the same liability as any other shipowner or cargo owner or owner of an aircraft. The principal distinction between a salvage claim against the Crown and a salvage claim against any other person is that the Federal Court has exclusive jurisdiction in respect of salvage claims against the Crown, while the Federal Court has "concurrent jurisdiction" with the provincial courts in respect of all other salvage claims.

An important difference is that no claim against the Crown can be brought *in rem.* Section 6 of the *Crown Liability Act* declares that:

Nothing in this Act authorizes proceedings *in rem* in respect of any claim against the Crown, or the arrest, detention or sale of any Crown ship or aircraft, or of any cargo or

---

18   *Crown Liability Act,* s. 3(3).

other property belonging to the Crown, or gives to any person any lien on any such ship, aircraft, cargo or other property.

Accordingly, the salvor's maritime lien, otherwise enforceable in the Federal Court, cannot be asserted against the salved Crown ship or cargo. On the other hand, if a valid salvage claim is established against the Crown, the judgment of the Federal Court, by virtue of section 57(3) of the *Federal Court Act*,[19] is a direct charge on the Consolidated Revenue Fund and is payable and paid notwithstanding that the Department concerned may have no appropriation out of which to pay the salvage claim.

(c) Salvage Contracts

There are very few cases of true salvage, which is awarded only to a third party independently of contract and is payable only when property has been salved.[20]

A large number of salvage services are rendered under the terms of Lloyd's Standard Form of Salvage Agreement, also known as Lloyd's Open Form (LOF), a commercial salvage contract based on the principle of "No Cure: No Pay" and governed by English law.

Under LOF the contractor agrees to use his best endeavours to salve the ship and/or her cargo and take them to a place of safety. Where the salvage services – which are rendered by the contractor and accepted by ship and cargo on the principle of "No Cure: No Pay" – are successful, the contractor's remuneration will be fixed by arbitration in London upon notice being received by the Committee of Lloyd's of a claim for arbitration from any party entitled to make such a claim.

The contractor has a maritime lien on the property salved for his remuneration. Where shipowners fail to comply with the requirements of LOF regarding the provision of proper security for such remuneration, the contractor may take steps to protect or enforce his lien as he thinks fit. LOF provides that, unless otherwise agreed, security must be provided in a form approved by the Committee of Lloyd's by persons, firms or corporations resident in the United Kingdom. The Committee is in no way responsible as to the sufficiency of any security given.

Once the arbitrator (or appeal arbitrator) has determined the award, the Committee will call upon the party concerned to pay the amount awarded. In the event of non-payment, the Committee may enforce the security and pay the amount awarded to the contractor.

From the Crown's point of view, the most significant provision of

---

19   *Supra* note 15.
20   *The Five Steel Barges* (1890), 15 P.D. 142; *The Hestia,* [1895] P. 193; *The Auguste Legembre,* [1902] P. 123.

the Lloyd's Salvage Agreement is the agreement to pay salvage in the amount determined by the Lloyd's Arbitrator.

Can the Crown agree to be bound to pay salvage in accordance with Lloyd's Form? The problem will not arise if the Crown and the salvor agree, but can the liability of the Crown be determined by such means? What happens if the Crown so agrees and is faced with paying an award which it thinks is excessive?

The problem is created by section 17 of the *Federal Court Act.* That section gives the Trial Division of the Federal Court original jurisdiction in all cases where relief is claimed against the Crown and in respect of any claim against the Crown arising out of a contract. The Trial Division is given *exclusive* original jurisdiction in all such cases.

This provision must be read with section 3(3) of the *Crown Liability Act.* That subsection states that all claims against the Crown for civil salvage must be heard and determined by a Judge of the Federal Court. One might therefore conclude that the salvor's only remedy against the Crown is to commence an action in the Federal Court. The question remains to be answered. There appear to be arguments both ways. It can be argued that, if the salvage contract itself provides its own remedy, the Federal Court would only intervene if the Crown failed to comply with its term and the salvor brought an action in the Federal Court for damages for breach of the salvage agreement.[21]

3. SALVAGE CLAIMS BY CROWN

(a) General Rule and Exceptions

One might think that, if the Crown is liable to pay civil salvage, it follows that her Majesty would have an equal but opposite right to claim salvage in respect of salvage services provided by the Crown. However, that is not the case. In England, the matter was settled in 1947 on the basis that the Crown paid salvage and claimed salvage in all cases.[22] In Canada, the Crown pays salvage but can only claim salvage for services provided by certain classes of ships. The general rule is that the Crown cannot claim salvage at all for salvage services rendered by government ships.[23] However, there are two important exceptions to this general rule:

---

21   *Cf. B.V. Bureau Wijsmuller v. United States,* 702 F 2d 333 (1983), where the U.S. government refused to participate in a Lloyd's Salvage Arbitration claiming sovereign immunity. It was found that the government was not a party to the salvage agreement.

22   *Crown Proceedings Act,* 1947 (10 & 11 Geo. 6, c. 44), s. 8 [ext. S.I. 1979/305].

23   *Canada Shipping Act,* R.S.C. 1970, c. S-9, s. 531. For a discussion of the "general rule", see *Kennedy's Civil Salvage* (4th ed., K.C. McGuffie ed., London, Stevens &

(a) The first exception is in section 531 of the *Canada Shipping Act,*[24] which enables the Crown to claim salvage for services provided by any salvage ship or tug belonging to Her Majesty. It is established that the salvage ship must be "especially equipped with a salvage plant". This exception has been strictly construed by the Admiralty Court.[25]

(b) The second and more important exception, at least at the present time, permits claims by the Crown for salvage services performed by vessels or aircraft belonging to or in the service of Her Majesty and used in the Canadian Forces.

This second exception from the general rule is contained in section 223(1) of the *National Defence Act.*[26] Subsection (7) of section 223 expressly overrides section 531 of the *Canada Shipping Act* insofar as Canadian Naval ships are concerned. The requirements of section 223 are that the salvage services must be rendered by or with the aid of a vessel or aircraft

(a) belonging to or in the service of Her Majesty, and

(b) used in the Canadian Forces.

The phrase "Canadian Forces" is defined in sections 14 and 15 of the *National Defence Act* in the following words:

> 14. The Canadian Forces are the armed forces of Her Majesty raised by Canada and consist of one Service called the Canadian Armed Forces.

> 15.(1) There shall be a component of the Canadian Forces, referred to in this Act as the regular force, consisting of officers and men who are enrolled for continuing, full-time military service.

(b) Background

Historically, there was no claim by naval forces for salvage services.[27] Wartime conditions during World War I demonstrated that salvage facilities offered by private contractors were inadequate to meet salvage needs. To solve this problem, in the United Kingdom, the *Merchant Shipping (Salvage) Act*[28] was passed in 1916, enabling claims to be made in respect of salvage services by naval ships and personnel but, as we have seen, this only authorized claims in respect of ships

---

Son Ltd., 1958), pp. 25 *et seq.* ; pp. 77 *et seq.* The Crown is regarded as being under a pre-existing duty to protect life and property; therefore the basic salvage requirement of "voluntariness" is generally held not to be met.

24 *Supra* note 23.

25 *The Morgana,* [1920] P. 442.

26 R.S.C. 1970, c. N-4.

27 *The Valverda, supra* note 1; *The Sarpen,* [1916] P. 306, [1916-17] All E.R. Rep. 1132 (C.A.).

28 1916 (6 & 7 Geo. 5, c. 41).

especially equipped with salvage plants or which were Admiralty tugs.[29]
During World War II, when control of all salvage operations was again
vested in the Admiralty, the *Merchant Shipping (Salvage) Act, 1940* [30]
stated that the Crown

> shall be entitled to claim salvage for these services and for the same rights and
> remedies in respect of those services as any other salvor would have if the ship, aircraft
> or property belonged to him.[31]

These provisions were re-enacted by the British *Crown Proceedings Act,*
1947.[32]

In Canada the legal position was altered by Orders-in-Council
passed under the *War Measures Act* [33] suspending the operation of
section 534 (now section 531) of the *Canada Shipping Act.*[34] These
Orders-in-Council enabled the Crown, as well as officers and crew of
Crown ships, to claim salvage with the consent of the Governor-in-
Council. These Orders-in-Council were repealed by an Order-in-Coun-
cil on December 8, 1947, and replaced by section 211 (now section 223)
of the *National Defence Act,*[35] with section 211 being made to operate
retrospectively from December 8, 1947.

In respect of the Commander, officers and crew of Crown ships,
their conditional right to claim salvage does not depend on the class of
ship in which they serve. Their right to claim salvage, however, is
conditional on obtaining:
(a) in respect of Naval ships, the consent of the Minister of National
     Defence;[36] or
(b) in respect of non-Naval ships, the consent of the Governor-in-
     Council.[37]

The necessary consent can be given at any time before "final
adjudication" but if the consent is not proved, the salvage claim must be
dismissed with costs.

As far as it is known, there have been no recent cases in which the
consent of the Governor-in-Council has been sought or obtained, but
there have been a number of cases where the consent of the Minister of
National Defence has been sought and obtained.

---

29 *Ibid.,* s. 1.
30 1940 (3 & 4 Geo. 6, c. 43).
31 *Ibid.,* s. 1(1).
32 *Supra* note 22.
33 R.S.C. 1927, c. 206.
34 S.C. 1934, c. 44.
35 S.C. 1950, c. 43.
36 *National Defence Act,* R.S.C. 1970, c. N-4, s. 223.
37 *Canada Shipping Act,* R.C.S. 1970, c. S-9, s. 531.

The restriction on the Crown's right to claim salvage, save for a tug or salvage vessel, cannot be overcome by the use of a salvage agreement. In the *Valverda* case,[38] the Admiralty in 1935 attempted to get around the existing restrictions in the *Merchant Shipping Act*[39] by asserting that a claim under a salvage agreement (Lloyd's Form) was not barred by the prohibitions in the 1916 *Merchant Shipping (Salvage) Act*.[40] In that case two Admiralty tugs and two warships of the Royal Navy had come to the rescue of the burning *Valverda*. One warship – HMS *Frobisher,* a Royal Navy Cruiser – had towed the *Valverda* about 900 miles to Bermuda. The Lloyd's Form had been entered into voluntarily and it was common ground that the services rendered by the two warships, HMS *Frobisher* and HMS *Guardian,* were difficult and dangerous and involved serious risk to those vessels.[41] The owners of *Valverda* admitted salvage services were rendered by *Frobisher* and *Guardian* and the two Admiralty tugs but denied that any salvage could be claimed in respect of the services of *Frobisher* and *Guardian.* Claims by the officers and crew were, however, admitted.

Notwithstanding these facts, the House of Lords decided that the salvage agreement could not override section 557 of the *Merchant Shipping Act* and that, on its true construction, it was intended to exclude and did exclude all claims whatsoever by the Admiralty, including claims for the use of the Royal Navy warship as a salving instrument.

(c) M.V. Partnership Salvage Services

A recent example of salvage services rendered by a Canadian warship is the case of the *Partnership.*

1. At about 15:00 local time, March 17, 1979, M.V. *Partnership,* a Danish general motor cargo vessel of 14,998 tons gross and 3,456 tons net register, sent out a distress signal. At the time she was laden with a cargo of used drilling equipment consigned to the Port of Saint John, New Brunswick. The ship was headed for that port when part of the cargo shifted and she began to take on water.

2. In the first instance, HMCS *Skeena* responded promptly to the distress call. She dispatched her helicopter with one gasoline-powered Coventry Climax pump to the casualty. The pump and the seaman were lifted onto the casualty at 16:20 hours. *Skeena* arrived at the position of the casualty at about 17:00 hours and observed that the vessel was listing about 15° to starboard, taking on water in

---

38   *Supra* note 1.
39   1894 (57 & 58 Vict., c. 60), s. 557.
40   *Supra* note 28, s. 1.
41   *Supra* note 1, at p. 175 [A.C.].

hold No. 2 and rolling in a laboured way. The weather was deteriorating with increasing winds, west-northwest 25 knots, and seas and swell of approximately 13 feet.

3. At about 17:55 a Buffalo Military Aircraft from Summerside, P.E.I. arrived over the casualty with a portable pump which was dropped into the sea close to *Skeena,* which recovered it and then transferred it, not without difficulties, by line to the casualty. There attempts were made to get the pumps working to control flooding in the No. 2 hold.

4. HMCS *Assiniboine* arrived at the casualty at 20:40 hours and took over from *Skeena* which had been keeping station on the casualty. The attempts to set up the pumps on the casualty had been unsuccessful because there was too great a distance from the pump over the side of the casualty to get proper suction.

5. Throughout the night the convoy remained in close company heading westerly at a speed of about 12 knots while attempts were made to control the rate of inflow of water. The weather remained the same.

6. At first light on March 18, *Assiniboine* transferred engineering personnel and another pump to the casualty. The transfer was completed using *Skeena's* helicopter. The weather had improved with the wind northwesterly ten knots in a three-foot sea over five-foot swells. The temperature had dropped below freezing.

7. At 09:12 the Master of *Partnership* informed the Captain of *Assiniboine* that he had very little fuel left to continue steaming. The pumping operations had been unsuccessful. It was therefore necessary for the *Partnership* to be taken in tow and instructions were relayed via Maritime Command for additional pumps to be transferred to the scene of the casualty as quickly as possible.

8. At approximately 11:15, the Master of the *Partnership* transferred the majority of the members of his crew to *Assiniboine* because he was concerned about their safety and the safety of his vessel.

9. During the afternoon of March 18, equipment was prepared and, at approximately 15:00 hours, the tow was connected between *Assiniboine* and the casualty. Once the weight had been taken on the tow, the *Assiniboine* was able to increase speed to 12 knots on a course of 260°.

10. The tow headed for Chedabucto Bay, Nova Scotia. There were reports of heavy ice conditions close to the coast. The tow continued in increasingly adverse weather conditions. The wind increased to 30 knots.

11. At 20:00 hours, the Coast Guard Cutter *Alert* arrived and transferred two additional submersible pumps, together with an en-

gineer, to the casualty. Throughout the night the three submersible pumps operated well, discharging approximately 50 tons per hour. The situation on board the casualty stabilized and began to improve.

12. On March 19th, at about 08:00, the list on board the casualty had been reduced to about 7°.

13. The tow continued towards Chedabucto Bay where it arrived at approximately 22:00. There the tow was slipped and the casualty proceeded to an anchorage in Inhabitants Bay.

14. Overall *Skeena* had been engaged for approximately eight hours. She had run out approximately 80 miles to meet the casualty and had escorted her for about 20 miles. *Assiniboine* had been engaged overall for about two days and six hours, had towed the casualty and the cargo a distance of about 220 miles and had successfully brought her to safe anchorage after a tow of about 30 hours.

15. The sound value of the ship was valued by David & Newman at $2.75 million U.S. The cargo, owned by Dome Petroleum Limited, had a value of approximately $2 million Canadian and was insured by Scandinavian underwriters.

16. The claim by the Department of National Defence on behalf of the Captain, officers and crew of the two naval vessels engaged was eventually settled. Of the amount accepted by the Department in settlement of the claim, one-quarter was apportioned among the Royal Canadian Navy personnel on board the two vessels involved in providing salvage services.

17. The Department of National Defence calculated that on a purely cost basis, and in relation only to the services of *Assiniboine,* the Department's costs were: Military Personnel – $56,217; direct operating costs – $35,125; and indirect operating costs – $17,110; a total of $108,452.

4.   CAN THE CROWN BE A VOLUNTEER?

(a) Analysis of the Crown's Duty

If a salvage claim is put forward by the Crown, it may be argued that the Crown is not a volunteer and that any assistance rendered was in accordance with some pre-existing duty owed by the Crown or the Crown ship to the owner of the ship and cargo saved.[42]

The principle that the salvor must be a volunteer is the cornerstone of the law of salvage.[43] Voluntariness is an essential element of salvage in

---

42   *See Kennedy's Civil Salvage, supra* note 23.

43   *Ibid.* at 25.

the sense that, if the service is rendered solely under a pre-existing contractual or official duty owed to the owner of the salved property, or solely in the interest of self-preservation, it is not salvage. As previously noted, the cases involving true salvage are few. For every case in the Federal Court, there are probably ten cases of "contract salvage" where the salvor is a contractor under Lloyd's Form and not a volunteer.

It would be difficult to say that the professional salvor is a volunteer in any ordinary sense of the word. He stations his ocean-going tugs in various critical parts of the world for the primary purpose of providing towage and other salvage assistance to vessels in distress. In fact, Lloyd's Arbitrators have for years operated on the premise that liberal awards should be made to professional salvors in order to give them an incentive to maintain and operate their highly specialized vessels.[44] It would be rare for these professional salvors to undertake any salvage work except on a Lloyd's Form "No Cure: No Pay" basis.

In the recent cases involving salvage claims by the Crown, it has not been argued, except in one case, that the Crown had a pre-existing duty to render the services for which salvage was claimed. In that case, it was contended the Navy tugs in question owed an official duty to assist in the rescue of the salved property, either by virtue of their status as vessels owned by the Department of National Defence or by virtue of the applicable Harbour Contingency Plan. The point was not pressed and the case was settled.

The fact remains, however, that the argument will be made and will have to be answered if the Crown is to be successful. The basic distinction that has to be made is between the saving of life at sea and the saving of property in peril.

As will be shown below in the analysis of the government search-and-rescue policy, the Government of Canada has assumed an obligation to aid in the search and rescue of life, but that policy does not extend to creating any duty on the part of the Crown or on the part of officers and servants of the Crown to save property.

We are not concerned with the Crown acting under some statutory authority for the removal of wrecks as contemplated by the *Navigable Waters Protection Act*[45] or Part X of the *Canada Shipping Act*. It seems to be recognized that the Crown only resorts to those powers when it is agreed by all interested that the ship and cargo in distress has no salvage value whatsoever and the only issue is whether the underwriters or the

---

44   The courts have held similar views: *e.g. The Tantalus v. The Telemachus,* [1957] P. 47, [1957] 1 All E.R. 72; *The Glengyle,* [1898] P. 97, on appeal [1898] P. 97 at 104 (C.A.), affirmed (*sub nom. Glengyle v. Neptune Salvage Co.*) [1898] A.C. 519 (H.L.).

45   R.S.C. 1970, c. N-19.

taxpayer is to be charged with the expense of removing or destroying the wreck.

Certainly Parliament has contemplated that the Crown can assert salvage claims in the same circumstances as any ordinary salvor can assert a claim for similar services. If the services are rendered in accordance with a Lloyd's Form or other salvage agreement, one would have thought that if the agreement was entered into voluntarily, the execution of that agreement should preclude any argument that the Crown has some pre-existing obligation to provide the services in question. It has been recently suggested that the execution of a Lloyd's Form is not a complete answer to such a contention,[46] but it would probably be a very unusual case where such a contention could successfully be made.

(b) Zapata Scotian Rescue

An example of "pure" salvage is the rescue of the *Zapata Scotian:*

1. On March 5, 1982, the barge *Seacamel* 393-11 broke loose from her moorings at Pier 21 in Halifax Harbour, Nova Scotia, and drifted in a northwesterly direction up the harbour towards the Angus L. McDonald Bridge. Laden on board the barge was the jack-up drilling rig *Zapata Scotian.*

2. The moorings of the barge parted at about 10:45 when the Superintendent, Naval Auxiliary Vessels, Captain Brick was on the rig with Captain Mayo, Master Attendant.

3. Captain Brick was on the rig on behalf of the Department of National Defence to supervise the use of the Department of National Defence Crane YD251-253 in the removal of wedges from the oil rig. As soon as he realized what had happened and that the barge and rig were drifting in the harbour towards the bridge, he took charge immediately and ordered every available tug in the harbour to the position of the rig.

4. Both civilian and Department of National Defence tugs came to the assistance of the rig. In all a total of seven tugs operated by the Department of National Defence were involved in the services, one for only a short period. The services themselves were performed and largely completed in a period of one hour.

5. The value of the barge and drilling rig was agreed to be $52,700,000 U.S.

6. Legal proceedings were commenced in the Federal Court of Canada to pursue claims for salvage on behalf of the Crown, on behalf of the masters and crews of the tugs themselves and on behalf of the two individuals who took control of the operation from the rig. Proceedings were also commenced by the owners of the civilian tugs.

---

46   See Brice, *supra* note 2, at p. 249, para. 564.

7. To assist in settlement discussions, the matter was referred informally to a Lloyd's Arbitrator in London who was asked to express an opinion as to the likely amount of the aggregate award had the matter been referred formally to arbitration in London under the terms of Lloyd's Form. All the salvage claims were subsequently settled and the apportionment between the salvors was agreed.

It would appear that the Crown is entitled to be awarded salvage on the same scale as a commercial salvor. In *The Queen Elizabeth*[47] Willmer J. declared:

> Lastly, I think I should say this in relation to the Admiralty tugs. As I understand the meaning of the Merchant Shipping (Salvage) Act, 1940, which repealed the 1916 Act, the Admiralty is placed, in relation to salvage claims, exactly, and for all purposes, in the same position as ordinary commercial owners of tugs and vessels. I have, therefore, given no consideration to the fact that these Admiralty tugs are maintained at the public expense, or anything of that sort. It seems to me that the Admiralty is entitled to a reward for rescuing property on exactly the same scale as is an ordinary commercial tugowner or shipowner.

5. THE ROLE OF GOVERNMENT IN SEARCH AND RESCUE AS COMPARED TO THE ROLE OF GOVERNMENT IN SALVAGE

(a) Background

By way of historical background,[48] the first authenticated lighthouse in what is now Canada was erected by French military engineers at Louisburgh in 1733. This has since disappeared, but the lighthouse erected in 1758 by the British on Sambro Island near Halifax, a classical stone tower rising 140 feet above sea level, is still in use today. Since those early days, when the lighthouses were built as part of a defence policy, great strides have been made throughout Canada to improve the safety of ships and seamen through the fixing of lights in the Maritimes, in the St. Lawrence, in the Great Lakes and on the Pacific Coast.

On the Atlantic Coast developments in the early years of the establishment of British North America included the building of humane stations. (One on Sable Island was occupied in 1801.) In those days, strategically placed humane stations were set up throughout the Gulf of St. Lawrence, on Seal Island, the Island of Anticosti and other places.

---

47 (1949), 82 Ll.L. Rep. 803 at 822.
48 Material for the following historical background is taken from *Canada's Contribution to Safety of Life at Sea,* The Neil Matheson McWharrie lecture by Thomas E. Appleton, P.Eng., MEIC former historian, Marine Administration, Ministry of Transport, Ottawa, delivered to the Commonwealth Section of the Royal Society of Arts, May 2, 1974.

They were usually unmanned and consisted of huts stocked with food and clothing which were inspected from time to time.

After Confederation, when the Department of Marine and Fisheries took over all shipping responsibilities, the system was expanded to include shore-based lifeboat stations with paid crews drawn from local fishermen. The first such station was at Hamond Point on Lake Ontario in 1871. Instruction given to the coxswain and crew was based on the Royal National Lifeboat Institution Procedures and the boats were based on two designs, both from the United States Lifesaving Service, built in Canada.

In the Gulf of St. Lawrence, the dangers resulting from ships being frozen into the ice demanded special measures. Ten life-saving canoe stations were in service in 1875. The canoes could hold up to 30 people and a crew of 6. They could be used either paddling in open spaces or by hauling out across the ice floes. Canoe stations were discontinued in 1890.

Serious problems in relation to competency and certification of masters and mates for Canada's huge fleet of wooden sailing vessels and in relation to shifting cargoes resulted in the evolution of regulations for shipping. Canada, for example, influenced changes to the *Merchant Shipping Act* by regulations for the carriage of deck loads and bulk cargoes.

According to Professor Appleton the two tributaries to the main river of Canadian safety legislation – the *Merchant Shipping Act* and the Board of Steamboat Inspection – were brought together in 1906 with the passing of the *Canada Shipping Act*.[49] Thereafter a third tributary flowed from the International Convention for the Safety of Human Lives at Sea held at London in 1914 as a direct result of the *Titanic* disaster. Canada was an original participant.

Today the original portfolio relating to shipping, including lighthouses, lifeboats and maritime safety in general remains firmly under the administration of one Department, the Ministry of Transport. Canada now has an extensive fleet of search-and-rescue vessels, lighthouse and buoy tenders, ice breakers and support ships administered by the Canadian Coast Guard and working across the vast marine areas under Canadian jurisdiction.

The development of civil air transportation has proceeded independently and a vast network of routes and airfields has been developed across Canada. Under the *Aeronautics Act*[50] the Minister of Transport has been given responsibilities relating to the control and regulation of

---

49   R.S.C. 1906, c. 113.
50   R.S.C. 1970, c. A-3.

air navigation over Canada, including the territorial sea. There has, in the context of this legislation, been some uncertainty as to who has the overall responsibility for search and rescue in Canada relating to civil aircraft. It is the opinion of Mr. Justice Charles L. Dubin[51] that the responsibility rests with the Minister of Transport, and his report recommends that:

(a)   The Department of Transport assume the overall responsibility for search and rescue.

(b)   The search and rescue operations be carried out by the Department of National Defence.

(c)   An agreement between Transport Canada and the Department of National Defence with respect to their respective roles in the field of search and rescue be formalized.

(b) Cabinet Directives and Other Policy Documents Relating to Search and Rescue

Under Cabinet Directive 18, dated September 26, 1950, the Cabinet agreed that the Royal Canadian Air Force should continue to provide search-and-rescue services on behalf of the Government of Canada under the International Civil Aviation Organization Agreement.

Cabinet Directive Circular No. 22, dated July 12, 1951, sets out regulations of the government relating to search-and-rescue services. All government Departments operating ships must have issued clear instructions that their vessels are to be part of the general marine search-and-rescue organization and are to render every possible assistance in the event of a marine casualty. The then Royal Canadian Air Force was designated as the agency co-ordinating all marine search and rescue services through its Rescue Co-ordination Centres.

Today, the Canadian Coast Guard provides the marine element of Canada's National Search and Rescue (SAR) committment. Part of the Canadian Coast Guard fleet is allocated solely for SAR and is backed up by every government-owned vessel, the resources of the Canadian Armed Forces and, when called upon, any Canadian ship in accordance with s. 445 of the *Canada Shipping Act.*[52] In addition, input is received from volunteer rescue agents, private citizens working without remuneration who provide a valuable service by keeping in touch with local boats and checking on missing persons. These individuals work under the supervision of Rescue Co-ordination Centres (RCC). There are four of these centres located across Canada at Victoria, Edmonton, Trenton and Halifax. Each centre is responsible for a SAR region. Each Rescue

---

51   Report of the Commission of Inquiry on Aviation Safety, 1981-82 Supply & Services, Canada.

52   R.S.C. 1970, c. S-9.

Co-ordination Centre can call upon government vessels and aircraft which are available for SAR activities and it is to the appropriate Rescue Co-ordination Centre that the Department of Transport gives reports of any missing aircraft and aviation distress calls.

On the question of salvage, Cabinet Directive 22, dated July 7, 1951, referred to above, specifies:

(f) Instructions to vessels owned by the Government are to clearly indicate that

(i) the immediate action required is that necessary to ensure safety of life and, if possible, prevention of damage to or loss of any ship or its cargo until such time as private or commercial salvage is available for this purpose; and

(ii) any action taken by Government-owned vessels is of a purely interim nature and should not be competitive with commercial interests.

Treasury Board has approved the procedure for SAR operations by government vessels in the following terms:

(a) Any Government vessel (or aircraft) must be considered as being available for SAR activities and must inform the appropriate rescue co-ordinating centre if it is at sea or at short-steaming notice. Cabinet Directive 22-51 states that all Government vessels must consider themselves available for SAR activities, and section 446 of the Canada Shipping Act requires any ship to respond to a call for assistance. Departments must terminate or truncate departmental program activities (such as Fisheries inspection) to respond to SAR calls from the Rescue Control Centre, and absorb any incremental operating costs.[53]

Maritime Search and Rescue Services and Salvage: The Standing Instructions of the Canadian Coast Guard relating to SAR provide that the Canadian Coast Guard has a special obligation to provide assistance to ships and aircrafts in distress at sea. In particular, the instructions provide:

... Masters must endeavour to earn respect for the service by displaying initiative, resolution and efficiency in all matters connected with search and rescue.[54]

Reflecting the Cabinet Instructions on the matter, the Canadian Coast Guard Regulations provide that, while it is the duty of all Canadian registered vessels to render assistance to vessels in distress, it is the particular duty of the Canadian Coast Guard and other government-owned vessels to do so. However, government policy dictates they should not compete with privately-owned ships in salvage work: see Instruction 13.10, which provides:

Canadian Coast Guard ships should therefore only undertake towing or other salvage operations when safety of life may be involved. It may at times be necessary to haul or hold a vessel off a dangeous lee until privately owned towing or salvage crews can

53   Treasury Board Minute.
54   Canadian Coast Guard Standing Instructions, s. 13.1.

reach the vessel. In this case steps should be taken to check the fact that a tug or salvage vessel's services have been requested and arranged.

The annual edition of the Notices to Mariners describes the search-and-rescue services available in Canadian and adjacent waters. In dealing with the topic of salvage, the Notice to Mariners specifies:

> The Canada Shipping Act does not authorize the Rescue Co-ordinator to order vessels to undertake salvage but the RCC will inform the stricken vessel of nearby vessels and attempt to inform the owners. Government vessels will only undertake property salvage when salvage is incidental to rescue, or is trivial or unobtainable from the private sector or is likely to cause undue hardship through delay.[55]

In summary, it can be concluded from the above-quoted provisions of the *Canada Shipping Act* and the *National Defence Act,* cabinet directives and governmental (*e.g.,* Coast Guard) regulations that the government gives clear priority to national search-and-rescue services co-ordinated under the direction of the Department of National Defence.

All government departments controlling ships and/or aircraft are required to engage in search-and-rescue operations. In this context the Canadian Coast Guard provides a marine element.

There is a clear emphasis on the saving of life only in such operations and, to the extent that the SAR Co-ordinator may call upon DND-owned vessels, ships used by the Canadian Armed Forces may find themselves in SAR operations that develop as well into ones containing the necessary elements of salvage in respect of which a claim can be made. The prevention of damage or loss to property is permitted only:

(i)   where the same is possible after the saving of life; and
(ii) until such time as private or commercial salvage operators can take over the operation.

As the Cabinet Directive stipulates, the operation by government-owned vessels to prevent damage or loss of property is to be only of a purely interim nature.[56] This applies equally to vessels owned by the government and used in the Canadian Armed Forces.

---

55   Notice to Mariners No. 36, para. 6.
56   Cabinet Directive Circular No. 22, July 12, 1951.